BEING-HERE

EASA Series

Published in Association with the European Association of Social Anthropologists (EASA)

Series Editor: Aleksandar Bošković, University of Belgrade

Social anthropology in Europe is growing, and the variety of work being done is expanding. This series is intended to present the best of the work produced by members of the EASA, both in monographs and in edited collections. The studies in this series describe societies, processes and institutions around the world and are intended for both scholarly and student readership.

For a full volume listing, please see back matter.

BEING-HERE

Placemaking in a World of Movement

Annika Lems

berghahn
NEW YORK · OXFORD
www.berghahnbooks.com

First published in 2018 by
Berghahn Books
www.berghahnbooks.com

© 2018, 2022 Annika Lems
First paperback edition published in 2022

Library of Congress Cataloging-in-Publication Data
A C.I.P. cataloging record is available from the Library of Congress
Library of Congress Cataloging in Publication Control Number:
2017053737

British Library Cataloguing in Publication Data
A catalogue record for this book is available from the British Library

ISBN 978-1-78533-849-6 hardback
ISBN 978-1-80073-440-1 paperback
ISBN 978-1-78533-850-2 ebook
https://doi.org/10.3167/9781785338496

The world is large, but in us it becomes deep
as the bottom of the sea.
—Rainer Maria Rilke

Contents

Illustrations

Acknowledgements

First and foremost, I would like to express my deep and heartfelt gratitude to Halima Mohamed, Omar Farah Dhollawa and Mohamed Ibrahim, whose stories have filled this book with life. There are not enough words to thank them for their generosity, for their readiness to let me into their lives and for all the time and effort they invested in this project. I also want to thank Klaus Neumann and Peter Browne, my dissertation supervisors at the former Swinburne Institute for Social Research in Melbourne, who travelled this journey with me from the very beginning. Their encouragement to explore and challenge my writing allowed me to open my mind to new possibilities, and to gain strength and confidence in my ability as a storytelling academic.

Like any academic work, this book did not grow in solitude. Rather, the many conversations and discussions I had with colleagues, friends and family members also formed my thinking and have left their imprints on this book. I would like to thank all participants of Klaus Neumann's residential seminars and Sandy Gifford's writing group for their generous and constructive feedback to some of my draft chapters. A thank you goes to my friends and colleagues in Australia, Zoe Robertson, Stefanie Scherr, Josefine Raasch, Robyn Sampson, Jasmina Kijevcanin, Michaela Callaghan, Katherine Wilson, Skye Krichauff and Caitlin Nunn. I am particularly indebted to Sandy Gifford for the time she dedicated to reading and commenting on my chapters, but also for her readiness to share some of her own experiences as an anthropologist with me. Furthermore, I want to express my gratitude to Sabine Strasser and Kathrin Oester for their persistent encouragement in pursuing this book project and to all my colleagues at the Institute of Social Anthropology at the University of Bern, who formed an invaluable support base – both academically and socially. A heartfelt thank you to Jelena Tošić,

Gerhild Perl, Julia Rehsmann, Veronika Siegl, Darcy Alexandra, Martha-Cecilia Dietrich, Laura Coppens and Michaela Schäuble. I was lucky enough to have two anthropologists whose approaches to ethnographic theory and writing formed a great source of inspiration to my own thinking examine the thesis underlying this book project. I thank Michael D. Jackson and Ruth Behar for their careful reading and commenting of my work. I would also like to thank Veena Das for the inspiring and encouraging exchange throughout her stays in Bern, allowing me to sharpen my analytical focus on the everyday. This book project would not have been possible without the generous encouragement and advice from the EASA book series editor Aleksandar Bošković, as well as three anonymous reviewers, all of whom took the time to read and comment on my manuscript. In times of accelerated academic pressures I do not take the labour going into such thorough feedback for granted, and thank them for their support.

Finally, I want to thank all those people close to my heart who have travelled this journey with me: Sahra and Sagal Mohamed for becoming my sisters; Christine Moderbacher for late-night or early-morning Skype sessions and for accompanying me throughout the way; Eva Lindtner, Abdi Mujeeb, Christine Esterbauer and Ursula Wagner for friendship and inspiration; Debbie Welsh for providing a home base in Melbourne; and finally my husband Paul Reade for being there with me and for me and for making me laugh when I felt like giving up. Last but not least I want to thank my family, who have let me move to the other end of the world and to whom so much of my writing is directed: my father Dennis Lems, my mother Ingeborg Lientscher and my brothers and sisters Florian, Eva, Lisa, Christian and Jonathan Lems.

Introduction
Greeting Xamar

After Mohamed disembarked from the plane and set foot in the city he had left behind thirty years ago, he knelt down on the tarmac to kiss the ground. Fellow passengers gave him puzzled looks, awkward giggles, smiles. It was his way of greeting *Xamar*, 'the red one', as Somalis often like to call Mogadishu.

Figure 0.1 *Stray bullet on a stony path. Image courtesy of Mohamed Ibrahim*

Over the past two decades the colour red has come to take on a new symbolic meaning for Somalis. It represents the violence, fear and terror that have devastated the country, driven more than a million people out of Somalia and led to the breakdown of the government, as well as to ever-shifting alliances, and attacks and counterattacks, among clans and sub-clans. In 1981, only nineteen years old, and after months of struggling to gain a passport, Mohamed migrated to Australia – partly because he had met an Australian woman, a young nurse who had come to Somalia as a member of a health team assisting internally displaced refugees, and partly because he sensed the upcoming civil war. Mohamed was amongst the first Somalis to settle in Melbourne. In the thirty years that followed he married the Australian woman he had fallen in love with, had four children with her, studied, became a telecommunications expert and made Melbourne his home. During this time, with the war uprooting his elderly parents and his brothers and sisters, many of whom he brought to Melbourne, Somalia as a place that lived and breathed had slipped away into a shadow area of his mind. While not entirely out of his life, Somalia had taken on the shape of a *somewhere*.

Around 2009, however, something changed. Somalia began crawling back into Mohamed's thoughts. Its aches and pains began to preoccupy him. It was time, he thought, to look for cures – and such a search needed the strength and energy of every Somali, old and young, man and woman, in the country and outside of it. He gave up his job in Melbourne in exchange for the (financial and personal) insecurity that came with the role of an IT advisor to the Somali transitional government. This government was in desperate need of educated people like Mohamed, driven by the motivation to rebuild Somalia and holding a passport from a Western country that allowed them to travel, connect and negotiate with other countries. From now on Mohamed was constantly on the move: from country to country, from UN conference to UN conference, from one international meeting to the next. But despite leading the life of a globetrotter, none of his travels took him back to the place all his thoughts and effort were directed towards. Because of the continuous instability in Mogadishu and the risk for politicians to move about freely, most Somali ministers operated from neighbouring countries. So although Somalia was at the centre of Mohamed's thoughts and actions, initially his position did not require him to return to his country. In 2011, however, he was overcome by an urge to see and confront Mogadishu as it had become. Despite the dangers of travelling in such a lawless place, and despite the continuing threat of attacks by Islamist al-Shabaab and Hizbul Islam rebels, Mohamed decided to embark on this return journey. Walking through the devastated streets and buildings, he took photos – images he would take back with him to Melbourne.

Back in Australia, sitting in a small coffee shop at Melbourne University, Mohamed showed me these photos. In 2009, when I was trying to find my way around Melbourne and looking for Somalis interested to work with me on their life stories, he was amongst the first people I had met. In fact, he was amongst the first people in Melbourne I became friends with. Looking for organizations to provide an entry point into the community, I had come across Mohamed as the chairman of the Somali Cultural Association. While none of the organizations I contacted paved my way into the field, my friendship with Mohamed marked the beginning of my research taking shape. The photos of his journeys he shared with me during his stays in Melbourne, or in emails laconically signed 'the nomad', began to form a bridge between us and shape some of the main themes that would come to preoccupy me in my research.

Sitting in the university coffee shop, flicking through the photos he had taken in Mogadishu on his laptop, he paused and pointed. 'Look!' he said to me. 'I really like this one.' I was surprised that he said he *liked* the photo. It depicts one of the many bullets that, as he told me, cover the city's ground. Against the backdrop of a grey gravel road, the bullet looks tiny, almost lost and innocent. Laughing, he explained that because of their whistling noise people in Mogadishu have jokingly come to call them 'Yusuf'. Ssuf, ssuf, ssuf they go …

But for Mohamed the bullet was not what moved him about the picture. 'Look at the ground it lies on,' he told me and pointed at the road. 'These rocks, they are so special, so specific for this part of Mogadishu, that even if I hadn't been the one to take this photo, I would have recognized it.' 'And the bullet?' I asked. 'They are everywhere', Mohamed said. 'Even if you are not looking for them, you will find them everywhere.'

While I had read the photo as another testimony to the destruction of Mogadishu, Mohamed was preoccupied with the sense of place it depicted. The stones that moved him to take the picture are the stones that cover a road that leads from the city to the ocean. That road stands for the light and easy times Mohamed experienced in Mogadishu as a teenager, a time before the Barre regime's violence against dissident clans, and a time he remembers in terms of the city's beauty and sophistication. It was the road he promenaded along with friends on warm summer evenings, when people flocked towards the beach for picnics and games. Because the beach was such a popular place for all inhabitants of Mogadishu to meet and spend time together, and the road the best way to walk there from the city, Mohamed stresses that anyone who has lived there will recognize the stones as part of the road that leads towards the Indian Ocean. Far from being another sad document of the breakdown of Somalia, the photo evokes a sense of past unity, of the days when people from all clans literally walked down the same path. It calls upon the memories of all Mogadishians, those who still live there and those whom the war has displaced, and it does so through *place*. Just as Mohamed, much to the bewilderment of the people around him, had kissed the tarmac to greet the city he had left behind, so did his photo embrace the sense of place that had carried his being-at-home in Mogadishu.

If a stony road in a city left behind so many years ago has the power to evoke such a strong sense of attachment to (or perhaps even love for) place, what is it that underlies this feeling? Is it what some theorists have described as 'the power of place' (Agnew and Duncan 1989; Hayden 1997; De Blij 2009)? Or is it, perhaps, the opposite? Does the strength of Mohamed's image derive from the very sense of displacement it depicts? In a world in which people like Mohamed (the 'nomad') can be in Geneva today for a conference and in Mali tomorrow, at another, and at a meeting in Dubai the day after, and in which people like me can move to the other side of the globe to do research with people who have also left their home-places behind, are homelessness and uprootedness, as John Berger (1984: 55) has suggested, the 'quintessential experience' of our time? Then again, how can *dis*placement in and for itself explain the abiding strength of stones on a road in a place like Mogadishu that has witnessed so much grief?

Mohamed's story of the image draws attention to the complex dynamics between emplacement and displacement as lived and felt in people's everyday lives. It raises questions about the links between place and the sensual, place and memory, place and movement, and place and the larger world. Mohamed's strong attachment to place also evokes questions about the common portrayal of people who have experienced displacement as homelessness as a being out of place, or, literally, as placelessness; it challenges us to ask how people actually shape and reshape places, particularly in the face of displacement, and how they negotiate their position in relation to the wider world.

Storying Place

Mohamed's photograph evokes a sense of the lived tension between emplacement and displacement. His image and reflections form a direct link to the two people whose lives and stories form the core of this book: Halima Mohamed and Omar Farah Dhollawa, two Somalis, who, over the course of two years, have told me their life stories. In weaving its way through their ups and downs, victories and losses, hopes and bereavements, this book looks at how emplacement and displacement are felt and understood in the everyday lives of these two individuals.

In many ways this book is anchored in the power of storytelling. It is through stories that humans travel their inner landscapes with others and thereby move them beyond their inner selves, and it is through stories that these landscapes morph and transcend and receive a presence in the here and now. I was not just a silent listener, the passive recipient of life stories. Rather, in travelling through these landscapes together, in letting them leak into the present, we allowed our lives to touch each other. Storying, the means through which we bring our inner world out and take the outer world in, has the ability to form, transform and change our experiences of things. It is through storying that we overcome our separateness, that we work towards common ground and that we rework reality. Through telling each other stories, through walking and talking Melbourne, Mogadishu, Puntland, Dubai and Vienna together, my understanding of emplacement and displacement took shape. In order to attend to this crucial moment of ethnographic work – to come to an understanding of meaning as a lived intersubjective reality, as the product of a dialogue that includes the material, imaginative and emotional landscapes of human relationships – some of my own stories will inevitably come to enter this book.

In sharp contrast to the grand themes, statistics and models that mark much research in the field of forced migration, the zooming in on two individuals' lifeworlds allows for a close look at the particularity and everydayness of being-in-place. This is not to suggest that Halima's and Omar's stories do not have the power to speak for more than themselves. As philosopher Jeff Malpas stresses, 'for the most part, it is the place of the ordinary and the everyday in and through which what is extraordinary shines forth' (Malpas 2012: 14). The following travels through stories will show how, through an engagement with the ordinary activities around which human life takes shape, the world at large comes into view. Throughout this journey, Mohamed's photographs accompany and pave the way for my thinking, writing and storying. The sensitivity, beauty and poetry of his way of seeing and depicting Mogadishu form junctures, or crossroads, between chapters that allow for a moment of reflection and a chance to gather, let go of or re-emplace thoughts. Above all, Mohamed's images of all the lost, ruined, reawakening and stubbornly persisting places he came across work as a skilful reminder of some of the deep-seated layers of emplacement and displacement that cannot always easily be expressed in words. Yet, it is perhaps through stories of displacement that emplacement best comes to the fore. In the last stanza of his poem 'Little Gidding', T.S. Eliot suggests that it is in the human nature to venture out into the world and explore it. He notes that it is precisely because of these outward movements that we are able to look at the place we have left behind with new eyes and understand it 'for the first time'.

Two People, Two Places

Australia and Somalia, two countries which, each in their own ways, have movement and migration at the core of their foundation stories, are intriguing places around which to frame a project that examines the dynamics of emplacement and displacement in a world of movement.

Somalis are often pictured to represent a double sense of movement: with around 60 per cent of the population organized along nomadic, non-sedentary clan-structures, identifying a place of 'original' territorial and cultural belonging takes on an entirely new meaning. With nomadic pastoralism and trade as the main forms of livelihood, mobility has been a crucial element for the Somali-speaking region over many centuries. In traditional stories and oral history accounts, migration is narrated as central to Somaliness itself. In these stories, Somalis speak of their migration from Aden to the Horn of Africa about one thousand years ago, but also of migratory movements within the country (Lewis 1999: 21–23; Kleist 2004: 2). Thirty years of war have led to the movement of a large number of Somalis all over the world. Ever since the breakdown of the military government of Siyaad Barre in 1991, Somalia has been without a central government. Warlordism, famine and ethnic conflict have turned more than one million people into refugees, with a third generation of Somalis growing up in exile. Because of the (historical and present) importance of migratory movement in the lives of Somalis, many scholars have highlighted the ways mobility determines questions of identity and belonging (e.g. Griffiths 2002; Horst 2006; Huisman et al. 2011).

In Australia, a nation of migrants that was built on the back of the violent displacement of its indigenous inhabitants, the search for an understanding of emplacement also needs to dig deep. For while Australia likes to celebrate itself as an immigrant nation, the question of who is allowed in and who has to stay out, who can lay claim to the place and who cannot, is highly contested (Hage 1998). Australia is amongst the few countries worldwide committed to resettling a substantial number of refugees living in protracted situations every year, but the question of who of the 22.5 million refugees worldwide is 'deserving' of resettlement in Australia has become a highly politicized issue. Forced migrants, who cannot or do not want to await the highly unlikely chance of being amongst the 1 per cent selected for resettlement by the UNHCR every year and take charge of their situations by coming to Australia (be it on leaky boats or by plane on tourist visas) and applying for asylum onshore, are portrayed as security threats and as queue jumpers who take away places from the deserving. Indeed, Australia has gone to great lengths to keep asylum seekers, marked as the ultimate outsiders, from laying claim to the place. Since 2001, the country has used draconian measures to prevent boat refugees from entering Australian territory. Reflecting a longstanding fear of invasion from the north, government responses treat asylum seekers arriving by boat as a serious threat (Mares 2001; Neumann 2015). Boat refugees are intercepted at sea and either turned back or sent to offshore detention centres on remote islands beyond the Australian migration zone, where they languish under extremely harsh conditions for indefinite periods of time. The treatment of refugees in Australia is thus marked by a sharp divide between people coming through the government's official resettlement programme and asylum seekers arriving by boat. While the former are deemed deserving the protection and attention of the Australian public and receive generous support, the latter are treated as threats in need of control and containment.

That Somalis were permitted to immigrate and that Halima, Mohamed and Omar made their way to Melbourne were the result of a complex set of political processes. It was only from the 1990s onwards that a shift in policy focus allowed for the resettlement of refugees from the Horn of Africa, most of whom settled in the state of Victoria, specifically in and around Melbourne. The 2011 census showed the number of Somalia-born living in Victoria to be 3,061, an increase of almost 17 per cent to the census figures from 2006 (ABS 2012). With the backlash against Muslim migrants after 9/11 (Poynting et al. 2004) and the complication of family reunion processes, however, the possibilities for Somalis to migrate to or become resettled in Australia have increasingly narrowed. Those who try to circumvent these exclusionary policies by embarking on perilous journeys to reach Australia by boat are confronted with the flipside of Australia's Janus-faced approach to refugees, as they are shipped to offshore detention camps or returned to Indonesia, Sri Lanka or Vietnam.

The two main places this book moves in and around, it seems, are united through images of displacement; Halima's and Omar's stories, however, suggest otherwise. While born in Somalia, neither of them lived the life of a nomad, not in Somalia, and not during the many years they spent on the move, looking for a place to settle down. Although both were admitted to Australia on humanitarian grounds, neither of them regarded themselves to be refugees. Refugeeness, Omar often told me, was nothing more than an obstacle, an extra weight that kept dragging people down. From the very first time I met Omar, he told me that Australia was his home. He arrived in Melbourne in 1989, shortly before the outbreak of the civil war in Somalia. Like Mohamed, he left the country with the combination of an adventurous spirit and fear that the already precarious political situation would deteriorate. In Australia, Omar studied international development and married a Somali woman from Mogadishu. Together with their five children they live in Hopper's Crossing, an outer suburb about 30 km south-west of Melbourne's centre.

Melbourne is where Omar locates his home now – and he invests all his time and effort to shape the place in ways that will allow him and fellow Somalis to become an accepted part of it. After years of struggle to find employment and watching many of his highly qualified Somali friends getting turned down time and again, Omar founded an NGO, Horn-Afrik, an employment, training and advocacy organization. He also works as a freelance interpreter, translating Somali documents into English, or government announcements into Somali. Because of his ability to articulate his community's concerns, and also because of his considerate nature, he has become a well-respected elder and spokesperson within the wider community of Somalis in Melbourne.

Like Omar, Halima is also actively involved in making the Somali community feel at home in Melbourne. She arrived in Australia ten years ago with three of her children and her adopted son. Because of her involvement in the government, she had been forced to leave Mogadishu in 1991 when the Barre regime collapsed and guerrillas from rival clans began to systematically target members of her clan. In the chaos of fleeing Somalia, Halima lost her husband, and for over a decade she did not know that he was still alive. Her own exodus led her, her four children and her sister's son through many different countries and finally to the United Arab Emirates, where she stayed for twelve years. After years of being in a constant state of limbo in a country where she did not have a legal status and on the verge of being deported back to Somalia, she was granted a family reunion visa to live in Australia. Over the past ten years, she has developed a strong sense of connection to her neighbourhood in the suburb of Maidstone, an area that is often portrayed as conflict-ridden and unsafe. All these problems, however, do not keep Halima from being attached to this place. Soon after her arrival in Melbourne she began looking for ways to help and strengthen the Somali community in her corner of the city. Once a week Halima works for a multicultural children's playgroup. She has also set up a small group of Somali women to run the canteen in a school in Kensington, a suburb close to where she lives, and organizes sewing classes for African women.

Without anticipating the details of the stories that form the heart of this book, these brief profiles of Halima and Omar and the places in which they are located already foreshadow some of the core dynamics. The efforts Halima and Omar invest in making Melbourne their home suggests that it is not their experience of displacement but rather their relentless struggle for *emplacement* that links them. These movements towards emplacement underscore Tim Ingold's suggestion that life is a movement of opening, not closing. Rather than getting stuck in a state of inescapable displacement, Halima's and Omar's narratives speak for the power of the story to move beyond these limitations. Life, Ingold (2011: 4) writes, 'just keeps on going, finding a way through the myriad of things that form, persist and break up in its currents'. It is exactly this, human life in its openness, in all its ambiguities and potentials, which forms my interest in anthropology. In a similar vein the tensions between people's need for attachment and boundedness, on the one side, and movement and openness, on the other, mark the main threads that run through this book.

The Topos of the Field

If I were to map out the site where my fieldwork took place, my field would not have much in common with the ethnographic field in the traditional sense of the term: rather than going on a journey to study 'a people' in their home-environment, my research only moved within the realms of three people and their lives. Not only are their original home-places far away, but the fact that they have been transformed, if not destroyed, by decades of violence complicates the concept of home as rooted in place.

While my research took place in Melbourne, Halima, Mohamed and Omar, in telling me their stories, moved the field beyond our immediate location and towards places they had left behind, but which, despite all, had not left them yet. Through their stories, these memory places were reawakened; they came back to life and in the moment of their telling often felt present and formed a lively part of the here and now. This here and now could be in Halima's living room, with her daughters Sagal and Sahra pottering around the house and joining us every now and then. This here and now could also be in Omar's small office at the ground level of a twenty-odd-story housing commission flat in Melbourne's inner suburb of Carlton, the photo of his children on top of the filing cabinet, like silent observers of the stories their father told me. Sometimes this here and now was at a Somali wedding or a fundraiser Halima or Omar had invited me to join, or in a mall in Footscray, where Halima and I were looking for herbs that smelled of Mogadishu. Sometimes, this here and now was in an email from Mohamed, 'the nomad', sending me photos from Tokyo or Abu Dhabi. Or, on Mohamed's occasional visits to Melbourne, this here and now could take the shape of a walk through the very mall I had strolled through with Halima, the 'Somali mall', a place that, as he told me, made him feel like at home – home in Somalia, and not home here, where we were walking and talking.

The multilayered character of the places where my research took place raises the question of how far we can actually speak of an ethnographic field. Alongside which boundaries or limitations does it constitute itself? Where can it be placed? The question of the whereness of the ethnographic field is complex and needs to be spelled out in more detail, as it is intimately linked to notions of place. In anthropology, the question of the topos of the ethnographic field has been discussed intensively over the last two decades by many different writers and from many different angles (e.g. Fog Olwig and Hastrup 1997; Gupta and Ferguson 1997a, 1997b; Coleman and Collins 2006). They tried to critique the way the field had been thought of previously – a self-imagination, which, although deeply rooted in place, did not take itself very seriously.

A famous line in the introduction to Malinowski's *Argonauts of the Western Pacific*, a book that lay the grounds for anthropology as a 'fieldwork science', has much to say about the discipline's strong, yet ambiguous and often unarticulated, connection to place:

> Imagine yourself suddenly set down surrounded by all your gear, alone on a tropical beach close to a native village, while the launch or dinghy that has brought you sails away out of sight. (Malinowksi 1932: 4)

'Imagine yourself', Malinowski tells his readers, and thereby invites them to join him in a timeless landscape that seems to mirror the people that inhabit it. At the same time, Malinowski's 'Imagine yourself' invites the readers to join him on a journey that has taken him away from the familiar and known hereness of home and towards the distant, exotic thereness of a tropical island-world. The island-world, an unnamed village somewhere in the Western Pacific's Trobriand Islands, is where the 'natives' seem to have their 'proper' place. At the same time, the remoteness of the island, the strenuous effort it took to get there, and the lonely researcher, who was thrown into the unknown and watches his last connection to home sail out of sight, map the anthropologist into his proper position, too. As Arjun Appadurai (1988a: 16) points out in his critique of the ethnographic fieldwork tradition, the field of the classical anthropologist is defined by his own voluntary displacement, while those he sets out to study are pushed into the position of the involuntarily localized 'other'. Malinowski's introductory notes suggest that the people he had come to study had their proper place in the 'native village', but that it may in fact have been the anthropologist who was in desperate need of the mappable and calculable boundaries of the 'terrains', 'regions', 'areas', 'landscapes', 'environments', 'centres', or 'peripheries' he had set out to study. For without the 'natives' mappable position and the anthropologist's displacement, what is it that defines (and confines) the field?

Before anthropologists came to ask this question, however, generations of ethnographers followed in Malinowski's footsteps, celebrating their journeys in and out of the field as a rite of passage, an initiation ritual into the academic ranks (Gupta and Ferguson 1997a: 16). With his famous introductory lines, Malinowski created an image of the lone, white, male fieldworker, living among native villagers, an image that had the power to form the discipline's self-imagination to such a degree that George Stocking (1992: 218) has described it as an 'archetype'. Within this vein, culture came to be seen as something fixed into a specific territory, and place became merely a tool for poetic reminiscences, or a backdrop of ethnographic accounts. While place has played a fundamental role from the beginning of anthropology as a discipline, it did so more as a framing device. As a concept, however, place was not critically scrutinized for a long time.

With the growing importance of global mobility and with the critique of the colonial nature of the ethnographic field tradition, the simple dualism of 'them' being there and 'us' being here came under scrutiny. The end of colonialism, the increasing number of 'them' being among 'us' and the problematization of this 'us' threw anthropology's self-conception into question. Key publications from the early 1980s, such as Edward Said's *Orientalism* (1979) and Benedict Anderson's *Imagined Communities* (1983), as well as the turn towards interpretation and reflexivity, led the discipline to rethink its traditional placement within the field – and also within the wider world.

From the early 1990s, and inspired by the spatial turn in human geography, a number of anthropologists began to explicitly tackle concepts of space and place. Following on from first discussions that focused on the intersection of place and representation, there emerged a distinct group of thinkers who came to be the face of the spatial turn in anthropology, a turn that unfolded across the social sciences and humanities (Warf and Arias 2009). These thinkers include Arjun Appadurai, who kicked off the debate on the boundedness of the ethnographic field and who subsequently studied mobile and global phenomena (Appadurai 1988a, 1988b, 1996); Akhil Gupta and James Ferguson, whose critique of the location of the anthropological fieldwork tradition lay the groundwork for an investigation of the links between power and place in anthropology (Gupta and Ferguson 1992, 1997a, 1997b); Margaret Rodman, who in taking a 'hard look' at places, showed them as politicized, culturally relative, historically specific, multiple social constructions (Rodman 1992); Liisa Malkki, who in studying refugees threw anthropological ways of creating intimate and 'natural' links between people and places into question (Malkki 1995a, 1995b); and Renato Rosaldo, who voiced an early critique about the way anthropologists, in constructing a field, had come to map certain problems or themes onto specific places and peoples (Rosaldo 1988). While the body of work they produced was diverse and cannot be subsumed under the label of 'anthropology of space', it signalled the beginning of a new focus (Ward 2003: 86).

In stating that this book cannot be anchored in a field in the classical ethnographic sense of the term, I am not positioning it outside the boundaries of the anthropological discipline. Rather, these boundaries have shifted and transformed to such a degree that by now the topos of the field almost needs to be looked for in its very displacement. Yet, to think of this book as grounded in a free-floating or placeless ethnographic encounter would not do justice to the importance of immediate physical and material settings on social life and thus to the way research takes shape. To speak of a fieldless ethnography would therefore go too far and deny the power and strength of being-in-place.

The ethnographic field that Omar, Mohamed, Halima and I were moving this research through must not be thought of as confined by boundary-lines in the way one would imagine the lines that mark the edge of a sports ground. Building on the existential tradition that considers place in its lived immediacy, I suggest imagining it as the conglomeration of specific places, confined not by a border, but by a horizon. A horizon, Martin Heidegger stresses, much like the boundary in the classical Greek sense of the term *(peras)*, is not the point at which something stops. Instead, the boundary 'is that from which something *begins its presencing*' (Heidegger 1975: 154). To think of the field as confined by the openness of the horizon, which allows for things to be moved, formed and understood rather than incarcerated, is to allow for movement to be an intrinsic part of it. At the same time, however, such an understanding must not lose sight of the very physical settings from where things take place or, as Heidegger puts it, '*wo etwas sein Wesen beginnt*' (from where something begins its presencing).

In locating this book within the settings of a topos, enclosed along the line of a horizon, I am moving within and beyond the field as it is currently being thought of in anthropological debates. For the spatial turn in anthropology had two core effects: on the one hand, it allowed for a profound problematization of the field as the pregiven locus for anthropological research, the settings of which I have attempted to outline. Following on from Appadurai's (1988b: 37) suggestion that much ethnographic writing tends to 'incarcerate natives' in places, anthropologists began to concentrate on the constructedness of the field and look for alternative methods – methods that would not, by default, root people in places (Malkki 1992; Fog Olwig and Hastrup 1997; Gupta and Ferguson 1997a, 1997b). As a result, anthropologists began to loosen the fixation and boundedness of the field and let movement become an intrinsic part of their self-understanding.

The spatial turn also opened the doors for a new theoretical and empirical focus on the connections between space, power and identity. Directly related to the project of dislocating the anthropological field, some anthropologists opted for a close look at the production of space through questions of power, domination and territoriality (e.g. Bammer 1994; Malkki 1995a; Appadurai 1996; Castells 1996). Inspired by philosophers such as Michel de Certeau (1984), Michel Foucault (1986) and Henri Lefebvre (1991), who wrote about the use of space as a technique of power and social control, anthropologists began to question the meaning of place. They called for a change in focus from stable, rooted and mappable identities to fluid, transitory and migratory movements. The result of this development was the acceptance of *displacement* as the new trope through which anthropologists came to look at the world. Because this focus played a major role in the way space and place have come to be dealt with in anthropology, and because it can be seen as the premise from which much of my thinking in this book departs, I continue sketching the field by outlining some of the main ideas and debates that delineate it.

Space Travellers

Our age has often been characterized in terms of relentless movement and displacement. In *The Origins of Totalitarianism*, Hannah Arendt (1971: vii) describes the physiognomy of the twentieth century as typified by 'homelessness on an unprecedented scale' and 'rootlessness to an unprecedented depth'. Exploring this feeling of rootlessness as a theoretical opportunity to move beyond rigid and exclusionary political realities, many modern thinkers have described themselves and their work in terms of borderless movement. In this vein, Ian Chambers (1994: 14) suggests that in 'the extensive and multiple worlds of the modern city we, too, become nomads', and in the same spirit Zygmunt Bauman (1992: 693) stresses that we live today 'in a nomadic world, in the universe of migration'. Being in the late modern age, Angelika Bammer (1994: xii) claims, is by definition 'to be an Other: displaced'.

The uprootedness often connected with forced migration has led some intellectuals to celebrate the refugee as paradigmatic for a time of deterritorialization (Deleuze and Guattari 1986). Refugees have come to be the symbolic figures of an age of movement and fluctuation. They challenge established notions of a 'national order of things' (Malkki 1995b), of a world that can be neatly mapped and of cultures that are deeply rooted in places that 'belong' to them. Within these lines, the refugee has come to be celebrated as a figure that embodies a sense of nomadic movement and who resists any form of categorization. In anthropology, the symbolic power of displacement has come to be of paradigmatic importance for the way place is conceptualized. From the 1980s onwards, and with the growing acceptance that the idea of studying people in their stable, 'local' environments did not meet the reality of the encounters ethnographers had in the field, the number of publications on refugees and migrants increased. In focusing on hypermobile people, anthropologists have attempted to move beyond the discursive conventions that see people as rooted in place and describe the loss of home as an incurable ailment. Refusing to be pinned down, refugees dismantle the national metaphysics and challenge cultural and national essentialisms (Malkki 1992: 36). Moving away from static and essentialist understandings of space and place, the figure of the refugee symbolizes the idea that people are more mobile and interconnected than ever. Rather than yearning for an immutable original place of belonging, in the last decades refugees and migrants have therefore come to be depicted as active agents whose rhizomic identities allow them to move beyond the incarceration of 'natives' or 'citizens' in places. With the spatial turn the metaphor of the root has become replaced by the image of the rhizome, a stem that is capable of producing the shoot and root systems of a new plant. In *Capitalism and Schizophrenia*, Gilles Deleuze and Félix Guattari develop the idea of the rhizome as a means of working against the metaphor of a tree setting roots, which represents the search for the original source of things. Rhizomes, then, stand for a way of positioning ourselves in the world that overcomes the immovability of the firmly rooted tree:

> We're tired of trees. We should stop believing in trees, roots, and radicles. They've made us suffer too much. All of arborescent culture is founded on them, from biology to linguistics. Nothing is beautiful or loving or political aside from underground stems and aerial roots, adventitious growths and rhizomes. (Deleuze and Guattari 1987:15)

Inspired by this 'treeless', rhizomic imagination of our age, many anthropologists focused on movement, deterritorialization and globalization. Thinking beyond rigid national and territorial boundaries and the search for other, more flexible or nomadic ways of being has not just become a theoretical task, but also a political project.

In a world that continues to be interspersed with exclusionary practices, anthropological debates have moved their attention away from roots and towards global space or global flows. Manuel Castells (1996), for example, speaks of the 'network society', in which the 'space of flows' begins to overtake the 'space of places'. In such a society everything is ordered through flows – of goods, of people, of services and of geographic regions. And in such a society, Castells argues, places cease to exist, because their inner meanings become absorbed by the network. In a similar vein, Arjun Appadurai (1996) famously speaks of 'global ethnoscapes' to describe the slippery and non-localized social, territorial, and cultural reproduction of group identity in an age of globalization. According to Zygmunt Bauman, this age of globalization can be characterized as a 'liquid modernity'. He imagines the stage of modernity we are currently living through in terms of fluids that constantly change their shape and can neither bind time nor space. In such a world of fluids, Bauman (2000: 2) argues, places lose their inner meaning because after all, they only exist 'for a moment' until they change shape again.

The shift to seeing contemporary people as 'migrants of identity' (Rapport and Dawson 1998), marked by the fluidity of time and space, has led to the loss of place as a metaphor for identity and culture (Escobar 2001: 146–47). Rather than being bounded to a timeless and unmovable place, people are now thought of as continuously moving through a flexible, open-ended and contested *space*. Humans and their lives have been set in motion; they have become space travellers – to such a degree that Slavoj Žižek (2007) poses the question of whether we are actually still living in a world. In an age in which subjectivity is celebrated as rootless, migratory, nomadic and hybrid, Žižek argues, the links that attach the mind to its fixed material embodiment seem to have become replaced by the logic of the computer, which allows us to migrate between endless possibilities.

The spatial turn in anthropology quite literally did what the term announces: it led to a radical shift towards space – and thereby lost sight of place. The de-essentialization of place was crucially important for the reformulation of a discipline wary of being complicit in the creation of exclusionary boundaries and practices. Yet, the question arises of what happened to place within the fluid space of a late modern world, a world in which trees have become boring and anthropologists look at the earth from outer space. In the wake of a deterritorialized dream of (non)belonging, we all seem to have become displaced. But are we really all refugees, as philosopher

Giorgio Agamben (1995) famously suggested? Where would this leave people like Halima and Omar, who came to Australia as so-called humanitarian entrants, yet refuse to see themselves as refugees? If displacement hits the nerve of our time, this should encourage questions about how it is constituted – not just as a theoretical and analytical category, but as lived and thought of in people's everyday lives.

The persistence of places in Halima's and Omar's stories and everyday lives moved my thinking away from an anthropology that locates humans in the blurry vastness of space. Their stories led me to move back towards a – albeit re-conceptualized – place-based focus. While places cannot be seen as bounded, immobile territories, place must not be disregarded altogether. This perspective is informed by the recognition that as place continues to be of such importance in people's lives, anthropologists cannot bypass it by creating ever-tightening theoretical categories. My perspective on place can be read within the lines of existential and phenomenological thinkers such as Martin Heidegger, Edward Casey, Jeff Malpas and Gaston Bachelard, who, by focusing on lived experience, have all embraced the idea that there is no being outside of place. This book can also be read within the context of a wider anthropological revalidation of place (e.g. Weiner 1991; Basso 1996; Feld and Basso 1996; Kirby 2009; Gregorič and Repič 2016). In recent years, a noticeable number of anthropologists writing on global and migratory phenomena, including prominent authors associated with the spatial turn, have called for more balanced views on place, movement and deterritorialization (e.g. Appadurai 2006; Rapport and Williksen 2010; Coleman and Von Hellermann 2011). Yet, while there has been talk about an impending 'topographic turn' (Hastrup 2005: 145) in anthropology and while the voices calling for a stronger focus on phenomenology and materiality in migration studies are becoming louder, anthropologists still seem to be reluctant to initiate a full-fledged shift from space to place. Part of this might have to do with the sense of backwardness and exclusion place has become associated with. While in anthropology the turn towards space was of crucial importance for the de-essentialization of place, it came with the side effect of creating a deep chasm between theory and lived experience. For although researchers have gone to great pains to develop theoretical concepts that emphasize the importance of globalized, transnational, rhizomic or nomadic spaces and identities, this treatment of space is essentially metaphorical and is often bypassed in migrants' everyday lives, where the particularity of place continues to be of importance.

Towards a Topology of Being

Sitting in the famous Melbourne coffee shop Brunetti on a busy Saturday afternoon whilst discussing the photographs Mohamed had brought with him, our conversation touched upon his migration to Melbourne. Sipping on his coffee, he tried to convey to me what it had been like to leave his home country and move to an unknown part of the world. One particular memory of this time, he said, had never left him. In 1981, waiting for a connecting flight to Melbourne after disembarking in Singapore from his first ever flight, Mohamed was struck by the strangeness of the place. Stepping outside the airport building, he could feel the heat clinging to his skin. 'I felt the wind and the humidity,' he told me. 'And I never knew what humidity was – all these little things you get used to. Where I grew up there was no humidity because it was dry in the morning and in the afternoon it got cooler. So to me, I couldn't understand: what was this? Why am I feeling sticky?' Laughing, he added that upon leaving Somalia, even little things like the sunset reminded him of the fact that he was somewhere else. Looking at the sun going down in Singapore, he was so overwhelmed by its size that he thought he must have come to the end of the world. 'I guess that was because I was close to the equator,' he explained. 'Anyway, this thing was huge and red, and all this comes to me when I think about it now.'

This brief, seemingly banal moment, which Mohamed told me that afternoon in the coffee shop, has much to say about the perspectives on place, displacement and storytelling that frame this book. When Mohamed stepped out of the world of the airport, the place immediately made itself felt. Through the humidity on his skin and the wind in the air he encountered some of its features and habits – habits he did not yet grasp. At the same time as the place made itself felt, it also created an utter sense of displacement within him. *All these little things you get used to* but were so strange and unknown made him realize how much he had been part and parcel of another place, a place he had left behind. And all these ways of being – the being-in-place, as well as the being-out-of-place – were so strong that thirty years later, sitting in a Melbourne café, they came back to him. Mohamed's story suggests that place does not cease to exist, even if it is experienced as a sense of deep and utter disruption (or displacement). It is always there, where we are. Because we cannot escape its presence, it plays into the way we see and engage with the world. We come to the world and keep returning to it, Edward Casey

(2000: 17–18) suggests, as already placed there. Humans, he stresses, are always already in place, never not emplaced. So what, then, is place – or the *in* of being-in-place?

Although the spatial turn in anthropology, as well as in the social sciences and humanities in general, set out to re-conceptualize space and place, it did not make the two terms any clearer. Trying to grasp the concept of place after the spatial turn, Edward Relph (2008: 5) notes, is 'like walking into the aftermath of an academic explosion'. While there has been much talk about place, the focus has tended to be not so much on place itself, but on the boundlessness of space and time and on the spatial politics place is believed to be a result of. With its main interest in power dynamics, space is often seen as the unarticulated assumption of a neutral and pregiven tabula rasa onto which the particularities of culture and history become inscribed, and of which place is the result (Casey 2000: 14). Following Casey's suggestion of a paradigmatic shift towards space in modern thinking, the current fascination with homelessness, exile and displacement is perhaps not surprising. He points out that the disregard of place in modern philosophy had massive impacts on Western theoretical thinking and specifically on the way the human became imagined as an inconsequential dot within the immensity of the universe (Casey 1997b: 292). In a world that is made up of fluid, boundless and indifferent open space, humans have become space travellers. Roots have become replaced by routes (Friedman 2002) and the human subject is left moving back and forth within the vastness of the universe without any abiding place to rest or dwell. Yet if, as in Mohamed's case, even the stickiness of humidity on the skin, a sunset, or stones on a path can have such a strong effect, how then can we think of this world as an indifferent space, as a placeless universe? Does not such a view also preclude the intimacy of *all the little things you get used to* – and with it the possibilities for people like Mohamed, Halima and Omar to feel a meaningful part of anywhere again?

Just how quickly people are capable of turning the strangeness of an unknown place into something meaningful became apparent as Mohamed told me about his first months in Melbourne. Sitting in the Brunetti café, he told me how he had arrived in winter, and not being used to the cold and the language, he had felt isolated and lonely. He said that he feared he would never be able to understand this place, that he had felt intimidated by the smallest things, such as the public transport system. The sheer incomprehensibility of the way the trams, trains and busses created a web of links from one part of Melbourne to the other had made him feel lost. Rather than letting these negative feelings overtake him, however, he felt the urge to leap into action and work against this sense of alienation. He managed to do so by taking on a job that required expert knowledge of the city. 'Looking back at it now, I don't think I could do that, but I managed to do it,' Mohamed said, laughing. 'I worked on the tram. After just four or five months I started to work on them.' I asked Mohamed what kind of work he did on the tram. 'Before the trams became automated like they are now, there used to be conductors who sold tickets in the tram. So I did that,' Mohamed said. 'It was an amazing job. But I was reflecting on it the other day. I thought: Could I do it now? I don't think I could. I had such a big confidence, because I didn't know the place and to do that job you have to know the streets by heart. Because people would ask me: "Can you please tell me when we are at Smith Street?", or something. But I didn't know! I myself didn't know where Smith Street was.' Looking back at his first moves through Melbourne, Mohamed was amazed by how confidently he had tackled this new place. By addressing the incomprehensibility of the place directly, by unravelling its different parts through his daily journeys on the tram, he actively combated the sense of displacement that had engulfed him upon arriving in Melbourne. Within a few months of taking on the job, he knew Melbourne's inner city and suburbs inside out.

Mohamed's story of fervently tackling his feelings of displacement indicates a key theme that spins its way throughout this book. Rather than using displacement as a metaphor for a sense of alienation from society, the stories that form the heart of this book show the different ways people actively make sense of new, left behind or lost places. In focusing on the felt, experienced and storied dimensions of place, rather than reducing it to its analytical and structural properties, this book can thus be read as a perspective on displacement that attempts to 'get back into place'. In doing so, I can build on Edward Casey's (1993) attempt to write the importance of place back into philosophy. His efforts to write the body back into place and place back into theoretical consciousness offered an important entry point for my own understanding. Building much of his work on Gaston Bachelard's phenomenology of intimate spaces, Casey adopts the idea of topo-analysis, which, for Bachelard, is 'the systematic psychological study of the sites of our intimate lives' (Bachelard 1994: 8). In examining the intimate and often unconscious dream-like experience of the houses we inhabited (or still inhabit), from their cellars to their attics, from their furniture to their doors, Bachelard lays open a topology of the self. This topology is close to what Martin Heidegger called a '*Topologie des Seins*' (topology of being) (see Heidegger 1977 [1956]: 32; 2003 [1977]: 41). It hints at being-in-the-world as something that is always emplaced. The links between self, place and experience are so crucial that throughout this book these three thinkers – Casey, Bachelard and Heidegger – play an essential role. They have informed my conceptualization of place as something that is not rigidly shielded off or enclosed, but as something that is essentially open – something *of* and *in* the world. While place is closely connected to being, this does not suggest that it is static – for being itself is always moving, always a form of becoming.

In developing the idea that place and being are intimately connected, yet not in ways that exclude the possibility for movement and change, I can draw on the work of Martin Heidegger. While *Being and Time* features sections on the spatiality of being *(die Räumlichkeit des Daseins)*, the idea of place is not spelled out in detail and priority is given to existentiality and temporality. In his later work, however, Heidegger abandons this position and begins to focus on the topological character of *Dasein* (being) instead (Malpas 2012: 16). Indeed, the German term for being, 'Dasein', underscores the intimate relationship between being and place. While Dasein is rendered into English as 'being', it actually merges two words – *da* (here) and *Sein* (being). Dasein, then, literally means being-here. In the English reading of Heidegger's work, this inherently spatial character of being is commonly lost in translation. Rethinking being as being-here is a shift I found important for my own understanding of place, as it emphasizes the connection of being with the particularity and materiality of here. Being, this suggests, is intimately interwoven with the textures and dynamics of place. In turning the links between being *(Sein)* and here *(da)* into explicit objects of ethnographic inquiry, this book sketches an existential anthropological approach to place and placemaking.

This turn towards the lived experience of place should not be regarded as a reactionary turn backwards. As I will show in more detail in chapter one, a critical existential approach to place takes into account both the everyday practices that shape our engagements with places and the structural forces that inhibit and control our actions and movements within them. And as the stories of departures, arrivals and homecomings in this book will show, there is no such thing as a stagnant, immovable place. The idea of place not as an imprisonment, but as something that reaches out into the world whilst not losing its possibility as a dwelling for humans, has shaped my understanding of emplacement. Throughout Omar's and Halima's stories, place features as something that contains and sets free at the same time, as something that is always moving, or 'on the way' *(unterwegs)*, as Heidegger (1962: 110) puts it. In their stories, the process of taking roots does not take on the suffocating character of immobility. Reflecting on his own experience as a migrant in Australia, Ghassan Hage writes that rootedness should not too easily be mistaken for a sense of being stuck or immovable. He suggests that many people experience the opposite, 'roots often are paradoxically experienced like an extra pair of wings' (Hage 2013: 149).

Human beings are essentially terrestrial beings; they cannot but travel through place. If we accept this thought, then we also need to view displacement differently. In such a reading, place becomes something particular, yet outward bound, something that has a material, physical presence and is yet open to change. Ingold uses the term 'wayfaring' to describe the embodied experience of place. It is as wayfarers, he writes, that human beings inhabit the earth. Ingold's wayfarer does not view the world as a surface to be traversed. Her movements form a thread *through*, rather than *across* the world, for the wayfarer is a terrestrial being and must travel over land (Ingold 2009: 37).

In framing a topology of being that begins and ends in place, yet in places that are always on the way, the strength of storytelling comes to the fore. It is through stories that people order, characterize, create and overrule places. And it is in places that stories come to life – that they, quite literally, take place. In 2009, when I moved to the other end of the world in order to write about other people's displacements, I could not have foreseen that my research would reveal people's continuous movements towards *emplacement*. It was by being-here in Melbourne and with Halima, Mohamed and Omar, and by telling each other stories, that I came to understand the continuous importance of place in their lives. They made me see that even people on the move, whether on the run from war, hunger or destruction, or simply looking for greener pastures elsewhere, do not move through an indifferent space. Rather, they travel through places – and in moving through, shape them and are in turn shaped by them.

Chapter Outline

It is along these horizons that the architecture of this book takes shape. The core themes of storytelling, emplacement and displacement form building blocks to the three parts. At the heart of the book are the lives and stories of Halima Mohamed and Omar Farah Dhollawa, as well as the visual stories of Mohamed Ibrahim. Besides a chapter that fleshes out the existential dynamics of life storytelling, the book is structured into two core parts, each of which is centred on a set of stories and events that marked crucial moments in Halima's and Omar's lives. Each sub-chapter begins with a short first-person account by Halima or Omar that defines the tone and theme of the chapter. My interpretations of the stories are interwoven with interactions, conversations and moments that occurred as I was accompanying them in their daily pathways. By bringing Omar's and Halima's everyday engagements with places in a conversation with their narratives, I emphasize the ways place is experienced both immediately and bodily as well as in terms of reflected imaginary, memorial and storied layers.

Before I turn to the life stories, however, I deepen the problem of life storytelling and its links to experience. The idea that stories can reveal deep-seated existential questions requires careful unpacking, as there is nothing simple about the suggestion that stories have the ability to shed light on lifeworlds, or about the idea of the lifeworld itself. Part I therefore centres on the question of how the stories in this book came about and on how far they can reveal lived experiences. By drawing the contours of an existential anthropological approach to ethnography, it aims to bring more depth and complexity into heavily overused yet epistemologically underdeveloped notions such as 'experience', 'existence', or 'existential'. Following Hannah Arendt's call to approach theory as 'thinking what we are doing', I sketch my move from ethnographic fieldwork to anthropological meaning-making. By shedding light on the dynamics of the life storytelling sessions, I will complicate the dichotomy between narrative and experience. I will suggest that while fictionalization is an important ingredient of life stories, this should not lead us to believe that life stories do not have the ability to shed light on the teller's experiences. Rather, the intersubjective moment of the telling allows for experiences to be shared, felt and understood in new ways. In doing so, life stories allow us to constantly create new versions of ourselves, thereby giving deep insights into the ways individuals actively make sense of their being-here.

Part II focuses on Omar's life story. Meandering through a set of narratives, each of which discusses a different phase in his life, it aims to come to an understanding of the ambiguity and complexity underlying the experience of being-in-place. Whilst touching upon different times and places, Omar's stories are linked through the overarching question of whether 'home' is located in a specific place and how people make sense of the places they find themselves at. Focusing on five stories that represent critical moments in Omar's life, I will engage with the historical, political and emotional dynamics shaping places and placemaking practices. Part III is built around Halima's stories and experiences and centres on the meaning of displacement. Thinking through the importance of emplacement and place-attachment in her narratives, the links between being-in- and out-of-place, past and present, and movement and stagnation come to the fore. The common thread going through all of Halima's stories is her tireless attempt to understand and befriend the places she finds herself at. Her stories suggest that even in the face of the disorienting feeling of displacement, and despite years spent on the move or caught in limbo, the intimacy and immediacy of place never ceases to be of critical existential importance. By engaging with four stories that stand for important events in her life, I will shed light on the interplay of time and place and suggest a new, place-based reading of displacement. While the theme of emplacement runs more strongly through Omar's stories, and displacement through Halima's, there is no strict thematic divide between the chapters. The openness of the storytelling approach allows me to stay *unterwegs* (on the way), even in my writing, and to expose the complex movements, tensions and interrelations between the two phenomena. Mohamed's photographs and stories will be woven throughout the book. They will form 'Junctures', brief interruptions between chapters that stand by themselves, but that nevertheless provoke reflections on some of the core themes that have been or will be touched upon in the chapters before or after.

More than anything else, this book can be read as a dialogue. In finding ways of not just retelling the stories Omar, Mohamed and Halima had told me, but also bringing the intersubjective dynamics of the storytelling moment into my writing, it became crucial to make myself part of the book. This was not a means of demonstrating reflexivity; rather, it grew out of the dialogical and conversational nature of the fieldwork condition. Ghassan Hage (2009: 62) has commented that 'drowning oneself in a sea of self-reflexivity' is hardly more anti-colonial than the 'desire to *seriously* reach out for otherness'. I agree with him and would add that this otherness can become a meeting point and common ground in that, albeit in different ways, we are all *other* and, in many ways, we are *same*, too. In embarking on a poetics of storytelling I needed to make this dialogical situation, this back and forth, this moving towards a shared understanding part of the writing of this book. The task was to find ways of weaving in and out of what Michael Jackson (2010: 49) describes as the three horizons of the hermeneutic circle: that of one's own world, that of the society one seeks to understand, and that of humanity. This book can be read as a dialogue between these three horizons, as it interweaves the stories of Halima, Mohamed and Omar with my own experiences, resulting in a constant movement towards the existential dynamics of emplacement.

PART I

Thinking What We Are Doing

Mohamed took this photo while driving through the heart of Mogadishu. The image's dreamlike mood, its multilayered perspective, its sense of rhythm and its exceptional framing immediately captivated me. Before knowing the photographer's account, the image stirred something inside me. It told me stories of the faceless

Figure PI.1 *Civilians driving a military truck through Mogadishu. Image courtesy of Mohamed Ibrahim*

people sitting on and in the truck, stories of the dusty roads they were travelling through, stories of their journeys, and stories of the onlooker behind the window of another car, capturing this blink of a moment.

'There are a lot of things you can comment on this,' Mohamed, the onlooker, explained later, when I asked him what had moved him about that very moment. 'First of all what I noticed was that this was no civilian truck. It's a military truck. Who am I to ask those questions? But if you really asked the proper question than you would have to ask: "How comes that these guys are using government property?" They would say: "But what government? Who cares?" So that's one level. One can actually say that things are so chaotic that now these guys can drive a stolen military truck in the middle of the town and nobody even recognizes it. Nobody cares. I care, because I can tell.'

Mohamed paused and gave me a knowing look. He could *tell* and with him I could *see*. But who were we to question the habits of a place we did not *in*habit? Mohamed continued: 'That's one thing. The other thing is the wood it's carrying. Even now, despite the famine and the lack of rain, they are still cutting down the trees. And then on top there are people sitting, these people are probably traders. So within this image there is so much that summarizes the problem in Somalia: The stealing of the national asset, the national resources, the safety issues, because they are sitting on top, and probably, if you look at the whole picture you might even find some people with guns, also sitting somewhere. So that alone gives us a snapshot of the whole problem.' Mohamed shook his head at the idea of this snapshot. It contains so many displacements: a truck, stolen from a state whose very existence seems to have become questionable, carrying wood from a mangrove forest that is dying through the middle of a town that has lost its balance. And capturing all these displacements is the eye of the man behind the camera, Mohamed, who remembers the city from times when things were in their proper place.

Yet for the people sitting on top of the truck, life goes on. Somehow, for them, things are in their proper place now, for they deal with the place as it happens. With all the displacements that have led to the disintegration of the place as Mohamed remembers it, to the people who live there it is a reality they have to live and deal with. So who is he to ask them questions about it? For the photographer, the returnee who positions himself strangely within and yet outside, the place depicted becomes something that is at once alienating and touching. The image captures place in all its material, storied and disputed dimensions. At the same time, it gives room to the many displacements that are also part of the photographer's ways of seeing the place.

And thus the question arises: How to approach place in a way that takes all these layers into account? How to approach it in its lived, sensed, felt density? How to find ways of understanding *Dasein* in its openness of being-here, even if this *here* is shattered by painful, violent or disorienting events?

1

Walkers of the Everyday

What always struck me as peculiar about Melbourne was the fact that so many birds, rather than flying in the sky or perching in the trees, inhabited the ground. Proudly and confidently they strutted on the ground, a world that was fully theirs. Their territories were the open spaces in the large parklands or the backyards where people planted herbs and held barbeques. I faced these tough little creatures, who seemed fearless even as I stepped close to shoo them away, with a mixture of amazement and horror. I encountered them when riding on the bike trail along the Yarra River; they paraded on the concrete path, not making the slightest move to get out of my way, so that I felt I had to swing my bike around not to hit them. Waking up to the peculiar warble of the large black and white Australian magpies often made me feel strangely foreign.

While living in Melbourne I was frequently asked about my background. Whether ordering a cup of tea, chatting about the weather to the staff at the local bottle shop, or responding to someone asking for directions, my accent stirred up a lot of curiosity. Once I had explained that I had moved from Austria to Australia in late 2009 on a scholarship to conduct research on Somali refugees, I was often asked how I liked Melbourne. When this happened I was always tempted to talk about the birds and how they reminded me of living 'down under' (or maybe rather 'upside down') every day. I wanted to say that even the blueness of the sky and the greyness of the clouds were so typical for Melbourne that they gave my being-here a specific texture. But instead, I fell back into the rehearsed everyday tales people like to repeat to reassert each other. 'People are friendly here,' I heard myself saying, 'it's easy to settle down as a foreigner in such a multicultural city.'

Yet there is much more to be said about the way I experienced Melbourne. By experiencing I do not just mean a way of intellectually making sense of my surroundings; I am also referring to the slow process of getting to know a place, of befriending it, of becoming emplaced. How to find words for the smells, the web of street names, or the sounds and unspoken rules that make up this sense of emplacement? And how to convey the timidity that accompanied my first steps through Melbourne, an utter feeling of strangeness – as if even my way of walking, the way I chose to step into the world, revealed the fact that I was not part of the wholeness to which everyone else seemed to belong?

In *The Practice of Everyday Life*, Michel de Certeau speaks of this wholeness of place when he thinks about the poetry of looking down at Manhattan from the 110th floor of the World Trade Centre. Looking down from so far above the city conveys a feeling of seeing the whole without its single parts:

> To be lifted to the summit of the World Trade Center is to be lifted out of the city's grasp. One's body is no longer clasped by the streets that turn and return it according to an anonymous law; nor is it possessed, whether as player or played, by the rumble of so many differences and by the nervousness of New York traffic. When one goes up there, he leaves behind the mass that carries off and mixes up in itself any identity of authors or spectators. An Icarus flying above these waters, he can ignore the devices of Daedalus in mobile and endless labyrinths far below. His elevation transfigures him into a voyeur. It puts him at a distance. It transforms the bewitching world by which one was 'possessed' into a text that lies before one's eye. (De Certeau 1984: 92)

Thus, the world turns into a text ready to be read and understood, while the ordinary practitioners of everyday city life are down below, 'below the thresholds at which visibility begins', as de Certeau (1984: 93) puts it. He calls them *Wandersmänner* (walkers), whose bodies follow an urban text they write without being able to read it. 'It is as though the practices organizing a bustling city were characterized by their blindness,' he notes. 'The networks of these moving, intersecting writings compose a manifold story that has neither author nor spectator, shaped out of fragments of trajectories and alterations of spaces: in relation to representations, it remains daily and indefinitely other' (De Certeau 1984: 93).

When Halima arrived in Melbourne on a winter evening in 2002, she was overwhelmed by the darkness of the city. Upon leaving the airport and driving towards the place that was to become her new home, she felt disoriented and confused by the sea of darkness that surrounded her. In the United Arab Emirates, where she had spent the last twelve years, the streets and buildings were saturated with such dazzling lights that even in the middle of the night there was no real darkness. 'So when I came here I thought: "What's going on? This is a developed country, what happened? Why is it so dark?",' Halima said.

Years later and drinking cups of sweet Somali tea in the living room of her house in Maidstone, she could share a laugh over the memories of her first encounters with Melbourne. Halima told me that driving through this darkness had made her question whether she had actually arrived in the right place. 'I thought I came to the wrong place, that it was not Australia,' she laughed. 'And my little adopted son, my nephew who grew up with my kids, he said: "Mum, I think we came to the wrong place, it's not Australia!"' Trying to describe this feeling of disorientation that accompanied Halima's first moves through Melbourne, she said that her experience of the place was strange, 'almost not real'. The silhouettes of the first suburban houses she could see made the order of this place even more ungraspable. 'I found that all the houses were small, small, small,' Halima said, 'because where I came from in Dubai I was surrounded by high-rises. Everything was very strange.'

It was from this feeling of strangeness, from the fear that upon awakening the next day the city would turn into an incomprehensible maze, that Halima's sister used all her strength to protect her. Sahra, who had arrived in Melbourne ten years before and already knew the paths and ways of the city, tried to loosen the sense of disorientation by being around her – day and night. 'For the first month she was with me,' Halima said. 'We were even sleeping in the same bed together.' And, thinking about it for a while she added: 'I don't think I could have survived if my sister hadn't been here.' It was by tackling the initial incomprehensibility of the city with someone else, by walking and talking through it together, that the feeling of alienation waned and Halima began to make sense of her surroundings. Beyond the Icarus-view of the city as a readable text, it was only in connection with others that Halima began to grasp rather than decipher the different parcels that constitute the wholeness of Melbourne and began to inhabit the place she had come to live in socially.

Consider the way clouds in the sky or birds on the ground filter into my way of walking through and perceiving Melbourne. And think of the way Melbourne's darkness occasioned a feeling of strangeness in Halima, a strangeness that only dissolved by beginning, step by step, to understand the way this place was organized. If the space of the city shapes us at the same time as it is shaped by us, then how can we come to an understanding of the fragile processes that form and shape place into a dwelling? How can we overcome the tension between the way we see, feel and live place and the way we come to conceptualize, think, decipher and read it? While de Certeau's observant eye deciphering the smooth wholeness of Manhattan from the top of the World Trade Centre suggests a clear and frictionless way of understanding place intellectually, in everyday life people do not lift themselves out of the city's grasp in order to interpret place as a text. Rather, the walkers of the everyday cannot but make sense of the wholeness of a place by walking, feeling, living, struggling in its manifold and ambiguous tracks.

This has important implications for me, the anthropologist, attempting to understand the ways people make sense of the places they live in, have left behind, lost, or are moving towards. Instead of becoming an Icarus, gliding over people's lives, deciphering the world from the skies above, it seems that I need to take on the role of a Daedalus, throwing myself into the mobile and endless labyrinths of everyday life. Yet, given everyday lives' ever-moving character, it is equally as important not to get lost in its maze of ambiguities and contradictions, thereby losing track of the sense of wholeness and direction that also constitutes our being-in-place. In the context of everyday religious practices Samuli Schielke and Liza Debevec (2012: 7) poignantly describe this tension as the interplay of 'ordinary lives' and 'grand schemes', posing the question of how we can 'account for the relationship of articulations of a coherent world-view and the practice and knowledge of living a life'.

My research was propelled by this question of how to find a balance between the everyday practices that shape our engagements with places and the larger structures that have the power to inhibit and control our movements and actions within them. Whilst trying to understand the particularities of the ways three individuals actively made sense of the places they had come to or left behind, it was equally important not to overlook the bigger political and historical processes that play into these dynamics. Like de Certeau, I came to see the importance of an approach to everyday placemaking practices that accommodates both – the larger structures that attempt to order and regulate places, and the walkers of the everyday, who constantly appropriate and challenge these efforts. This insight did not grow in isolation, but in direct conversation with Halima, Mohamed and Omar. It was by walking and talking our way through Melbourne together that I became aware of the importance of establishing an approach that would allow me to address both the Daedalus perspective, in which even the tiniest nuances of places such as the darkness of the sky or birds on the ground have such a force that they come to permeate and shift our lifeworlds, and the means people use to integrate such experiences into an Icarus view onto the world as a whole.

In this chapter I sketch the outlines of such an approach. By zooming in on the particularities of my work with Halima, Omar and Mohamed, I will show the interplay of the three core themes that came to shape my approach to place and displacement: experience, storytelling and existential anthropology. In a first step I will show the importance of developing a methodological framework that allows me to address the movements of the walkers of the everyday from an experiential perspective – to not impose predetermined explanations and theorizations upon the phenomena we aim to understand, but to focus on *what there is* instead. In a second step I will shed light on the dialogical nature of my collaboration with Halima, Mohamed and Omar to make transparent the at times complex and ambiguous processes underlying anthropological knowledge-production. This will lead me to reread important analytical categories, such as 'refugee', 'life story' or 'lived experience'. Finally, I will shed light on the politics and poetics of storytelling that shaped the stories that made their way into this book.

What There Is

From our first encounters, Omar told me stories about his life. He spoke about many details of his long journey to Australia at the end of the 1980s. He tried to explain to me what it means to see one's country crippled by war and famine from afar. He told me about his struggle to get his mother and siblings out of Somalia when the civil war broke out, and how he had met his wife, who had just fled to Nairobi, while he was waiting there for his family. During none of our first meetings did it occur to me that Omar and his family were not refugees. My project was to write about the life stories of Somali refugees and many of his stories dealt with the war in Somalia, so I never doubted that what I was attempting to understand had to be framed in terms of displacement. One day, however, when I used the word refugee to describe his situation, Omar protested. He told me

that he did not believe he was a refugee. He said it with such convic-
tion and sobriety that I realized I had stumbled upon something
important. Seeing my puzzled look, he laughed. 'Okay,' Omar said.
'I will explain it.' In order to understand him, he added, he needed to
talk about the Somali word for refugee, *qaxooti*:

> *Qax* means to run away. Qaxooti is the one who is actually doing that.
> So it's the one who's running away from something. But it never meant
> before to move from one country to another. Maybe it used to be from
> one place to another place in the same area. And that word was used
> when there was a fire and the people were evacuated, or there was a
> flooding and they ran away to a higher place for safety. It has never been
> to run from your own country to another country.

When I asked Omar what he thinks when people call him a refugee,
he said: 'Qaxooti has got one meaning: If you call me qaxooti, then
I'm qaxooti – qaxooti means running away from something. Am
I running away from something now? After twenty-three years in
Australia? No.' 'So you would say that this word only applies to
someone who is in the immediate action of running?' I asked Omar.
'Yes,' he answered. 'And afterwards – unless you still believe that I am
running away from something.' Thinking about the absurdity of this
idea we both began to laugh. 'Am I running away from something
after twenty-three years?'

That afternoon, we spent a long time talking about the power
of words. Omar struggled to find a suitable alternative to the term
qaxooti/refugee that was open enough to capture the complexity
of his experience. The verb Somalis use for travelling, he said, the
Arabic *safar*, did not fit. Safar, Omar explained, is an adventure
people choose, 'a kind of drifting', as he put it, out of the pure joy
of movement. His journey away from Somalia was partially driven
by a curiosity to see other places, but it was also prompted by the
instability in his own country. To describe his movement to Australia
as safar would therefore not capture the complexity of his lived
experience. Omar also rejected the label migrant, or *soogalooti*. He
explained that in the Somali context, the noun soogalooti is used to
describe 'someone who has come from a different culture or a different environment, or someone who is new to a particular place'. Like
refugee, he said, it had the potential to mark him as an outsider, as
someone who did not belong to Australian society. Being a migrant,
he said, had to have a limit. 'Because if you call me "migrant" then
what will come into my mind is: "I'm not like anyone else, I'm not
Australian, I'm not Aussie".' He concluded that he did not like to be

put into a box at all. Instead, he preferred to be accepted as a member of Australian society, regardless of what had brought him here in the first place. 'What I want to feel and what I want my children to feel is that we are Australian,' he said. 'Full stop. Nothing more, nothing less.'

As I cycled home that day, it struck me that none of the people who were telling me their life stories, neither Halima, nor Mohamed, nor Omar, and none of the members of their families, had ever referred to being a refugee. For me, I realized, the word had become a metaphor that embodied urgent questions of our time, such as the intertwined forces of inclusion and exclusion that mark the nation state, as well as the movement and general sense of homelessness that seems to characterize our era. To uncritically assume that my Somali friends would think likewise, however, would mean beginning with an intellectual structure and ignoring phenomena as they are actually felt, lived and experienced by the people who are labelled as such. When confronted with the absence of refugeeness in Omar's life-world, I was radically reminded that as an anthropologist I cannot set myself above what matters to the people I am working with. Instead of approaching my research from a pregiven analytical lens, I needed to develop a perspective that gives preference to the ways phenomena are lived through and made sense of by the people I worked with.

This is not to suggest an anti-intellectual stance that throws all established theories overboard. Analytical concepts such as migration or forced migration can be valuable tools to grasp complex and multilayered processes. Yet, I agree with Sonia Silva's (2015: 127–28) warning that we need to pay attention to the ways such concepts tend to become reified, leading scholars to lose touch with the realities of the people whose lived experiences they attempt to understand, thereby turning them into 'a lesser, one-dimensional version of themselves'. That afternoon when Omar told me that he was not a refugee, I came to see that if I were to keep this analytical framework, I would reduce the complexity and multidimensionality of his being-here to a simplistic, one-dimensional portrayal of being-out-of-place. To stay with Omar's analogy, if I continued describing him as a refugee/qaxooti my analysis would have been running away with him, while he himself was actually doing everything in his power to stay put. To keep on describing Omar as a refugee would have created an unbridgeable gap between my analytical thinking and the world it was attempting to understand. The conversation with Omar brought home to me the fact that I could no longer impose analytical concepts on the phenomena I was intending to understand whilst ignoring

my participants' own objections against them. Close to the phenomenological doctrine to return 'to the things themselves' *(die Sache
an sich)*, I needed to develop a methodology that would allow me to
attend to the ambiguities of being-here without, to paraphrase Hans
Lucht (2015: 122), 'squeezing the life out of it'. Instead of understanding anthropological knowledge as something *about* the world,
I needed to approach it as something 'urgently *of* and *for* the world'
(Jackson 1996: 37, emphasis added). In developing such a framework
I could take my cues from the phenomenological tradition.

Phenomenology, often described as the scientific study of experience, attempts to understand the given, 'the things themselves' as
they appear to our consciousness prior to theoretical abstraction.
It grew from a deep dissatisfaction with the abstract and rationalist
character of Western theoretical thought, which tended to tame the
unsystematic and messy reality of the world through well-ordered
and classified scientific models and schemata. The turn phenomenology initiated was towards the taken for granted and away from the
seemingly objective, fixed and intellectually ordered truth of positiv-
ist thinking. Edmund Husserl, one of the founding figures of phenomenology, spoke of the taken-for-granted world we all live in as
the *Lebenswelt* (lifeworld) (Husserl 1970a [1936]). He showed that
consciousness is never something that is closed up in itself but always
a consciousness *of* something (Husserl 1970b). This condition, he
suggests, this way that life is always straightforwardly directed at a
world that is already present, is the *natürliche Einstellung* (natural
attitude) (Husserl 1970a: 281). Maurice Natanson, who, along with
his teacher Alfred Schutz, elaborated Husserl's ideas for social
research, described this as the perception of what there is (Natanson
1973: 54).

For anthropologists to work with phenomenological methods,
entails a shift in focus from theoretical abstraction to the ordinariness
of everyday life. Through direct engagements with the lived experiences of particular human beings, phenomenological anthropologists
aim to develop a better understanding of the social quality of being.
Knowledge is no longer seen as something that belongs to the intellectual domain, for its very existence can only grow out of what
has been there (in the lifeworld) in the first place. Becoming closely
involved in Halima's, Omar's and Mohamed's lives, I moved away
from the idea that lives are ready to be read and deciphered by a
somewhat lonely and removed anthropologist. Walking the everyday
together, telling stories to each other, and moving through and within
places together, I began to see my role as an anthropologist in terms

of intersubjectivity. Anthropologists are not only researching other people's experiences. As researchers, we are part of the same world, a world in which meanings shift and new borders are constantly set up and crossed. Or, as Natanson (1973: 54) puts it, there is one world – and there are different ways of attending to it. By taking these crossing points seriously, by paying attention to the points at which differences fade, perceptions of the self are destabilized and lifeworlds begin to overlap, we can shed light on the complex dialogical process that is at the root of anthropological knowledge production.

While my epistemological framework grew directly from my involvement in the everyday lives of Mohamed, Halima and Omar, I think it is important not to portray this dialogical process as smooth and frictionless. As Omar's opposition against the term refugee shows, it confronted me with countless contradictions, misconceptions and seemingly unbridgeable divides. Yet, it is often exactly in the moments when we are overtaken by events we did not anticipate and our methodological preconceptions collapse that we are faced with the urgent need to question our pre-understandings, adjust our analytical frameworks and rethink what we are doing. Like Hannah Arendt (1998: 5), who approaches philosophy as 'thinking what we are doing', I believe that the theoretical knowledge we as anthropologists create should not be so far removed from the intersubjective dynamics it grew out of that all meaning or worldliness of the problems get lost. Rather than writing off moments when our methodological preconceptions break down, I suggest taking them as a starting point for thinking what we are doing.

On Methodological Mishaps

On a summer afternoon in March 2011 I met Halima in a small Iraqi kebab eatery in Footscray, a suburb close to her house. She had chosen this place as the location of our first recorded storytelling session. Because of its affordable halal meals and its closeness to the 'Somali mall' – an inoperative former shopping mall that had been taken over by Somali small businesses – the restaurant was a popular meeting point for many Somalis. As I entered the store a strong scent of meat wafted through the small, modestly furnished room. Halima was already sitting at one of the tables, a collection of shopping bags gathered around her. Laughing, she cleared a chair for me, explaining that she had hardly been able to carry all the groceries here on her own and that unless she wanted to set roots in this restaurant one of her daughters would have to pick her up later on. Remembering how much I had enjoyed her Somali tea the last time we met, she ordered two cups of strong Iraqi chai tea.

I had gotten to know Halima several weeks earlier at a community event she had organized. We had spent an afternoon together and had immediately taken a liking to each other. She had agreed to participate in my research project, and when I called her to arrange a date for our first recorded storytelling session she had repeated that she was eager to collaborate with me on her life story. As we were sipping our teas I pulled out the voice recorder, explaining how it worked and showing the red light through which she would be able to see whether the device was recording our conversations or not. The recorder fascinated Halima. 'It's beautiful,' she said, feeling it in her hands. 'Is it from your country or did you buy it here?' 'I brought it from my country,' I responded, 'but you can also buy it here in Australia.' For a while we talked about the recording device, about how it was going to pick up all our conversations so that I could transcribe and use them as the basis for writing down her life story later on. This all sounded reasonable to Halima, and after a while she indicated that she was ready to start. I told her that I did not believe we needed to organize the conversations too much. 'I think for the beginning it's maybe easiest if we begin with your life in Somalia and your childhood,' I said, asking her to describe the kind of life she was leading there. Halima gave me a puzzled look. 'Yes,' she said, hesitatingly, taking a sip from her tea. Then she started to narrate her life story. But her account did not carry any traits of the well-versed and gripping storyteller Halima was in everyday life. In a self-conscious and programmatic style akin to the ways students rattle out poems she talked about her life. Within the two hours we spent in the restaurant, Halima raced through her entire life, revealing some of its main twists and turns and a body of information, but leaving the contours of her experiences untouched.

This first attempt to work with Halima on her life story left me baffled. According to the methodological texts I had read, the conditions for working on her life story could not have been better. Not unlike the dynamics described by many anthropologists working with individuals on their life stories, Halima had found me rather than the other way around and had been keen to tell me her story (e.g. Behar 1993; Biehl 2005). We had built up a trustful relationship, chosen a place where she felt comfortable and discussed the technicalities of recording her narratives. Yet, the first recorded storytelling session proved me wrong. That afternoon in the Iraqi kebab restaurant, we were both guided by our own preconceptions about what such a thing as a life story could be. Our preconceptions, however, did not align. While Halima was guided by the idea that this was going to be something like an interview, a question and answer type of conversation, my understanding was based on a vague idea of modern autobiographical narratives, influenced, perhaps, by the seemingly endless range of biographical texts that have become an important genre within the Western literary world. I had assumed that the teller of an autobiographical account has the ability to make a story out of a life, and is able to talk about their life in a unified and chronological way (Langness and Frank 1981: 101). While I was expecting intricate and deep-reaching narratives, Halima was waiting for me to ask questions and trying to summarize her whole life as concisely as possible.

An even more dramatic methodological mishap emerged after my first recorded conversation with Mohamed. We had met in the Brunetti coffee shop in order to begin working on his life story. Throughout the hour we spent together he was struggling to find topics to talk about, nervously fiddling with the pen in front of him. In the end he told me that he did not want to have his life story recorded in future meetings and suggested we think of alternative ways of using his story. At this point I had already known Mohamed for almost a year. He had been sharing the many photographs he was taking with his small digital pocket camera that was his constant companion. He had invited me to comment on his images and taken me to places in the city where Somalis liked to hang out, all the while documenting our movements with his camera. This common enthusiasm for photography had created a bridge between us and paved the way for our friendship. Yet, when I introduced the voice recorder into our conversations these dynamics completely changed. I had not anticipated that the recorder would work as a distancing device that extinguished any sense of closeness between us. 'I don't know what exactly it is,' Mohamed said to me, 'it's just that I really dislike this feeling that my voice will be kept somewhere.' Embarrassed by my own insensitivity, I left the meeting disillusioned and puzzled about how to move on from here.

In these first encounters I was confronted with the need to free the life story from my preconceptions and take more seriously the uniqueness of the storytelling situation. Storytelling does not take place in the safe solitude a novel is created in. It is the product of a social interaction between the teller and her audience. I could not simply retreat into the role of a silent listener or removed inter-viewer. As Walter Benjamin (2007: 97) explains in his famous essay 'The Storyteller', the listener's relationship to the storyteller lies in his interest in retaining and retelling what is told. For the tellers to entrust me with their stories, stories that would be retold by me, we first had to create the common ground needed in order for the stories to become shareable. I was not just a silent listener, the passive recipient of life stories. Rather, I was an active part of the storytelling dynamics, bringing in my own accounts, reflections and reactions and participating in the creation of this common ground from where stories could be told and retold.

Like many other researchers deploying narrative methods in the context of forced migration, my interest in working with a small number of refugees on their life stories had grown from a deep frustration with the scholarly disregard for people's actual experi-ences and voices. My interest was with a body of research that uses individual life stories to communicate refugees' and migrants' own thoughts and experiences in direct and powerful ways (e.g. Eastmond 1996, 2007; Powles 2004; Alexandra 2008; Jackson 2013a), thereby hoping to overcome homogenizing portrayals of refugees as voice-less, apolitical and ahistorical victims (Malkki 1996). The increased importance of narrative ethnographic methodologies in the last few decades has formed an essential step in creating a deeper understand-ing for the complexity and multidimensionality of displacement.

In anthropology, this push for narrative approaches in refugee research can be linked to theoretical and methodological develop-ments in the 1980s and 1990s, when anthropologists began to question the sharp distinction between fiction and reality. With the publication of the landmark collection of essays *Writing Culture* in 1986, which reviewed anthropology's relationship with writing and especially with the production of ethnographic realities, this simple binary was eroding (Clifford and Marcus 1986). Researchers became critical of the realist approach of representing lives and cultures, and became interested in interpretative, narrative approaches as tools to explore people's lived experiences. At the same time, researchers also grew more sensible to the power relations that accompany the pro-duction of life stories (Eastmond 2007: 248). With the turn towards reflexivity, narration and interpretation anthropologists started to take the dynamics of storytelling more seriously. They began to reflect on the ways stories were produced in ethnographic settings, on the role of the researcher in the creation of the story and on the ways anthropologists themselves create stories through the texts they write (Crapanzano 1980, 1992; Abu-Lughod 1993; Behar 1993). Instead of working with life histories, scholars now focused on life stories, meaning that the constructed nature of the story was pushed into the academic spotlight. While life histories focus on diachronic change within anthropology's traditional paradigms of naturalism or realism, life stories focus on the cultural scripts and narrative devices that individuals use to make sense of experience (Frank 1995: 145). Over the past thirty years, then, there has been a methodological shift from the realist approach of life histories to a focus on experience. This change could be characterized as a shift from words to lives, from the verifiable recounting of the past to life stories as subjective documents (Lamb 2001).

Despite the rich and long history of anthropological engagements with stories and storytelling settings, nothing could have prepared me for the messiness of my first life storytelling attempts with Halima and Mohamed. Faced with their discomfort with the storytelling setting, I began to ask myself whether my intention of 'giving voice' to experiences of displacement had not been too simplistic. Indeed, the shock over these methodological mishaps was so strong that it took me a few months to lick my wounds. During these months, however, I became intimately involved in Halima's life, thereby moving my focus beyond the boundaries of the recorded life storytelling setting into the realm of everyday life. Having moved to a country where I did not have any family links, Halima and her family took me in as one of their own, treating me as a daughter and sister. I became so closely involved in Halima's life that by the time I picked up the recorder again she had already told me many stories of her life. I had become familiar with the 'critical events' (Das 1995) that had shaped her as a person, with the pace of her telling, the topics she struggled to talk about and the themes she did not consider appropriate for a story.

From Words to Lifeworlds

After our first confused attempt to work on Halima' life story, I came to understand that there was no such thing as *a* life story. Rather than telling me intricate details about her personal life along a chronologically ordered and well-structured plot that interweaves events into a unified life story, I had to make do with the lived messiness of the storytelling moment. Instead of framing her stories as one uniform and uninterrupted life story, Halima told me many stories through a multitude of different forms, including autobiographical accounts, but also through anecdotes, tales, poetry and songs. While the different narratives were propelled by the vague idea of portraying 'a life', they often lost track of this overarching idea and jumped between different lifetimes, places, people and events.

From a textual perspective the stories Halima told me could easily be discarded as inconsistent, fictional or unfinished. Yet, they were loaded with meaning. This became particularly clear to me when I finally forced myself to return to the notes of our first life story meeting almost a year later. At the end of our muddled attempt, when I had just switched off the recorder, Halima had told me a story, which, she said, was very important to her. At the very moment I did not understand why she was telling me this children's tale, which, I then believed, had nothing to do with her own experiences. Yet, despite my perplexity this story continued to work inside of me. It managed to work its way deep into my thoughts and ultimately came to shape my understanding of storytelling as an existential force.

Halima's story was set around the fireplace of a nomadic camp somewhere in Somalia. All the men had gone away for a few days to find pastures for the cattle. Only a mother and her small child were left behind. It was in the middle of the dry season, when people were often forced to go without a meal for many days. The boy was starving and kept asking his mother for food. But she had nothing to cook. He began to wail and weep bitterly. After listening helplessly to her child crying for some time, the mother had an idea. She took a pot and filled it with water. She collected firewood and made a fire. Once the fire was going, the woman placed the pot onto the fire. 'You see?' she said to her hungry child. 'I'm preparing the food for you now.' While the pot filled with nothing but boiling water was kept on the fire, she told her child stories. Every time he asked for the food, she would say: 'Just be patient, the food needs to be cooked first. Look, the water is already boiling!' She kept repeating this many, many times, until the boy fell asleep. The next day, early in the morning, the woman went around the camp, desperately looking for roots and leaves – anything she could cook. When the boy woke up, the food was already prepared. It was a meagre meal, but enough to feed him. The child, believing that it had been cooking all night, was happy.

A few months after our first meeting in the kebab eatery, when we were working on a body of stories about Halima's life in the United Arab Emirates, she told me that during times of extreme hardship she had often used this tale as a kind of guideline. When she was living in Dubai, with five children to feed, no knowledge of her husband's whereabouts, and the threat of deportation constantly looming, she used the mother's clever handling of the fearful and scary situation as a template to deal with an at times desperate situation in which she had no rights. 'Look,' she said. 'Sometimes I felt so hopeless and scared that I really wanted to give up. But I couldn't, I had my children to look after.' If her children asked for special food or things she could not afford, she would try to divert their attention, just like the mother in the story, by telling them that very soon she would get them what they were dreaming of. Whenever she felt like she could not handle the situation anymore she would go back to this story her father had often told her when she was a child. Far from my first perplexed reaction, Halima's story actually revealed something intricate about the links between storytelling and experience.

Anthropologists have long grappled with the question of how to understand or approach life stories. Many of the troubles they encountered arise from the question of whether stories have the ability to represent lives, or whether they are mere fiction. Sarah Lamb (2001: 16) locates the core problem in the difficulty for anthropologists to decide whether life stories speak of life as actually lived, or of life as constructed in narration. She describes these dynamics as the interplay between lives and words. Lamb points out that part of this problem arises from the fact that the life story cannot be taken as a direct, objective account of actual events that happened in an external and transparent past. Therefore, some of the most prominent anthropologists working with life stories have warned that researchers need to be aware of the distinction between life as represented through the story and life as actually lived (Crapanzano 1980; Bruner 1988; Behar 1990).

The children's tale Halima told me complicates this dichotomy between narrative and experience. It suggests that whilst narratives should not be mistaken as reality, they should also not be written off as mere fiction. In all their fictionality they have the capability to convey our experiences and create new and powerful versions of ourselves. Halima's tale highlights the capacity of stories to create a sense of stability, even when the whole world seems to be in a state of violent imbalance. In his path-breaking work on storytelling, violence and intersubjectivity, Michael Jackson (2002: 15) describes these dynamics. He emphasizes the existential importance of telling stories, particularly in the face of hardship and displacement. Jackson characterizes storytelling as a crucial human strategy for sustaining a sense of agency in the context of disempowering circumstances.

Focusing on stories from people in different parts of the world who
have experienced violence and suffering, he shows that the narrative
reworking of reality through storytelling can be a means to symbolically alter the balance between actor and acted upon, allowing
them to regain control over events that make them feel helpless
or lost (Jackson 2002: 16–17). Jackson (2002: 18) defines storytelling as a 'coping strategy that involves making words stand for the
world', which allows for experiences to be changed, reshaped and
lived through again, but in new ways. Storytelling as an anthropological method, then, has more to reveal than one individual's life.
The creative possibility of the story to remodel and retell, to meet
and overcome obstacles, to point at or transform conflict makes it
a crucial means for understanding the ways humans actively make
sense of their being-in-the-world. In this vein Sarah Lamb (2001: 16)
argues that just like other forms of talk or communication, telling
a life story 'is *part* of life as lived, for it *is* lived and experienced, at
least during the moments of telling'. Narrative and experience, this
suggests, are not two detrimentally opposed poles, but intimately
interwoven. While stories do not mirror the exact state of what we
lived through in the past they have the power to form and transform
our self-understanding in the present, thereby twisting our experiences into something new. This hints at storytelling as an existential
force: it is in the act of telling a story that words and lives melt
and create the possibility to not just narrate but also experientially
rework ourselves. Before further exploring the existential quality of
storytelling I will make a brief detour and spell out in more detail the
idea of experience it hinges on.

The Modalities of Experience

While since the 1990s the notion of experience has become increasingly important to anthropologists, and many rely on it for describing the realities of human existence, the roots and complexity of the
concept itself often remain unscrutinized. In this vein the famous
philosopher of experience, Michael Oakeshott (2015: 7), argues that
of all the words in the philosophic vocabulary the notion of experience is the most difficult to handle. He notes that every writer
'reckless enough to use the word' needs to do everything within his
possibility to escape its many ambiguities. Part of the problem is that
experience is frequently used in colloquial, taken-for-granted ways.
The relationship between the vernacular and theoretical use of the

term experience is often difficult to disentangle (Willen and Seeman 2012: 1).

Experience is a notion with a long and complex etymological history (Turner 1985: 221). The Webster English dictionary traces the word back to Middle English through Old French to the Latin term *experientia*, which translates to 'trial, proof or experiment'. According to Webster there are five modern meanings of the verb experience: the first meaning refers to 'direct observation of or participation in events as a basis of knowledge'. Closely linked to this meaning, the second use of the term points to the practical knowledge derived from direct observation of or through participation in events. The third sense of experience refers to everything that has happened to an individual and that makes up his or her life. The fourth meaning comes closest to the ways anthropologists often deploy the term: it defines experience as 'something personally encountered, undergone, or lived through'. The fifth definition of experience refers to an activity or a process through which we immediately perceive reality. These last two meanings of experience are of particular importance to anthropological uses of the term. They refer to the two modes of experience that often appear in anthropological texts: the act of living through something and the ways we are confronted with reality in an immediate and direct way. It was in this sense of the term that Victor Turner delineated the anthropology of experience, a project he embarked upon towards the end of his career (Turner 1985; Turner and Bruner 1986). In developing such an experiential approach, Turner expressed his lifelong discontent with anthropology's strong focus on social models and its neglect of people's everyday experiences and struggles (Bruner 1986: 3). Inspired by the work of German philosopher Wilhelm Dilthey (1906), the ideas of 'life' *(Leben)* and 'living through' *(erleben)* were key to Turner's anthropology of experience. While Turner emphasized experience's dialectical relationship with its expressions, the underlying idea of experience as the act of living through something came to shape and influence subsequent anthropological applications of the term (Turner 1985: 210–13). To insinuate the closeness between experience and life, the term experience is frequently used in combination with the adjectival modifier 'lived'.

Following on from this interest in experience as lived, there has been a strong preoccupation in anthropology with the bodily and sensorial dimensions of experience (e.g. Stoller 1989, 1997; Csordas 1994; Geurts 2002). When deployed in this way, the notion of experience appears as an act of living through something directly, as a bodily, sensory and pre-reflective means of encountering the world. Focusing on this dimension of experience was an important development in anthropological debates. It allowed scholars to move beyond the rigidity and immovability of scientific models of social life, and explore alternative, non-narrative means of knowledge production. Yet treating experience solely in an embodied and immediate way does not come without its own dangers. Tracing back this popular use of experience to eighteenth-century British empiricism, and particularly to the work of John Locke, David Carr (2014: 11) shows that it is closely linked to ideas of innocence and purity. Experience in this sense stands for our first, innocent encounter with the world, a 'plain confrontation between me and the thing' (Carr 2014: 11). In this reading, experience resembles the idea of an untouched, pure or uncorrupted mind. This particular use of experience was developed as a critical response to rationalist complication and abstraction, an aim, which, as I argued before, I share. Yet its reduction to a state of innocence brings the notion of experience dangerously close to the figure of the sensuous noble savage, a figure that stands for the processes of exoticization and othering of indigenous populations that anthropologists (including anthropologists of experience) have attempted to move beyond for several decades. Close to the sense of loss expressed by romantic thinkers bemoaning the end of a state of innocence and pure humanity through the influence of Western civilization, many important thinkers have lamented the loss of experience in the modern world (Jay 2005: 2). Reducing experience to a bodily, immediate encounter thus runs the risk of creating simplistic and essentializing views of people and their everyday lives. Robert Desjarlais and Jason Throop (2011: 93) warn that when used in an unreflexive way, the notion of experience 'at times presumes and promotes unexamined cultural assumptions concerning articulations of self, subjectivity, and social action that may blind us to other possible forms of life and ways of being'. As a result, a range of anthropologists have critically examined the concept of experience and urged for a more complex, multifaceted understanding of the notion (Desjarlais 1996; Mattingly 1998; Throop 2003, 2009). Indeed, Turner himself was careful not to frame experience as a self-enclosed unit. He argued that while experience is lived through in the present, it carries direct links to the past, thus tying it into a dialectical wider whole (Turner 1985: 211).

Besides the historical baggage that comes with this use of the term experience, treating it solely as an immediate and non-intellectual way of encountering the world would not have done justice to the complexity I was confronted with in my collaboration with Halima,

Mohamed and Omar. If I were to treat experience purely in terms of the immediacy it is lived through, the stories Halima, Mohamed and Omar told me would not have had anything to reveal about their lives. They are, after all, reflections on events they have lived through in the past. Yet, as the role of the children's story in restructuring Halima's experiences of displacement shows, narrative and experience are often intimately linked. I agree with Cheryl Mattingly, who has challenged the dichotomy between experience as narrated and experience as lived. She criticizes the notion that lived experience is solely a non-narrated 'prelinguistic bombardment of the senses' and stresses that 'narrative imitates experience because experience already has in it the seeds of narrative' (Mattingly 1998: 45). While the stories Halima, Mohamed and Omar told me were reflections on past experiences, the very act of storying allowed them to actively reshape and relive some of these experiences. Rather than reducing the notion of experience to one single modality, my focus needed to shift between its different modalities.

Two such modalities are captured in the notions of *Erlebnis* and *Erfahrung*, a distinction that has found its way into anthropology through the work of Wilhelm Dilthey. The German equivalent of the English term experience is comprised of these two words that carry very different meanings. While Erlebnis is immediate, unreflected experience, Erfahrung is the point at which experience is examined and articulated. In my collaboration with Mohamed, Halima and Omar I found that these two modalities of experience constantly overlapped, creating a situation where it was no longer possible to distinguish them. As a result, my focus continually moved between the immediate, pre-reflective and affective ways we live through something and the temporally extended means we use to encounter the world through reflection, experimentation and learning. As such, my use of experience comes closer to the initial, dialectical meaning of the term, where it refers to a venture, experimentation or risk. This meaning of experience is also contained in the German Erfahrung. Going back to *Fahrt* (journey) as well *Gefahr* (danger), Erfahrung connotes 'the progressive, if not always smooth, movement over time' that marks our being-in-the-world (Jay 2005: 11). It places temporality at the centre of the concept and emphasizes the know-how and savvy that plays into our everyday engagements with the world (Carr 2014: 18–19). My approach to experience is in close conversation with Veena Das' conceptualization of the ordinary. She argues that rather than looking for a unitary collective subject, we need to turn our attention to the everyday 'forms of inhabiting the world in which one tries to make the world one's own' (Das 2006: 216). To return to the example of Halima's children's tale, this use of experience is able to accommodate the remarkable capability of a seemingly banal story to guide and direct her in moments when she felt powerless. It shows the power of narratives to blur the boundaries between fiction and reality by allowing us to experiment with different versions of ourselves. By bringing to the fore the dialectical and experimental nature of experience, the example of the children's story allows me to raise broader questions about the ways humans struggle with and actively make sense of their being-here. In doing so, it has the power to lay bare the existential parameters that constitute the spatiality of being.

The Existential Parameters of Being-Here

Halima's telling of the children's story reveals the many layers of experience life storytelling is enmeshed within. While the story was not part of her autobiography in the strict sense of the term, it had a lot to say about her life. In conveying a sense of the moods, troubles and victories of being-in-the-world, it had become an intricate part of her seeing the world. This dialectical character of experience came to play an essential role in many of the stories Halima and I worked on after our first slippery attempt. The question of whether things had happened exactly the way she told them in her stories no longer took priority, for, as Vincent Crapanzano (1980: 9) points out, autobiography is essentially a process of self-creation. It gives an order to past events and tries to establish a link between what the narrator was then and what she is today (Corradi 1991: 107).

This is not to suggest that the act of telling stories effects a psychological resolution of deep-rooted problems or traumas. Rather, life stories allow us to shed light both on the teller's hopes, imaginations and ambitions, and on the reality of being part of a wider world that often contradicts and shatters these hopes. In the *Phenomenology of Perception*, Merleau-Ponty describes these dynamics as an essential feature of human existence. He observes that while every individual is acted upon, she or he is also open to possibilities. These situations define our choices: 'To be born is both to be born of the world and to be born into the world,' he writes. While the world is already constituted, it is never complete. 'In the first place we are acted upon, in the second we are open to an infinite number of possibilities.' Because humans always exist in both ways and *at once*, there is no such thing as absolute determinism (Merleau-Ponty 2003 [1945]: 527). While life as told should not be mistaken to be the equivalent of life as lived, I see the strength and value of the life story as a method in its ability to create an understanding of humans as being born *of* and *into* the world, as actors and acted upon. In the context of forced migration, it enables a movement away from 'refugee stories' as manifestations of trauma, instability and victimhood towards a more complex understanding of displacement. Halima's, Mohamed's and Omar's stories give an insight into both the struggles and violent forces that crossed their plans and hopes, and their innermost strengths and capabilities that allowed them to regain a sense of balance – at times even under the most destabilizing circumstances.

Martin Heidegger coined the term 'thrownness' *(Geworfenheit)* to capture this existential condition of our being-in-the-world (Heidegger 1962: 219–24). He stresses that humans find themselves thrown *(geworfen)* into a world that is not of their making. This does not mean that they do not have the means to leap into action or obtain changes, but rather that human life is never undetermined or neutral, that we are always already situated *in* something. This being *in* constitutes the setting and limits for our meaning-making (Withy 2014: 62). Close to Merleau-Ponty's suggestion that we are born of and into the world, Heidegger's thrownness allows us to look at experience as situated *in* something. Rather than viewing experience as closed up in itself, it embeds it in time and space, thereby emphasizing the acts of experimentation, trial and error that play into our daily engagements with our surroundings.

Unfortunately, Heidegger's work does not offer much guidance in spelling out the political, historical and economic dynamics that constitute this being-*in*. His work largely remains on an abstract level that is not grounded in specific experiences, histories or lifeworlds. A too narrow adaptation of Heidegger's existential thought onto anthropological settings thus runs the risk of producing romanticized and universalist portrayals of being-in-the-world. The recent publication of Heidegger's *Black Note Books* (Heidegger 2016), which proves his philosophical entanglement with anti-Semitic and fascist ideas, shows the danger of grand humanist ideas gone astray. Rather than throwing out the baby with the bathwater, however, I believe that we should take the difficult history of thought attached to Heidegger's work as a starting point to make the political an explicit part of a contemporary engagement with his philosophy.

While phenomenological and existential approaches have often been accused of creating intuitive, ahistorical and apolitical views of the world (e.g. Lèvi-Strauss 1973: 58; Geertz 1973: 12–13), I do not believe that there is a contradiction in being both existentially and structurally oriented. Indeed, my collaboration with Halima, Mohamed and Omar proved that an existential perspective that pays serious attention to people's everyday struggles for being cannot but take into account the political and historical. The power dynamics that had forced them to leave their home-places and the spatial tactics that had enabled them to enter some places or blocked them from others formed a crucial element of their lived experiences of place. At the same time, my focus could not solely rest on the structural constraints that undercut their ability to act. Halima's and Omar's stories and Mohamed's photographs also talk about the sometimes playful, sometimes very serious strategies they deployed to contest the politics of place they encountered in Australia, Dubai or Saudi Arabia. When applied to the everyday life contexts anthropologists study, a critical rendering of Heidegger's notion of thrownness thus can be a helpful means to understand the ways power dynamics constitute the settings our interlocutors find themselves cast into. Rather than keeping the focus solely on these structural constraints, however, thrownness also allows us to shed light on the means and strategies people deploy to actively deal with the situations they find themselves in. If applied critically, thrownness strikes a balance between people as actors and acted upon, as born of and into the world. In attempting to achieve this balance, my approach echoes the work of existential anthropologists who work along the lines of a critical phenomenology (e.g. Desjarlais 1997; Jackson 2011, 2013b; Lucht 2011; Gaibazzi 2015; Schielke 2015). While such an approach stays true to the phenomenological call to describe the 'things themselves', it simultaneously asks why things are the way they are (Desjarlais 1997: 25).

One of the most crucial themes existential anthropologists explore is the question of how people deal with the tension between personal choice and external circumstances that restrict their possibilities to act. Existential anthropologists hold that individuals are never entirely reducible to an ascribed identity. Instead, they work with the tension that arises between the two conflicting poles of being a 'who' and a 'what' at the same time (Jackson and Piette 2015: 3). Moving away from social scientists' longstanding focus on the collective, existential anthropology seeks 'to capture the human presence in its manifold and elusive modes of engagement' (Jackson and Piette 2015: 19). Such a perspective actively works with the ambiguities of lived sociality: while individuals are intimately involved in collective issues, there are other layers of being that lie outside of what could be captured through static concepts such as 'the social' or 'the cultural'.

For researchers working with life storytelling as a method, an existential perspective entails an awareness that people never live in stable states and with fixed identities, but that they 'live experimentally', always on the move between different narratives, world views and modes of being (Jackson and Piette 2015: 9–10). As such, the focus moves from the interpretation of the life story to the transitive, ambiguous and multilayered nature of life itself. My collaboration with Halima confronted me with the need to move away from my focus on the life story and towards the dynamics of the telling. Rather than solely looking for meaning in the stories themselves, I turned my attention towards the social process of the telling, thereby putting the spotlight on everyday acts of meaning-making (Jackson 2002: 18). With this shift in perspective, small, seemingly banal moments in everyday life (like the story Halima had told me at the end of our first meeting) turned into crucial entry points into the nuances of human existence. Not dissimilar to Albert Piette's (2015a: 185–86) focus on the 'minor modes' of being, I came to see the inconsistencies, interruptions, fragments and silences, the 'small bits and pieces' that make up individuals' everyday engagements with their surroundings, as essential gateways to a more nuanced understanding of the role of place in a world of movement.

Albert Piette coined the notion of the minor mode to capture the small gestures, behaviours and attitudes that appear when individuals are engaged in a situation. These fragmented and incomplete expressions often go unnoticed or are treated as unimportant, as they cannot be ordered and quantified. However, as Piette (2015b: 39) points out, these details are important exactly because they are deemed not relevant and are inextricably linked to individual lifeworlds. In paying attention to minor modes of existence, he urges anthropologists to resist the compulsion to subordinate individuals to groups, cultures or societies. Instead, they should study humans 'one at a time' (Piette 2015b: 12). When Piette speaks of an existentially oriented anthropology he has in mind an anthropology that analyses the singularity of individuals in the act of existing. While I share with Piette an interest in the particularities of human existence, I believe in the importance of understanding how the singularity of being-here is linked to a shared and relational being-with-others. In this vein, Heidegger emphasizes that our being-in-the-world is marked by the continuous attempt to strike a balance between *Mitsein* (being-with-others) and *Selbstsein* (being-oneself) (Heidegger 1962: 149–68). It is only by reaching out into the wider world, by encountering others, that we can grasp the notion of our own self (Weiner 2001: 6). Going back to the metaphor brought up at the beginning of the chapter, I concur with Piette that anthropologists cannot reduce their role to that of an Icarus observing life from above, thereby only picking up on the bigger picture of life as a whole. But also they cannot reduce their perspective to that of a Daedalus, thereby getting lost in the ambiguous and never-ending parts that make up daily life. I agree with Victor Turner's (1985: 190) warning that we need to create a balance between these two perspectives, because while 'extreme individualism only understands a part of man', 'extreme collectivism only understands man as a part'. The existential anthropology I embark on, therefore, attempts to strike a balance between these different parameters of existence: between wholes and parts, structure and agency, an Icarus and Daedalus perspective, the individual and the relational, trial and error, and thrownness and picking oneself up.

That afternoon in the Iraqi kebab restaurant, when my methodological preconceptions collapsed like a house of cards, I was forced to confront these dynamics. While I could not grasp the full meaning of this story straight away, sitting in that restaurant with the smell of the kebabs cooking on the spit and the chatter and laughter of people eating their lunch surrounding us, Halima's telling of the story moved something inside me instantaneously. This movement inside of me, a movement that grew out of an emotional involvement, was, I now think, a first step towards the beginning of a dialogue between us. Just as the story cannot grow in utter silence and privacy, so does ethnographic reasoning not just *happen* in the mind of the scholar. Rather, Halima's story and my reaction to it show that such reasoning is created through and in relation to the outside world, a world we share with others. Instead of writing off the methodological mishap that marked my first conversations with Halima, it formed a crucial starting point for understanding and finally theorizing the entanglement of storytelling and experience.

Visual Storytelling

After Mohamed had so clearly stated that he felt uncomfortable in the recorded storytelling situation, I completely dropped the idea of collaborating with him on his life story. This time coincided with a period of great change in Mohamed's life. He had just started his position as adviser to the Somali transitional government and was about to embark on a long trip that would take him to many conferences all over the world. During this extended period abroad he would also return to Mogadishu more than thirty years after he had last set foot in it. Throughout this time we stayed in contact. Mohamed kept me updated about his whereabouts through Skype or emails, often by sending me images. It was the small, intangible things he came across during his journeys that compelled Mohamed to take photographs: the statue of a Hindu goddess surrounded by offerings amidst the soulless scenery of an airport shopping mall, a brief video clip of a patch of blue sky peeking through the mist of thick fume caused by a smoke-bomb somewhere in Tunisia, a snapshot of himself against a mirror that had broken during an earthquake in Tokyo (Figure 1.1.), or an image of himself pretending to throw a letter into a completely demolished letter box in Mogadishu. When I received the email containing the latter image, Mohamed had just left Mogadishu for Tanzania. I asked him to describe what it had been like, but he replied that he could not do this in writing. 'But I have very important photographs I want to discuss with you,' he wrote. 'I have been to Geneva … then Kenya, Somalia, South Africa … and now in Dar es Salaam until the 10th I will be in Dubai/ Abu Dhabi for 3 days, then to KL/ Singapore until 22nd. I hope to see you after that. Tell me how r things with you; I'm actually missing your adventure stories …' Weeks later, when Mohamed returned to Melbourne, I received

Figure 1.1 *Self-portrait in front of a broken mirror. Image courtesy of Mohamed Ibrahim*

a message: 'Am back in town till the 10th ... let us catch up when convenient.'

When I first saw the photographs Mohamed had taken in Mogadishu I was struck by their narrative strength. They showed skeletons of bombed out houses, gusts of dust in deserted streets, sheep grazing in the middle of the city and people rushing through the remnants of destroyed buildings. Going beyond the places' bleak and sad surface, however, Mohamed began telling me stories of their former grace and beauty, and of moments from the past his images evoked. Through the photos, Mohamed was able to *visually* tell of experiences that were otherwise hard to find words for. This was a crucial insight for me that changed the shape of my methodological approach. When I first saw the photos he had taken in Mogadishu, I was struck by their ability to shed light on the ways Mohamed actively dealt with his sense of displacement. I came to realize that he had been giving me profound insights into his experiences through his photographs all along. These insights were more than purely visual. Rather, the images he showed and the conversations we had around them involved visual, sensory, embodied and narrative dimensions of experience. The photos and short video clips of his journeys he shared with me during his stays in Melbourne, or in email or Skype conversations, gave crucial insights into his everyday engagements with his surroundings. Ultimately, the photographs and our conversations about them came to shape the core theme of the interplay of place and experience that came to frame my epistemological approach.

I found that Mohamed's engagement with place through photography was close to the dynamics Tim Ingold (2011: 178) describes when he writes that by making things people 'bind their own pathways or lines of becoming into the texture of the world'. When looked at as a practice, the act of taking photographs bears many resemblances to the existential dynamics of making as a means of actively carving out our place in relation to the wider world. Similarly, I would argue that through his camera Mohamed was taking in the places he was moving through and creating stories about them, which enabled him to invest his surroundings with meaning. This form of visual storytelling could be compared to the act of drawing oneself into the world, a comparison that is not as far-fetched as it might first appear if one looks into the roots of the word photography: it derives from the Greek *photos* (light) and *graphos* (drawing). Photography, then, literally means 'drawing with light'. In the photographs Mohamed took in Mogadishu the act of walking and taking photographs did not just allow him to draw himself into the world he was moving through, but also to tell stories that allowed him to overcome his feelings of estrangement from this place he had left so many years ago. That he used the camera as a tool for this was perhaps not a coincidence. As Susan Sontag (2008: 9) writes in her famous essays *On Photography*, the act of taking photographs helps people to take possession of spaces in which they are insecure. She points out that the tourist or traveller often takes photos, as the very activity of taking photographs is soothing and assuages the feeling of disorientation that is part of travelling. That Mohamed, travelling through the place he had left behind so many years ago, began taking photographs of his movements was perhaps part and parcel of the same dynamics. By putting the camera between himself and Mogadishu, he distanced himself from the things he was seeing while at the same time never losing sight of the place he was moving through. Again, his photographs do not speak of experience as a purely visual and immediate encounter with the world. The camera enabled Mohamed to not just look and experiment with, but also *interpret* the world around him. Within these lines, the great Hungarian photographer André Kertész once said: 'The camera is my tool. Through it I give reason to everything around me' (in Berger and Mohr 1995: 128). Kertész, who as a consequence of World War II experienced displacement first-hand, used the camera as a means of depicting his encounters with New York, the place where he had found refuge. The camera allowed him to express both his fascination with and alienation from his new surroundings. It is of such experimental ways of seeing and drawing his engagement with the world that Mohamed's photographs speak.

While through the photographs Mohamed was able to tell me stories of his life, we no longer aimed at working towards a coherent life story. The opposite was the case: my initial aspiration for narrative ordering was replaced by an interest in the disarray that marks everyday acts of meaning-making. Rather than making Mohamed order his experiences along the linearity of a story-plot, I integrated his photographic practice as a means of shedding light on the complexities and ambiguities of his placemaking practices. The interplay of walking, taking photographs and looking at them created a peculiar perspective through which Mohamed made sense of the world – not in terms of the smoothness of a story, but in terms of dialectical snapshots that represented past, present and future all at once (Lems 2017). Consequently, I have embedded Mohamed's experiences in the flimsy and unfinished ways they appeared in our conversations. Instead of producing a continuum between here and there, and now and then, his photographs form 'dialectical images' (Buck-Morss 1989; Benjamin 1999) – images that refuse to be woven into a coherent storyline. In doing so, the photographs and story snippets that form the junctures of this book have the power to shed light on the experimental character of experience – a characteristic that allows people like Mohamed who are confronted with the ruin- ation of their home places to create a sense of temporal and spatial continuity and bestow them with meaning.

Life Storytelling

The methodological mishaps that had shocked me so thoroughly out of my academic comfort zone revealed something deep – not just about the practical conundrums involved in narrating a life, but also about the politics of life storytelling. It forced me to see that while a focus on individual stories allows for a deep look into the particularity of being-displaced, it simultaneously runs the risk of romanticizing the outcome (the life story) of what is in fact the product of a complex process (the telling of the life story). Rather than melting the different set of stories, practices and dialogues into a coherent life story, my focus shifted towards the storytelling moment and its lived messiness. This messiness has a lot to say about the ways different modalities of experience continuously overlap. By actively working with the ambiguity that marked many of Halima's, Omar's and Mohamed's engagements with place – an ambiguity that enabled them to constantly shift back and forth between actor and acted upon, between being born of and into the world – I came to understand the experimental nature of experience.

While my collaboration with Mohamed had shifted to his visual acts of storytelling, Halima, Omar and I continued to work on their life stories. Both of them chose different means or genres for narrat- ing them. Omar captivated me with the political power of his words. In line with the great storytellers from different parts of the world, he embodied the characters that appeared and used the story to make the listener travel with him between places, countries and lifetimes. The main theme that ran through all of his stories, however, was an urge to understand the social, political and emotional downfall of his country. In telling me his life story, he was not only telling me his own story, but the story of the Somali community in Melbourne and the fate of his people in Puntland. In formulating such a comprehensive portrayal, Omar was careful to create a balanced view, one that did not feed into the poisonous interclan dynamics that have created so much friction amongst Somalis – in Somalia as well as in Melbourne. At the same time, the telling of his story was also driven by the hope that it would work towards creating a place for Somali-Australians in the wider national narrative.

After our first somewhat confused attempt to work on Halima's life story, I became so closely involved in her life that by the time we started to work on her life story again she had already told me many of the stories that were to become part of this book, lending the storytelling setting an intimate strength. Halima often said that telling me her stories gave her a feeling of relief. At the same time, her stories were also directed towards a very specific goal. She was telling her story for a younger generation of Somalis (especially women) growing up outside of Somalia, whom she wanted to understand the many struggles she had been through and the tactics she adopted to overcome them. Halima hoped that her stories would convey the sense of a Somaliness she was proud of to a younger generation that had never encountered it – a Somaliness that was marked by peace and interclan solidarity and that had allowed women like her to participate in political life. But like Omar, she also told her story for an Australian audience whom she wanted to understand better the complex journeys of Somalis in Australia. Halima's story can be likened to what Lidwien Kapteijns (2009: 105), in the context of her work on the life story of the Somali woman Maryan Muuse Boqor, describes as an 'exemplary narrative', a story told by the narrator to serve as an inspiring example for others.

While each storytelling session began with the rough idea of a specific time in the lives of Halima or Omar, none of the life stories developed chronologically or as a singular narrative or text. Instead, they were told to me in fragments, sometimes in the form of anecdotes, sometimes prompted by specific questions I had after recapitulating things we had spoken about before, sometimes in relation to a story I had told about myself. Mostly, however, they were told as stories in their own right that in many ways linked back to other stories that had already been told. Linguist anthropologist Charlotte Linde (1993: 25) proposes that a life story is not simply a collection of stories, but that they relate to each other. She stresses that 'when any new story is added to the repertoire of the life story, it must be related in some way to the themes of the other stories included in the life story, or at least it must not contradict them'. As a result, the stories that make up a life story are undergoing constant changes in order to express our current understanding of what our lives mean. In

Halima's and Omar's case, the life storytelling process reflected some of the dynamics Linde identifies. Rather than framing their stories as one uniform and uninterrupted life story, they told me many stories. All these stories, however, were linked by the all-encompassing objective to create a picture of the experiences that shaped them into the persons they had become. At the same time, Omar and Halima also used the stories as vehicles to create a sense of coherence in their own lives. Through the act of telling they came to relive moments and events in their lives that had shaped them – and by reliving them, these experiences were reshaped or re-emplaced in the here and now. Their stories were aimed at giving a sense of what moulded them into the people they had become. The vague idea of portraying 'a life' or 'a person' can thus be seen as the glue binding the many stories that spanned different lifetimes, places, people and events into something 'whole'. At the same time, however, each story was important in itself; it allowed for the sense of wholeness to become interrupted by the many shifts, twists and movements that form our being-here. In doing so, their stories show how Omar and Halima actively made sense of the world. This, again, points towards the importance of creating a balance between an Icarus and Daedalus perspective in the storytelling setting: while life storytelling requires an understanding of the wholeness of a storied life, its genres, and the set of cultural rules and responsibilities that can guide both the teller and the listener, it is also crucial to value its parts. As I will demonstrate when I present Halima's story, in the context of displacement and traumatic experiences it is equally important to respect missing links, silences and fragments. As Elinor Ochs and Lisa Capps (1997: 3) point out, a story is not just a story; 'it is a struggle to formulate a life, a history, an ethics, especially a justification for actions realized and to come'.

The idea of a life story as chronological and whole from the outset thus does not match the reality of a life storytelling setting. Most life stories are partial, and this partiality, and the missing links and contradictions, need to be respected as an essential part of their inner workings. It is not up to the researcher to become engaged in a forensics of storytelling that attempts to meticulously piece together stories of a life into the fluent wholeness of a text. As Gaylene Becker (1997: 28) points out in her work on the role of storytelling in the context of disrupted lives, there are good reasons for not telling everything there is to tell. Life stories are always accompanied by an internal editing process that works as a means of lending the story a greater sense of coherence and wholeness. This, in turn, also leads to a greater sense of self-consistency. What is edited out or left in, however, is often intimately linked to the cultural background of the narrator and to what she thinks can or cannot be part of a coherent story. The themes and events that found their way into Halima's and Omar's stories, as well as those that were left out, had much to do with their ideas of what constitutes a good or shareable story.

The Poetics of Life Storytelling

In Somalia, storytelling is at the heart of the country's self-identification. As the growing number of Somali poems distributed and disseminated worldwide through the internet and on CDs and DVDs shows, the role of poets and poetry in Somalia might have changed but they have not lost their crucial importance, specifically in the face of war and destruction (Andrzejewski and Andrzejewski 1993; Kapteijns 2010; Andrzejewski 2011). Often in the form of poems, the Somali orature goes beyond a mere retelling of historical events. As Said Samatar (1982: 55) shows in his book on the role of poetry in the making and remaking of a Somali national identity, poems play such an essential role in Somali society that people attach to it the 'highest measure of importance'. Poets are not seen as esoteric people, or as outsiders to society, whose poems are recited solely to inspire through the lyrical and beautiful. Instead, they are at the centre of political and social action and are drawn upon for their ability to inform, persuade and convince. Traditionally, poetry was used as a principle vehicle of political power in Somalia.[1] While there are specific poetical genres that give expression to personal emotion or passion, the ultimate concern of the Somali poet is 'to influence the opinions of others towards a certain vital issue' (S. Samatar 1982: 57).

Although Halima and Omar grew up as part of the educated elite and although both of them were also influenced by Western ideas of autobiography, the politics of a Somali way of storytelling informs their stories. That Omar's stories were so self-confident and often evolved around core political questions concerning Somalia's condition can partly be explained by his position as a spokesperson and elder within the community of Somalis from the Puntland area in Melbourne. It is in this position that he regularly publishes articles disseminated through Somali websites, which describe, analyse and comment on current political developments in Somalia and in the Somali diaspora. Like the most serious and politically loaded form of Somali poetry, the gabay, which is only performed by men and representatives of a clan, his stories reflect a persuasive effort to create political stability and harmonious relationships. Driven by this core effort, Omar's stories paint nuanced pictures of the sociopolitical, historical, religious and economical dimensions that have shaped his personal trajectories. In taking on the role of the politically minded storyteller, however, the emotional dimensions of life were pushed into the background: in his stories Omar rarely revealed his innermost feelings, creating the picture of a somewhat removed onlooker or commentator on his own life. This absence of emotionality might be related to the fact that in the Somali storytelling setting, speaking of personal emotions without making a politically, socially or universally relevant point is generally not seen as acceptable, specifically when the stories are told by older and respectable men (Kapteijns 2010: 30). At the same time, in the Somali context, stories usually do not focus on the inner life of the storyteller because they are told to persuade and effect changes or forward solutions that go beyond the life of one individual (Kapteijns 2010: 31).

For Omar, who does not only tell the story of himself but of his community, and who spends all his time and effort in finding ways to make Melbourne a home to this community, there were more important questions to dwell on than his inner life. Similar to the dynamics Renato Rosaldo (1976) described in his work on the life story of Tukbaw, a member of the Ilongot society in the Philippines, it was much more important to Omar to focus on his public self and on the role he represented within wider political and social realms. Instead of centring his stories on groundbreaking emotional events in his life, such as his marriage, the birth of his children, or the arrival of his elderly mother in Melbourne, he found it more important to convey a sense of the overarching political and social dynamics he was confronted with and the ways he chose to deal with them. While he was keen for the readers of this book to understand the struggles of Somalis in Australia, he often told me that he did not want his written story to deteriorate into a form of navel-gazing.

Halima's stories, on the other hand, do not shy away from entering emotional territory and also give insight into her inner life. Her stories bear the characteristics of the main genre of women's storytelling in Somalia, the buraanbur. Whereas male storytellers are expected to contain their private feelings, emotional dimensions are an accepted feature of female storytelling in Somalia. Women often use poetry and songs to speak of their hopes and dreams, struggles and fears. Halima's stories were steeped in a poetics and rhythm that reflect many of the buraanbur's conventions. The poetic tone in her stories can be linked to the fact that ever since the outbreak of the civil war she has been composing her own poems and songs. Just as the life storytelling session gave her a sense of relief, writing poems helped her to communicate the hardships she had experienced and to make sense of the political disintegration of Somalia. As I show in more detail in Part III, her poems sometimes found their way into the stories she told me. In letting her emotions become part of her songs and poems, Halima was able to reflect on her innermost feelings without turning her story into a confession – a mode of storytelling she found deeply embarrassing for the teller's willingness to lay bare their most personal thoughts.

Although Halima gave insight into her inner life, there were also aspects she did not consider appropriate for a story that would be read by people she did not know. Stories that touched upon emotionally charged topics were often told to me as a friend, but underwent editing processes in the course of turning her stories into written texts. When reading a first draft of my selection of stories, Halima felt uncomfortable. There were moments in our conversation when she had become oblivious to the fact that her stories would be shared with a wider audience in a written text. When reading the written stories, she became distressed about the idea of sharing some details with a wider audience. In the Somali context, certain topics are acceptable to be discussed within the settings of a very specific audience (usually other females or family members), but in a public setting such topics are not tolerated as part of a 'good' story. During the act of the telling I had been Halima's audience, and the intimacy of this setting allowed for aspects to be told that, in the context of the written text and its more public orientation, could not be part of the story. As a result, we spent many hours going through my drafts, rephrasing some sentences and, on two occasions, editing out sections. Because of these editorial processes, a few stories lost some of the intimate depth and details they had first carried. This was a price I was willing to pay. As Ruth Behar (1993: 273) so eloquently put it, in the context of her collaboration with Esperanza, a Mexican street peddler, I was determined to respect Halima's silences 'as though they were her fiercest words'.

Because Halima and Omar did not necessarily aim for a coherent grand narrative representing *a* life story but told me many stories about themselves instead, I found it crucial to let these dynamics also enter my writing. As a result I have not attempted to edit the many stories into a singular life story. Instead, I chose to focus on a selection of short stories, centred on crucial moments or experiences that shaped and defined Omar's and Halima's lives. In my attempt to strike a balance between an Icarus and Daedalus perspective, however, I tried not to over-concentrate on the stories as singular parts and thereby lose sight of the sense of wholeness of 'a life' or 'a person' both Halima and Omar, in telling their stories, were also trying to convey. I therefore ordered the stories that became part of this book chronologically to allow the reader to literally follow Omar and Halima through some of the ups and downs of their lives and gain a stronger sense of them as persons.

Not all the stories made their way into this book, and the decisions about what to leave out were sometimes painful and hard. But the act of retelling stories in a written form must follow its own poetics of storytelling. In the context of her work with Esperanza, Ruth Behar (1993: 19) describes this process as cutting Esperanza's tongue, which she subsequently patches together to form a new one. This process of patching together a new tongue, however, required Omar's and Halima's input. Both of them read and commented on the versions I had written, suggested changes, and, in Halima's case, also asked me to take out things that she felt misrepresented her, and sometimes added layers that she thought were needed. Halima's and Omar's verbatim stories that became part of this book are thus not exact reproductions of the stories I recorded. While I was determined to stay as close to the transcripts as possible, I was confronted with the difficulty that sometimes elements that work well in the telling of a story do not translate easily into a written text. Omar, who had read transcripts of the recorded storytelling sessions from the first day we met, pointed out the necessity for editorial steps early on. He wanted to have his story written in a comprehensive and balanced way, to eliminate grammatical mistakes, repetitions and unnecessary detours, which, as he found, weakened his voice.

The different poetic conventions deployed by Halima, Omar and Mohamed draw attention to the importance of creativity and aesthetics in life storytelling. As Mary Chamberlain and Paul Thompson (1998: 1) point out, any life story is not only shaped by the reworking of experiences, but also by art. My role as an anthropologist thus goes beyond that of a responsible listener. In the writing and retelling of life stories an awareness of the *politics* of life storytelling is clearly essential, but I suggest that a *poetics* of storytelling is just as important. That very first afternoon when I met Halima in the Footscray café to begin working with her, when for a split second I feared that my idea of life storytelling had ended before I had started to understand it, the subtlety and beauty of the children's story Halima shared with me gently brought me back again. Rather than looking for a grammar or language to translate the inner workings of stories, I recognized an obligation towards Omar, Mohamed and Halima to find a way of developing a poetics of ethnographic writing that would allow me to convey the beauty and strength of their stories. Such a poetics of ethnographic writing also needed to capture the politics of storytelling and make transparent the (inner and outer) dialogues that had led me to grasp the continuing role of place in a hypermobile world.

Note

1. As John William Johnson (1996) and Lidwien Kapteijns (2011) have shown in their work on the Somali popular song, Somali modes of story-telling influence the political sphere – not only in a 'traditional' context. They were utilized by the anti-colonial national liberation movement in Somalia, as well as by the governments that followed. While the popular song is a relatively new development, it bears many resemblances to traditional oral poetry. Both are characterized by a commitment to persuade, inform and aim for action and change.

PART II
Emplacement

Returning from Mogadishu, Mohamed often talked about how strange it was that everyday life seemed to continue as normal – that people, in the midst of all the conflict, the chaos and the fear, still inhabited the place. Over the years of war, the once unified city had disintegrated into a series of embattled clan enclaves. Every step in the

Figure PII.1 *A market in the centre of Mogadishu. Image courtesy of Mohamed Ibrahim*

wrong direction, every crossing of an invisible boundary, every word to the wrong person was potentially dangerous. The place seemed to have broken into countless parts, as if it had become de-placed. And yet, life unfolded in the strangest ways and under the greatest pressures. With the persistence of people, with their stories, their hopes and imaginations, places like Mogadishu, places that appear so lost, do not simply disappear.

Mohamed took this photo driving past a little market in the middle of Mogadishu. Because he took the image from a moving car, it carries a strange sense of fleetingness – as if not only the photographer but everyone in the picture is ready to pack up and run off at any moment. 'I was interested in this, because with all the chaos and destruction – this still goes on,' Mohamed explained. 'People are still buying and selling.' Although the traders have to make do with the few things they could find to sell, the sight of the few humble stalls gave Mohamed the impression that at least in some corners of the city life went on as normal. Pointing at the children gathering around the table on the left-hand side of the image, he noted: 'For someone like this kid, for all these kids in fact, probably this is all they know. Because they were born at a time when all they experienced was this. So to them it's normal. But to me it's abnormal because I remember what this place was like.'

To Mohamed, who had left the place so many years ago, this corroded Mogadishu and its inner workings felt alien. What had become normal to its inhabitants was abnormal to him. What had become normal to Mohamed was out of reach of the normality of those living in Mogadishu. Still, coming past the little market place, seeing people setting up stalls, selling the few things they could find, let some of the habits of the place he remembered, the inhabited place, shine through. It reminded Mohamed of the liveliness of Mogadishu, a place that somehow, despite all its brokenness, was still home. He was nineteen when he had last seen the city. 'And look at my age now,' Mohamed said. 'I was not even half of my age now, so it was not significant – but it is because it still is home.'

So what is this, 'home'? What allows a place like Mogadishu to remain significant in Mohamed's life after so many years, despite all the changes that have made it hard to comprehend the place and its inhabitants the way he once used to? What, in the end, does it mean to be emplaced?

2

Placing Somalia

Meeting Omar

I was waiting for Omar in front of the blocks of council flats in Melbourne's inner suburb of Carlton. He had instructed me to wait for him at the front gate, as it would be difficult to find my way on my own in the large building. I looked around, wondering what it must be like to live on the twentieth floor of one of these buildings. The old 1970s-style towers had a strange presence, their greyness making them stand out from the neatly renovated Victorian terrace houses that surrounded them. Hundreds of windows gave a hint of the many people that lived there. And yet, the windows appeared to be empty, as if the building was jealously making sure that it disclosed no one but itself.

A tall, friendly man came up to me. 'Hello,' he said, 'Welcome to Australia. I'm Omar.' Omar is a spokesperson for the Somalis living in and around the Carlton flats. His NGO, Horn Afrik, is based in an office on the ground floor of one of the council buildings. As we walked into the dim, almost windowless room at the back of the office space, where Omar had placed his desk and laptop, he told me about his work. 'Whenever there are problems or requests, be it from the police, the government or other organizations, they come and speak to me,' he explained, inviting me to sit down. I had received his phone number from a community worker who had told me that Omar might be able to help me find Somali participants for my project. He had many questions about my research and about my own journey from Austria to Australia. 'Life story, can you explain to me what that means?' he asked me. I told him that I would meet up with the participants often, that I would ask them to tell me about their lives, about their childhood, their journey to Australia and anything that was of importance to them. 'So you don't just ask questions for once and then we never hear from you again?' he asked. He told me about the many researchers who had come and gone, leaving the community without ever letting them know about the results of their research. I told him that I was planning to work with only a small group of people, who I wanted to get to know well and acknowledge their stories.

'All right then,' Omar said. 'Do you want to start the interview?' Having come with the expectation that he would help me to find others to interview, I was surprised by this turn. I told him that I was not prepared and suggested that it might be better for me to come back in a couple of weeks to give him time to think about a topic we could start with. 'That's right,' Omar responded. 'Because I have a lot to tell you. So many countries I went through, Saudi Arabia, India, Australia … I have a lot of stories to tell you.'

I was born in Puntland in Somalia.[1] Particularly, I was born in the north-east of Somalia, in a town called Gardo. I grew up in an area where most of the people were from my clan, or my sub-clan, the Majeerteen. The people who lived on the right side were from my clan; the people who lived in front of our house were from my clan; the people who lived behind our house were from my clan; the people who lived on my left side were from my clan. And I grew up with the attitude that there is nothing in this world except my clan.

And I didn't open my eyes properly until I moved to Mogadishu, where there are so many different clans. Then I went to the Middle East, to Saudi Arabia, and I learned more about Somalis and their culture and where they come from and that there is nothing like a group that is more superior than others. In fact, where I grew up the majority was Majeerteen, who are a sub-clan of the Harti or Darood. My main clan, the Darood, is divided into sub-clans of which the Majeerteen is one. The Somali clan system is like an onion: when you take one layer, there is another layer, you take that layer and then there's another layer, and so on.

The Darood happened to be those who used to run the country for a long time. I think what really helped them to emerge stronger than others was their relationship with other civilizations. If you check the map, the north-east of Somalia has a close proximity to the Middle East. So people from my region used to travel to the Middle East, and they used to go to Asia, to Indonesia and Malaysia. When the Europeans arrived in Somalia they started to work with the local authorities. The Darood's cooperation with the newly arrived Europeans gave them more power and more openness to governance, administration and so forth. And eventually, when the Europeans left the country, they handed the power over to them. Unfortunately the colonial system didn't help anyone. What really transpires now is that the territory mainly occupied by the Darood is more stable than the south, where they are actually fighting over the power.

So that's the kind of life I come from. However, if you read in the history books, you will see that the dictator Siyaad Barre, the leader of the regime from 1969 to 1991, was also Darood, but that he started to turn against the Majeerteen, who were a sub-clan of the Darood, purely because the Majeerteen were running the country before him.

Where I grew up, some people were fishermen, and some were farmers, but the main income came from livestock. They exported livestock to all Middle Eastern countries and that was their major income. Now fishery came into life because in the north-east of Somalia we've got the largest stock of tuna in the whole world. Recently you could see the price for tuna going up in Europe after the pirates started to operate in Somalia. And actually the pirates originally came from the fishing people whose business was destroyed by large European fishing trawlers.

I had sixteen brothers and sisters. My father married more than two wives. Even though polygamy was very common, I think my father was more energetic compared to many other people. He also was wealthy, so he was capable to marry more than once. But in accordance with the religion he was never married to more than four women at the same time. My mother was from a different sub-clan than my father. When I was a child it was very common in Somalia to marry a woman who didn't belong to your immediate clan. The reason was to bring the clans together. So the woman used to be the bridge between the clans, because intermarriage brings the people together – in-laws, nephews, all these create a situation where regardless which clan you are from, the people are becoming closer.

My father was a businessman. He used to work for different companies that were running the fish industry in the north-east of Somalia, owned by the Italian and Somali governments. He was the CEO and used to go to the Middle East or Italy. He spent most of his time either in Italy, Yemen or Mogadishu. Because of his business duties I could hardly see my father until he retired.

So that's how the make-up of my family worked. We children are from different mothers, but we consider each other to be brothers and sisters. Many of my brothers and sisters have died.

I was born in 1960, the year Somalia became a nation state. So I grew up in a governmental system. But I can see now that why we have never been rule-abiding citizens is because of our background. There was no system that centralized us. It is the fragmented system that keeps us apart; everyone lives in his own world.

My father always advised me: 'You are Somali, that's the end of the road. Your main clan are the Majeerteen and that's all you have to learn about it.' He was always telling me that what you learn and what you achieve personally will help you and not what clan A or clan B has or has not. My father was different, but within the wider society the clan issue was always there.

I think that what put us into the position we are in today is purely the clan. If all the people who see themselves as Somali accepted anyone as a Somali, without any discrimination, without any further investigation of which sub-clan he is, we wouldn't be in the position we are in today. And it's also true that there was abuse in some of the clans. That's why the image of the clan was becoming an issue. The people were led to believe that the only way you can survive is to have a leader from your clan in the highest seat of the nation. That's why they're fighting over the power. Many of the clans, like my clan, they were not even allowed to have a passport let alone anything else. When I left Somalia, I changed my name and my identity to get a passport.

Somalia, it's not the Somalia that it used to be, the people are not the people that I used to know. The clan, it always used to be the clan but not the clan that created fences between the people. Now we've got clans that create fences when it comes to intelligence, when it comes to understanding, when it comes to assessing something.

I left Puntland to go to university in Mogadishu in 1976. I was studying fisheries. It's funny, there were two reasons why I chose to learn fisheries: one was that my family had a background in the fishing industry. But the main reason was that the university I chose was the only one where they taught English in the mainstream subjects. I was trying to find somewhere where I could improve my English skills. I had this dream that one day I will leave and work in a non-Somali speaking country.

For me going to university was a stepping stone. I didn't want to stay in Somalia, I didn't see Somalia to be a country that could respond to my needs. And also going overseas was very popular in my age. It was the talk of the day about who went where and who was doing what and the kind of life that they had.

We used to watch the *Dallas* movies all the time, movies about these American oil millionaires who put all values and morals aside and were more focused on money. This kind of Hollywood fiction impacted us to some extent. We were not necessarily impacted by their actions but by the life that they had: the roads, the lights, the shining things, the freedom, the fact that they lived in a clean, nice place. So we thought: 'This is what I want to get, this is where I want to go.' I wanted to drive that kind of car, I wanted to drive that car in that kind of road, that highway, I wanted to dress in that kind of way, with ties and shoes and shirts and jackets and all this. Why shouldn't I have this in my country? If I had that in my country I wouldn't need to go anywhere else.

And again, the country was not providing us young people with what we needed: the employment, the income, the stability, the discrimination against particular clans and so on. At that time Siyaad Barre was discriminating and arresting, and turning against all Majeerteen, especially after 1978, when they attempted to do a coup and the coup was not successful, so many of them were killed, many of them were arrested, many of them left the country.

So I was like someone who was in a cage. You know, if you have a bird in a cage, it always wants to get out of that cage. As soon as you open it: pieeeew, it will fly. That's exactly what happened to us.

I think in Somalia there were three categories of emigrants: those who smelled and started to run, those who actually became victims and as a result ran and those who finally got into the mess and tried to go somewhere else. I was in the group of those who smelled before the war actually started to come to the surface. And I left the country. I was nineteen years old when I left Somalia.

I left Somalia eight months before my graduation. That was very bad. Going north was more important to me than finishing university in Somalia, at least in my view at that time. It was wrong. Just because I had all these dreams you will never really experience – theoretically maybe, but not in reality.

My father died in 1991 in Mogadishu, in a natural way. The last time I saw him was in 1983 when I was leaving Somalia. He advised me not to leave the country and go overseas; he was not one of those people who believed that you should migrate to other countries because he believed you would become a minority. And he was right. I did my BA and Masters and the job I am doing is not the job that I should be doing. I wouldn't be doing this kind of job if I were in Somalia. I wouldn't be less than a minister in Somalia.

Creating Common Ground

When I began listening to Omar's life story, neither of us was sure how to approach the dizzyingly large task of storying one's life. I had the idea of letting the story unfold, letting it happen rather than making it happen, but I did not verbalize this idea in our first meetings. And Omar, who as a spokesperson for the Somali community in Melbourne is often approached by journalists, local politicians or community workers, had his own ideas about what he wanted to tell me. I had told him about the reasons behind my decision to focus on life stories, but we did not go much further in thinking about how and where to begin. Looking back now, I think that we were preoccupied with getting to know each other, which made the technicalities of planning what was to come seem out of place. Instead of discussing our ideas of life stories, we started by simply telling each other about our lives. I told Omar about my family, about our complicated history of movements between the Netherlands and Austria and about my impressions of Australia. Omar told me about his wife, who was working as a cultural mediator in Melbourne's main hospital, about his children, his work, his life in general. From our first conversations it became clear that while Omar was a very thoughtful person, he also liked to see things from a humorous side. We laughed about the fact that Somalis all seem to have such similar names. 'If you talked to another Somali here in Melbourne about me, he would probably have no idea which Omar Farah you are talking about,' he said. 'But people would immediately recognize me by my family's nickname "Dhollawa".' 'What does it mean?' I asked. Omar began to laugh. 'It means something along the lines of "the one with the chipped tooth",' he explained. His family had inherited the nickname from his grandfather, who had a missing tooth. Omar told me how in Somalia, people often received their nicknames after distinctive physical marks or events in their own or their families' lives. He told me that nicknames such as 'the one-legged one' or 'the one whose brother was killed in a car accident' were very common. 'Here in Australia that would be unthinkable!' he laughed. 'Imagine calling a disabled person "one-legged".' Sitting in his office, the soundscape of the busy Nicholson street intersection outside leaking through the little window and Omar joking about his nickname, we lost our initial insecurity over how to start working on a life story.

By sharing a few details of our lives with each other, by revealing some of the things that moved, amused and appalled us, we slowly came to know each other. By getting to know each other better we also worked towards creating the common ground mentioned in the previous chapter, where stories could be told and retold. Instead of letting Omar's story happen, we were both preoccupied with creating the conditions for making the telling of a story possible. This process

of creating common ground should not be thought of as an intellectual exchange, as something we consciously thought through. Rather,
it was shaped by simple things and habits we had to get accustomed
to, such as the spatial settings of our encounters in Omar's office, the
rhythm, language and tone of the telling and the moments when we
drifted from friendship-talk to recorded life storytelling.

The stories Omar told me in our first encounters were marked by
the dynamics of this search for common ground. Conversational in
character, they moved back and forth between different times and
places and painted a detailed picture of the complex and multiple
layers that characterized the Somalia Omar had grown up in. For
many hours he explained to me the different dynamics that had shaped
his hometown Gardo, the Puntland area and the Somali nation state.
He told me about the history of his clan, the Majeerteen, and how in
the eighteenth century it established the Majeerteen Sultanate, which
existed until the early twentieth century and extended as far as central
Somalia. He also told me about the complex interplay between the
different clans and how, growing up, he witnessed the slow disintegration of the Somali nation state. Yet, in the stories Omar told me in
our first encounters, he did not stage himself as the central character,
as the main subject of the narrative. In the two stories I chose for the
opening of this chapter, he provides a context for his childhood, his
family's makeup and his decision to leave Somalia, but he does not
offer much insight into his personal life. Instead, Omar was preoccupied with placing himself within the broader political and social
forces that formed his personal journey. His story travels from the
way his clan shaped him, and how the clan was in turn shaped by the
outside world, to his desire to leave Somalia, a place he feels has lost
itself. Touching on the traces left behind by pastoralism, colonialism, dictatorship and war, the narrative also travels through different
times. By telling the story, Omar takes us with him to the place of
his childhood Somalia, to different features of the social landscape
that formed him. In travelling through different times, he also takes
us to the lost place that Somalia has become for him. As he tells its
story, we are invited to follow Omar in his attempt to make sense of
the country's disintegration. At the same time, we begin to grasp the
importance of the specific places he mentions – Gardo, Mogadishu,
and the nation state Somalia – not just in terms of how they were, but
also their role in constituting who Omar has become.

I chose the two opening stories for their ability to place Omar –
within his family, his clan, his hometown, and within the different
dynamics that mark his relationship to Somalia. While they only

represent a fraction of the body of stories he told me in these first encounters, they are representative of the tone, themes and rhythm through which the storytelling began to take shape. When I listened to the stories Omar told me in our first encounters, I was struck by the detail and mindfulness that marked his telling. On the one hand, this emphasis might reflect the Somali politics of storytelling I discussed before, which, while acknowledging the importance of personal experiences, is bound to always return to wider communal or sometimes even universal questions. But similar to Mohamed, who used the camera as a distancing device, Omar's emphasis on wider sociopolitical events was also a way of trying to come to terms with the difficulty of telling stories about a place that has undergone such violent and destructive change. Omar could speak about growing up in Somalia, but he could not tell a story that is oblivious of the place it has become since then. He wanted me to listen carefully and understand that the Somalia he grew up in does not exist anymore, and he wanted me to appreciate all the complexities that led to his decision to leave.

I chose the two opening stories also because most other stories Omar told me in our first encounters were marked by large jumps between different times and themes, and upon reading the first

Figure 2.1 *Omar Farah in Melbourne, 2017. Image courtesy of Paul Reade*

transcripts Omar said that he felt uncomfortable with turning such unpolished narratives into written texts. Many of these stories evolved around the place that had become the embodiment of Somalia's forlornness for him: Mogadishu. Like Mohamed, he talked about the city's former beauty and sophistication, about its cosmopolitan flair, about the carefree and fun times he had there as a young student, strolling through the bustling streets and making new friends wherever he went. Yet, in his stories, nostalgic moments never persisted for long. Omar could not look back towards the past ignoring what had happened afterwards. He could not look at a then, disregarding the now. As a result, his stories constantly jumped back and forth. While this jumpiness does not read well in a written text, in the moment of the telling it opened a window for me to begin seeing some of the reasons behind Omar's focus on political and social dynamics rather than on personal events. It also made me understand the way displacement and storytelling can be experienced like two equal magnetic poles: whilst constantly trying to find ways to connect, the forces to drive them apart remain ever stronger.

Storying a Dust-State

The Mogadishu Omar's stories described was characterized by chaos, loss and displacement. It was a place that had become emptied of itself and its inner meanings to such a degree that he literally described it as dissolving into nothing but dust:

> Mogadishu used to be very nice. And when I see the documentaries from Mogadishu now, I really cry. If you watch Mogadishu and really know Mogadishu, you say: actually, this is a dust-state. It really is a dust-state. Because all the streets that you knew are gone, all the buildings that you knew are just rubbish, broken, the windows are taken, the roof has been taken. The nice roads that used to run through the middle of the city have become abandoned – trees have grown there. Instead of two ways, one on the right and one on the left, there's nothing left. The cars go their way, they just drive wherever they can find some space, because the trees are growing here or there. Hopeless! I cannot understand it.

While listening to Omar, the difficulty and pain of telling stories of a place disintegrating into dust was palpable. How to story such a place: where human habits and rules have made way for wilderness; where houses have been replaced by piles of rubbish; where roofs, built to protect and shelter people, have fallen down on them; and where there is no right or left anymore, for *there is nothing left*? The place Omar pictures, a place that ceases to have loveable habits, refuses narration. If, as Walter Benjamin (2007: 83–84) has suggested, stories grow from experience, the experience of being in a place like Mogadishu, a place where violence and destruction mark people's everyday life, cannot be shared. The 'dust-state' Omar describes reminds me of the *Gelände* (terrain) Paul Celan writes about in his poem 'Engführung' (The Straitening). In many of his poems Celan, a German-speaking Romanian Jew whose parents died in a Nazi concentration camp in the Ukraine, expresses the idea that after experiences of such destructive force, place and landscape cease to be narratable. As a result, he attempted to find the means to rewrite the genre of the landscape poem. In 'The Straitening' he writes about a soulless terrain 'with the unmistakeable track: / Grass, written asunder. The stones, white, / With the shadows of grassblades'. In this de-placed place, the contemplative distance between the self and the setting that makes experience possible is shattered (Baer 2000: 226), and Celan enjoins the reader to:

Read no more – look!
Look no more – walk![2]

The terrain Celan writes about refuses to be understood experientially in the way we make sense of a place. It carries the burden of a shattered self, a shattered place, a shattered world, where nothing makes sense anymore. This dark, lifeless terrain represents the opposite of the idyllic sense of *Heimat*, a rootedness in place praised in the work of so many German poets. Instead, it speaks of the destruction of the links between self, place and identity. Like Celan, Omar found it difficult to find words for a place that had been struck by such painful events – so difficult indeed, that he refrained from indulging in reminiscences of Mogadishu's past beauty. He told me that he and his Somali friends often remind each other not to get lost in nostalgic memories of the old Mogadishu, the Mogadishu they had loved so much and that, for so many Somalis, represents the hope of a unified nation.

People are telling me: "Look, the Mogadishu that you have in mind is not there anymore". It's gone. Dead and buried. Unfortunately the people who took over Mogadishu forcefully from Siyaad Barre did nothing except for physically burying the Somalis' name and reputation, putting it in a grave and then leaving it. Now anything and everything bad can be related to Somalia, anything and everything that you can think of. Why? Somalia used to be a well-respected country in the international community. Where is it now?

Omar's description of Somalia as an abandoned graveyard, and his question why this had happened made me shiver. At the same time I also grasped why he had spent so many hours telling me about the political and social order of the place he had left behind. Listening to his Mogadishu stories I began to understand that Omar had not just left Somalia behind. Somalia had also left itself and its inner workings behind. The place had actually completely lost itself and disintegrated into something he could not experientially make sense of anymore. It was exactly this – the urge to understand what had happened to Somalia, how a well-respected country could deteriorate into a 'dust-state' – that drove Omar's stories. Being *here*, in his office in Melbourne, and not *there*, where things were so violently falling apart, created a distance that seemed impossible to bridge. Rather than telling stories of his childhood, his family and his inner transformations, Omar's stories were attempts at bridging the gap between the Somalia he knew and understood by heart and the hopeless Somalia he did not understand anymore. By piecing together how Somalia had fallen apart, Omar was also piecing together his own sense of displacement from it. At the same time, his urge to understand the lost place Somalia had become to him can also be read

Figure 2.2 *Remnants of a demolished church in Mogadishu. Image courtesy of Mohamed Ibrahim*

as an urge to give it a new meaning, and by doing so to re-emplace it within the realms of his present life.

Following Omar's urge to understand Somalia's disintegration, I take the two opening accounts as a means of fleshing out some of the political and historical forces impacting on the places he was trying to picture. While his stories allow me to shed some light on the destructive struggle over places in Somalia he wanted me and the readers of this book to understand, they also allow for a better understanding of the historical context that sets the scenes for both Omar's and Halima's stories of emplacement.

Puntland

Omar's 'mother's backyard' was in Gardo, a town of about 47,000 inhabitants in the north-east of Somalia, in what is now known as Puntland. Omar tells how his clan, the Majeerteen, had been very active traders and travellers; bringing them in contact with people from other countries long before the first Europeans arrived. He also speaks about the ability of his clan to deal with the first colonizers, linking it to their experience with a more centralized form of power. In the mid eighteenth century, Omar's clan established the Majeerteen Sultanate, also known as Migiurtinia. When the Italian colonizers arrived in Somalia in the late nineteenth century, the sultan entered into negotiations, using the protection of the Europeans in the fight over power that had developed with competing sultanates.

During the colonial period, Somalia was divided among four powers: England, Italy, France and Ethiopia. The French established a trading centre and coaling station in Djibouti, the British founded British Somaliland in the north and the Italians aimed to establish a settler colony and develop commercial enterprises along the Juba and Shabeele rivers in the south. The arrival of the European colonialists coincided with the growing strength of Ethiopia under Menelik II. It began to extend its territorial control over Somali-populated areas that they claimed had once belonged to Ethiopia. Thus, the European colonizers found themselves negotiating with Ethiopia, which was the only Christian kingdom in Africa (Hough 2011: 11). The division between different powers with differing forms of rule left its traces on Somalia. Omar believes that the entirely different experience of colonial rule in the northern part of the country could explain why the north is generally more stable and was able to bury most of the interclan conflicts almost twenty years ago. British imperialism in northern Somalia was essentially reactive and mainly interested in coordinating long distance trade rather than claiming the territory itself (Prunier 2010: 36). This approach strongly contrasted with that of the Italians in the southern part of Somalia. When Italy began its colonial endeavours in 1880, it had itself only existed as a nation state for fifteen years. Up until World War I, Italy largely ignored its colony. In 1920 Rome estimated that only 30 per cent of Somalia was under its effective control (Prunier 2010: 40). The northern Sultanates of Obbia and Migiurtinia were only distant protectorates, and most of the areas populated by the Hawiye clans were in fact independent and barely controlled by the Italians. With the rise of the fascist regime in 1922, Italy's attitude towards its colony changed substantially. In 1923, Mussolini's close associate, Cesare Maria De Vecchi Di Val Cismon, became the new governor of Italian Somaliland. The changes he instituted have been described by historians as 'the second conquest of Somalia' (Prunier 2010: 41). He brought Obbia and Migiurtinia under close control and began to terrorize the population.

With the independence of Somalia in the year Omar was born, the area where he grew up was unified with the other Italian occupied areas in the south and British Somaliland in the far north. When all state institutions collapsed during the civil war in the 1990s, political leaders in the north and north-east of the country were able to establish a peace agreement between the different clans. As a result, Somaliland and Puntland declared themselves autonomous states in 1991 and 1998 respectively. The government of Puntland is seated in Garowe and based on an alliance of different Darood/ Harti sub-clans, such as the Majeerteen, Dhulbahante and Warsangali. While Somaliland presents itself as an independent state, claiming international recognition of its independence along the borders of the former British Protectorate, Puntland regards itself as part of the Somali state and works towards rebuilding the Somali government.

Politics of Place in Somalia

While Omar's life story begins as an attempt to shed light on the historical transformations that shaped Gardo, the place where he grew up, it can also be seen as an attempt to place Somalia at large by explaining the interclan dynamics that led to its current situation as a failed state without a functioning central government. The task of explaining Somalia's present condition is indeed daunting. As Said Samatar (2010: 209) argues, in a Somalia that has become barren, even the once so highly respected poets have fallen silent. Prominent among those few literary figures that still tell stories about Somalia is the writer Nuruddin Farah. Many of his stories deal with the displacements that marked his life. Forced to flee to Somalia from the Ethiopian-ruled and Somali-inhabited Ogaden region after Somalia's independence, and from there forced into exile in 1976, after upsetting the Barre regime, Farah has carefully analysed his country's demise. In his novel *Links*, he tries to describe the multiple causes that led to his country's destruction:

> A poet might have described Somalia as a ship caught in a great storm without the guiding hand of a wise captain. Another might have portrayed the land as laid to waste, abandoned, the women widowed, the children orphaned, and the sick untended. A third might have depicted it as a tragic country ransacked by madmen driven by insatiable hunger for more wealth and limitless power. So many lives pointlessly cut short, so much futile violence. (Farah 2004: 15)

Just like Omar in his opening story, Nuruddin Farah attempts to make sense of Somalia's situation by piecing together the interplay of different forces that left the place shattered. Colonialism, dictatorship and cold war rivalries have all left their traces on a country where the majority of the population shares a language, an ethnicity and a religion. But while Somalia is often portrayed as a unitary nation, the idea of the clan takes on an ambiguous role, with divisive effects. Omar says that he grew up believing that there was nothing else in the world except his clan. But he also wants to make it clear that his view underwent a substantial change, particularly after he had left his hometown of Gardo, where the Majeerteen formed the majority. Looking back at the Somalia he grew up in, Omar sees the clan as one of the major contributors to the country's demise.

Omar visualizes the Somali clan system as an onion, with the main clans forming the skin, which, when peeled back, opens up layer upon layer of different sub-clans that divide into smaller and smaller sections. Academics often make use of the symbol of the tree to explain the ordering of the Somali nation (Lewis 1978, 1994; Mansur 1995; Luling 2006). The top of the tree is formed by the mythological figure Hiil, to whom all Somalis are related through their affiliation to one of his two sons Samaal and Sab. The majority of the Somalis are Samaal, who are traditionally nomadic pastoralists from northern Somalia. The main clans that belong to this branch of the genealogical tree are Omar's main clan, the Darood, as well as the Dir, Isaaq and Hawiye. The sedentary Sab form a smaller part of the population and the second branch of the tree. They live primarily in the south as agriculturalists, with the Digil and Rahanweyn as the main agropastoral clans.

These boundaries are often blurred, however, as some pastoralists temporarily make use of cropping in times of hardship, while sedentary cultivators often also keep livestock (Horst 2006: 47). The boundaries are also blurred by numerous minority groups who exist beyond the main division, such as the Tumal, Midgan, Eyle, Yahar and Yibr in the north and the Jareer (or Bantu) in the south. The fact that many Somalis migrated to towns and cities and move between the boundaries of Samaal and Sab creates a more dynamic picture of the country. The often reproduced stereotypical image of 'the Somali' as a nomadic pastoralist, moving freely from place to place, ignores the changing realities of a nation that is fully embedded in global processes. Nor does it do justice to the many people who, like Omar, grew up in urban areas, or the many people who leave the harsh nomadic lifestyle behind and flock to the cities. As Cindy Horst (2006: 46) points out, this distinction does not acknowledge the fact that while it is possible to identify 'home areas' that form the strongholds of specific Somali clans, 'in actual fact there is a great mix of people from different clans living together in different places'.

The centrality of clanship in the depiction of Somali struggles over place has been greatly influenced by the work of British anthropologist I.M. Lewis. In his first article, published in 1957, Lewis characterizes the Somali genealogical system as 'total genealogy', a characterization that has since then dramatically shaped the way Somalis are seen (Lewis 1978 [1957]). Through the total genealogy every Somali can identify how closely or remotely they are related to other lineages on the family tree. Lewis suggests that civil associations along one's clan-lines and loyalty to one's lineage are the defining characteristics of Somali politics and social life. He stresses that while Somalis believe that they are one people with a shared origin and history, there are also cleavages, which often divide them in politics and everyday life. Lewis believes that in the harsh struggle for survival faced by Somali pastoralists, suspicion and at times hostility between lineage groups must be seen as a natural attitude, since the groups are competing for access to scarce pasture and water (Lewis 2008: 25).

Lewis' depiction of the role of the total genealogy in shaping a Somali politics of place has sparked a fierce debate between academics studying the roots of the war in Somalia. While Lewis' reading of the role of kinship was so influential that it became a point of reference for almost anyone writing or thinking about Somalia, it was also the topic that divided scholars. With the eruption of the civil war and the unprecedented forms of violence in the 1990s, the questioning of the anthropologist's views grew louder. An article by Catherine Besteman on the representation of the state collapse in Somalia in the US media sparked the controversy. Besteman attacked the clan-based explanation of warfare used by many journalists and policymakers. They had derived these explanations from Lewis' classical anthropological accounts of organization of pastoral societies in Somaliland, which, as she argued, oversimplified the complex and dynamic hierarchies of different patterns such as race and class (Besteman 1996a: 120). Lewis disagreed with Besteman's interpretation of the warfare in 1990s Somalia and wrote a critical response, provocatively titled 'Doing Violence to Ethnography' (Lewis 1998).

Lewis' interpretation of the eruption of the civil war in Somalia follows a primordialist point of view. He argues that the violence experienced today mirrors the traditionally aggressive nature of Somali culture. Besteman, on the other hand, sees tradition as more fluid (Besteman 1996b). She contends that the violence and fragmentation in Somalia are better understood by looking at twentieth century transformations, and criticizes Lewis for disregarding events such as colonialism, state building, the Cold War, international aid and the expanding global economy. She argues that while some aspects of the traditional kinship system have persisted, others have been transformed dramatically (Besteman 1996b: 110). Lewis, on the other hand, stresses that the conflict in Somalia today resembles what Somalis 'have always done – only with greater access to more lethal weapons' (Lewis 1998: 101).

Omar's story supports an understanding of Somalia's disintegration as the interplay of different forces. While the clan plays a crucial role in shaping the Somali people's relationship to place, he simultaneously emphasizes the importance of acknowledging the historical and political forces that play into these dynamics. The year he was born, he tells us, Somalia was born as an independent nation state. After years of division during colonialism, the areas that were under British and Italian rule were unified and many Somalis enthusiastically greeted the foundation of a pan-Somali state. His main clan, the Darood, played an important role in the formation of the first political party, the Somali Youth League (SYL), in the struggle for independence and in the formation of Somalia's first government.

Omar grew up with his father's advice to first and foremost regard himself as a Somali. This view could be closely tied to his father's social position as a wealthy and well-educated urban trader who embodied the ideals of nationalism and rejected the importance of the clan. Yet, as Omar's story also shows, this ideal never matched the reality of everyday life and clan affiliations never ceased to play a fundamental role in politics (Luling 2006: 475–76). Siyaad Barre's regime, which formed the political backdrop of Omar's youth, explicitly buried clanship. He came to power after a successful coup d'état in 1969 and adapted a quasi-socialist approach, including the nationalization of most industries and farms and a large-scale literacy programme. Although the regime forbade any form of clanism and attempted to foster a belief in a unified Somalia, Barre himself made use of the system and began playing one clan against another. Omar tells of the sudden change in attitude the dictator began to show towards the Majeerteen, regardless of their affiliation to the Darood. The prohibition of open references to clans, however, influenced the generation growing up under Barre. Being among the growing number of Somalis moving to Mogadishu and other towns, leading to a greater mix of people from different clans and sub-clans, Omar portrays himself as part of a generation that valued education and moved away from clan-thinking. Luling (2006: 476) describes it as 'a generation of young urban people to many of whom clanship meant little, or who were committed to rejecting it'.

In Omar's opening story, the clan takes on an ambiguous role: on the one side he sees the clan as the ordering principle for any form of social relation, which, as he shows in the case of the marriage of his parents, was not always exclusionary.[3] On the other side, he describes the breakdown of this positive and protective understanding of the clan into one 'that creates fences between people'. In Omar's story it is the rise of this form of clanism that leads to the demise of Somalia.

Discussing the many changes his clan went through – from pre-colonial, to colonial, and postcolonial times – Omar places Somalia's present state in a wider history. He refuses the stereotypical picture of Somalia as the land where the courageous, egalitarian nomads rule and proposes another, less homogenous understanding of the politics of place. And, as Omar emphasizes throughout the beginning of his life story, his journey started in Somalia but it did not end there. While the place called Somalia that still preoccupies him helped mould him into the person he has become, it was by leaving that place behind that he could encounter new places and be moulded by them. Commenting on the transcripts of the first storytelling session I had sent him to read, Omar said that the way he sees Somalia today had to be understood in the context of the different experiences he had after leaving it behind. It had to be read against the backdrop of his whole life story, of the many experiences he had had – in Somalia and beyond. 'All this has in one way or another shaped my life,' he said, 'it shaped the way I see things, shaped how I am seen by others or how I see them regardless of what I used to believe when I was growing up in my mother's lap, or my mother's backyard, or my clan's environment.' Thus in our first storytelling sessions – encounters that were marked by our attempts to find common ground – Omar wanted me to listen and understand the complexity of the many layers that led to his being *here*, in his office in Melbourne telling his story about a *there* that had become so ungraspable that it was present and distant at the same time.

Notes

1. To emphasize the verbatim character of the story fragments that were the product of my collaboration with Halima and Omar and indicate the change in authorial voice, they appear in a different font.
2. Translation by Ulrich Baer (2000: 221).
3. Indeed, marriages in traditional Somali society were by rule exogamic. As Kapteijns (1995: 246–47) argues, intermarriage was an important instrument to create political harmony and mutual economic support between different groups. Since the outbreak of the civil war, however, these dynamics have changed substantially, so that now many Somalis are expected to marry within their own clan (Gardner and Warsame 2004: 153–61).

3

Living One-Eyed

Making the Story Unfold

Sitting in his small office in Carlton, I had travelled with Omar from his hometown Gardo, through the changing city of Mogadishu to the moment he left the country against his father's will. Like any journey, this story-journey had not been characterized by stability but by shifts and ruptures in the act of telling, movements that mirrored the changing relationship between Omar and me. Since our first meetings, when we still had to get to know each other and Omar's stories seemed to be directed towards creating common ground in order to tell further stories, we had now grown more comfortable with each other, and with the growing closeness the pace of Omar's storytelling had changed as well. While his initial accounts of Somalia were marked by the difficulty of narrating a place that had undergone such violent rupture, the storytelling was slowly beginning to sharpen its focus. This shift, however, did not magically happen, as I initially thought it would.

At the end of one of our encounters Omar invited me to come to the launch of a report he had written together with people from the Carlton Neighbourhood Centre about creating employment opportunities for men from Horn of Africa countries living in Melbourne. As I followed a group of Somali men into the venue, the Centre's beautiful, old garden house, Omar spotted me. 'Annika, you came!' he exclaimed, sounding almost surprised that I had really come. He introduced me to a group of older Somali men, joking that I was his friend who had come all the way from Austria to find out what Somalis in Melbourne were up to. As he showed me to my seat, Omar told me that he would have liked to introduce me to his eldest son, who was supposed to be there for the presentation, but that he was obviously arriving in 'Somali time'. A few minutes later, when people began taking their seats, a tall boy entered the room. His father did not need to introduce us; he looked like a younger version of Omar. 'You're Omar's son, right?' I asked him as he sat down next to me. 'Yes,' he replied, shyly.

In his talk Omar summarized some of his findings. He explained to the audience the many challenges Eritrean, Ethiopian, South Sudanese and Somali men faced when settling in Melbourne. He pointed out that a high percentage of those who had been admitted to Australia on humanitarian grounds were highly educated, but that their university degrees were not accepted here. As a result, many former university professors and successful business men ended up as taxi drivers or factory workers, depressed about the lack of pathways into jobs befitting their skills and training. Omar said that those who could afford it often chose to remigrate to countries such as the Arab Emirates, Kenya or Egypt, where they felt more valued.

After his presentation, people were gathering around the buffet filled with injera-bread, fruit and Somali sweets. Omar was talking to the local politician who had launched the report. The Somali elders Omar had introduced me to were standing next to me, immersed in a lively debate. Omar's son and a group of other teenage boys were sitting in the garden, immersed in their mobile phones. A man, who introduced himself to me as Abdi, thanked an Ethiopian woman passing by for preparing the food. 'Oh, that's not my work,' she said, laughing. 'You know me – I'm a bad house-wife.' Standing by the window, chatting to Abdi, the spring sun warming us and looking out into the garden, where flowers and trees were in full bloom, I could see that the people who had come were appreciative of Omar's work. There were not many people of his calibre in Melbourne, Abdi said, who were capable of communicating with both their own and the wider community.

After a while, Omar joined us. We talked about his report, about how most employment policies for refugees in Victoria were aimed at integrating young people into the job market, whilst ignoring their parents' generation. Omar told us how unemployed Somali men came to ask him for advice almost every day and how little opportunities there were for them. He said that he himself was experiencing all these difficulties first-hand. Although he had secured funding for his project, his position was very insecure and always dependent on the goodwill of those administering the public purse. The idea of setting up his own NGO to look into employment pathways was, in a way, a reaction to the fact that he had not been able to find a job that suited his educational background. It was as he had pointed out in one of his stories: back in Puntland, he said, he would not have these struggles. There he would not be less than a minister.

As I was about to leave, Omar suggested continuing working on his life story the following week. He told me that he had read the transcripts of our first conversations, which I had emailed to him. Omar said that he was not happy about the way he was sometimes jumping from one stage of his life to another. He asked me not to use the stories that were marked by this jumpiness for the book. We agreed that I would not use these stories as verbatim texts. 'How could we solve this problem with the jumpiness?' I asked him. 'I think the structure of my past history may need more sharpening,' Omar said, explaining that upon reading the transcripts he felt that the stories he told me needed editorial work so that they also worked as texts. From then on he would read over all the transcripts and suggest changes, parts that did not work well, or ask me to rephrase. When we met again a week later, he also proposed that I take on a more directive role. 'Maybe it would be wise if you put the question in a different format so that I can stay in a particular time of my life and then move on from there,' he said.

So instead of just letting the story happen, I was now actively involved in making the story happen. From then on, our meetings would begin with my asking Omar to tell me about a specific time in his life. Although I sometimes interrupted to ask him to elaborate some aspects, or commented on things that interested, moved, or amused me, it seems that by reading the first transcripts Omar himself had become much more conscious about his voice as a storyteller. As a result, the leaps back and forth disappeared and my direction was no longer necessary. The disjointedness within the storytelling disappeared, it seems, by finding common ground, by sharing the responsibility over what was told and how. As part of this process we got to know each other, our interests and motivations better. By reading and discussing the transcripts, we began to understand the different natures of spoken and written stories. We came to agree on the aesthetic parameters that should guide the retelling of his stories in this book. As part of this process we also got to know our limitations and the unspoken thresholds within the storytelling setting that could not be crossed.

I left Somalia in 1983 and went to Saudi Arabia. In my view at that time there were many connections between Somalia and the Arab world. But when I got there it was different. I was seen as an African, I was seen to be black, and I was only allowed to legally stay in the country if I found a job. The system of employment was very, very poor. You had to aggressively go out and find the job yourself. I knew a few people in Saudi Arabia, but when it came to jobs they couldn't do much for me. So I had to do all I could to find employment.

The culture that I had grown up in and the culture that I started to experience in Saudi Arabia were different. The thing that really bothered me the most at that time was that if, for example, you visited a friend and that friend got into trouble and the police came to his house, they not only arrested the person that they considered to be their target but all the people who were there as well, and you were likely to be deported back to the country where you came from.

So the migrants were always living in fear. You could not talk to a lady who was not either your mother or your sister. And that was another problem because we Somalis came from a more liberal life and there were so many girls living in Saudi Arabia. So you sometimes had to ignore a woman walking by whom you knew, purely because you didn't want to be caught by the police. Or you had to wait until you could go somewhere where you could talk or even just say hello. So that kind of culture was there. The people there lived under the authority of a strong monarch. The king decided about anything and everything and all the people were expected to be loyal and behave well towards the royal family.

I lived in Saudi Arabia for four years. For the first year and a half I was trying to find a job. My plan was to get work there and to then either come back to Somalia to start some kind of business or to go somewhere in Europe. It seems that the latter option became more viable, because Somalia was getting worse year after year.

I always wanted to learn, because when I was leaving the country the first thing my father liked me to do was to study. My father was so determined to educate us, because he believed that our life and our success depended on our education. And he was really, really upset that I was leaving and he strongly believed that it would not be easier for me to go overseas to study there because he knew how hard it was to survive in another country. I promised him that I would make sure that I studied and that I would make sure that I achieved something. As a result, I did my best to finish my education. Here in Australia I did my BA in International

Studies and a Masters in International Development. That had so much to do with what I said to my father and the expectation of my father.

The money for my migration to Saudi Arabia was given to me by a friend. For someone to leave Somalia and to go to Saudi Arabia you had to spend thousands and thousands of Somali Schilling, at that time. My father did not in any way contribute to my departure or my travel to overseas. He was against it and he didn't want to be part of it. But I was always communicating with him on the phone when I was in Saudi Arabia and when I was here in Australia. I was always supporting him economically, especially in the last two years before his death, because the situation was deteriorating in Somalia, so his needs were much higher than before. So I tried to fill that gap and help him.

I found a job and began working for a hospital. Sometimes we used to get a patient from the royal family and the whole staff, particularly the Saudis and some Arabs, were becoming hysterical because they were having a patient from the royal family. It was shocking to me. Why this? Why does this bother you? The problem was that if I was seen by the Saudis to not be supportive then I was in trouble. And I was a different person: young, very energetic, someone who came from a liberal society who didn't care about all this. There were times when I was worried that what I was doing wasn't right.

I remember, one day we had a son of the current king as a patient; at that time he was Crown Prince. And someone came to me and said to me: 'Do you know this young boy?' I said: 'No.' And he said: 'He is better than you.' And I said: 'Why?' And he said: 'Because he is the son of the Crown Prince.' And I said: 'Hang on, he is not better than me, he might be better than you, but I don't care about what he is.' That guy, he was in shock, hearing someone saying these kinds of things. He didn't come to work for almost five days, worrying that he might be arrested as a result of the interaction between him and me. He was absolutely in shock.

There was a large Somali community of expatriates in Saudi Arabia, so I was associating with them more or less. There were Saudi colleagues I was working with but the interaction between the Saudis and me was limited, and I think it was coming from their side. I could be wrong but I think in Saudi Arabia for Saudis to interact with foreigners in their free time was not encouraged. They didn't want them to be exposed to other cultures, to hear other views. You know, someone like me who was anti-monarchy or didn't bother who they were. So the kind of relationship that we had was more job-focused than social.

Initially I was shocked by this treatment but later on I got used to it. I mean, it was common and you always accept what is common. What you can't accept or what you question is what is directed to you personally and not to others. So when I see that everybody is the same, I accept it. A Somali proverb says: *'Haddaad tagto meel il laga la'yahay ilbaa la iska ridaa.'* Translated it says: 'If you go into a society where they have only one eye, then you have to keep one of your eyes covered as well.' The issue is not the eye per se; it is that if they see the thing from a certain angle you have to go with the flow. Otherwise you will be wrong as all the others see the thing through one eye, not two eyes. So I used this proverb as a basis of me adapting to that life. It was the right time to use that proverb.

I think for many, many Somalis, Saudi Arabia was a springboard that they could use to jump to another place. So you just went there and earned money so that you could buy your ticket and then leave as soon as possible. I couldn't see a future in Saudi Arabia and I couldn't see a future in Somalia, so I decided to go somewhere else. I remember when I was in Saudi Arabia, in the last contract that I signed there was a clause that said: 'We will terminate your contract whenever someone who can replace you and who is Saudi is there.' At that time they were having what they called a Saudization programme, whereby the migrants had to give way to the Saudis. So every morning when I went to work I had to check the board to see whether I had been terminated or not. That was shocking, that means an uncertainty, you don't know your fate, you don't know what will happen to you tomorrow.

What really made me leave was to be ahead a little bit, so I terminated them before they terminated me. That's what I did. I first secured my visa to go to India and then I said, 'Good luck!' and left. I didn't want them to say to me 'you have to leave', because if they told me I had to leave I would have had to go back to Somalia. And that's what I was trying to avoid.

I wanted to go to India for two reasons: one, I could get their visa, and two, the money that I had collected was enough to pay for my education there. Coming from Saudi Arabia, India was a totally different issue. The life there, especially in my time in 1988, was very rough, the poverty was high, people were living in the streets. Actually you could find people who lived under a balcony! They were born there, they grew up there and probably they will die there. The mother conceived the child under that balcony. The poverty was enormous.

I was coming from Saudi Arabia, which was rich, shiny, clean, the latest cars, the latest high-tech, anything you can imagine, it was just clean and glowing. And to then come to India was shocking to me, more shocking than when I was in Saudi Arabia. So I decided to go somewhere else and I managed to get a visa to go to New Zealand. Actually, I first applied for an Australian visa, but it was denied because I was honest with them and confessed that my brother was there and had applied to become a refugee so they concluded that I would also apply for refugee status there. So they said: 'Sorry, we cannot give it to you.'

I stayed in India only for one month and a half. Then I decided to just try my luck and see New Zealand and see whether I could live there or not.

The Pirate-View on the World

When I was seven and in my first year at school in Eindhoven in the Netherlands, there was a boy in my class whose name was Hansje. We used to call him a pirate, because he wore an eye patch. The teacher explained to us that he had a 'lazy' eye, and that the doctors had decided to keep the well-functioning eye covered for a while so that the other one could catch up. I was fascinated by this boy's condition. When we were out in the playground I was observing him, trying to figure out how he was able to see things with only one lazy eye. Would he be able to play soccer without missing the ball? Would he be able to run without falling over? Discovering no obvious signs of difference, I closed one of my eyes, determined to find out what the world looked like for a one-eyed person. I soon realized that covering up one eye did not produce a remarkably different experience of the world. I now know that Hansje would have seen everything around him perfectly clear, but that he would not have been able to perceive distance and speed, and that he therefore would not have experienced space three-dimensionally.

Omar's story awakened long-forgotten memories of Hansje and his pirate-view of the world. After leaving Omar's office, they kept following me, even in my dreams. My memories of Hansje, the 'pirate', I realized, stood for more than my childhood experiments with seeing the world through one eye. Hansje also embodied my earliest and perhaps most deep-seated encounter with displacement. He was what parents and teachers called a 'difficult' child: he was wild, loud and rough. In fits of rage he destroyed whatever he could get his hands on, usually toys that he threw against the wall, pens that he broke and books that he tore into pieces. Most children – and, even more so, their parents – avoided him. He was hardly ever invited to birthday parties or sleepovers. Despite all this, Hansje and I became friends. I came to learn that he was loud and angry, but that he would never turn this anger against others. I also came to understand the reasons behind his anger: Hansje's parents had neglected him to such a degree that two years earlier welfare officers had put him in a children's home. From there a family with three children, keen to give a disadvantaged child a chance, had taken him into foster care. I still remember the moment when he told me that his parents and siblings, the people I had met so many times, were not his real parents. His real parents, he said, could not look after him. I still recollect talking to my mother about it. She told me that Hansje was sad and angry, but that his new family was trying to create a place for him to feel at home again.

One day, Hansje stopped coming to school. My mother told me that his foster parents had been overwhelmed by his outbursts of anger; that they did not know how to deal with the amount of aggression he showed. As a result, they had decided to return him to the children's home. I remember the anger and helplessness I felt over the way my friend was pushed around from one place to another. I was angry about the way the people who had invited him into their house to make him feel at home, had taken that very home away from him again. I felt helpless, thinking about his life in the children's home, and how I could not do anything to change the situation. And I thought that now Hansje's anger would only grow bigger. Although I never saw Hansje again, these feelings of anger and helplessness over his displacements have never left me. While Hansje's and Omar's stories are obviously dissimilar, there was something in Omar's telling that provoked me to leave these differences aside and think about the underlying existential theme of how humans experience and cope with displacement.

Omar's one-eyed look onto the world surrounding him in Saudi Arabia protected him from the hopelessness and rage Hansje felt over the impossibility of belonging somewhere and to someone. Omar made a conscious decision to live one-eyed. In an exclusionary society where he felt that he did not belong and far away from the protective reach of his family, he took an old Somali proverb as guidance. As he never felt that Saudi Arabia was where he wanted to stay, he was working his way out, towards 'somewhere else'. In the meantime, however, he decided that keeping himself from getting socially involved, from experiencing the place in all its dimensions, was the best way of weathering the storm. Experiencing the world one-eyed was a strategy, a way of dealing with a place that marked him as an outsider.

Omar's experiences in Saudi Arabia as an outsider and sharp onlooker, albeit with one eye, resemble someone retreating into his shell. In *The Poetics of Space*, Gaston Bachelard (1994: 105–35) writes about the ambiguous position the shell has come to take up in the human imagination. He suggests that empty shells, similar to empty nests, invite us to daydream about refuge. Yet hiding in a shell should not too easily be discarded as a passive act. As Bachelard (1994: 111) explains, someone who is hiding in a shell is always preparing a way out. By staying motionless in the shell, the hiding creature is preparing 'temporal explosions', or 'whirlwinds of being'. He stresses that the most dramatic escapes take place in cases of repressed beings, for by going inwards and postponing their action, they carry in them the potential for a type of action that is the most decisive of all (Bachelard 1994: 112). In a similar way, Omar's one-eyed look onto the world was not a passive retreat. In deciding to go with the flow and to keep himself from experiencing the world around him in all its dimensions, Omar was only preparing his way out and away from a repressive environment. While Saudi Arabia was the springboard he needed to leave Somalia, it did not provide the security and social features necessary for making it a home. During this time, it was not in place but in the realms of his inner self that he found security and protection. Rather than dwelling in place, Omar retreated and became a self-dweller. Where Hansje, in his helplessness over the way the world denied him a place to belong, turned outwards in the form of anger, Omar turned inwards, not letting the harshness of the surrounding world enter his inner world. While such a turn inwards does not, of course, exclude the possibility of directing any anger he might have experienced merely at himself, in his stories about Saudi Arabia Omar stories himself as a calm, distanced onlooker.

Given that the one-eyed look at the world deprives us of spatial three-dimensionality, the absence of a more detailed sense of place in Omar's account perhaps should not come as a surprise. Omar speaks about the four years he spent in Saudi Arabia, excluded as 'other', as 'black', as 'African'. He speaks of the pain of leaving Somalia against his father's will, thereby creating a rupture with his home-place. He also talks about the little victories he celebrated within the limits of an oppressive and absolutist system where every word could be turned against oneself. But while he pictures his everyday life and the limited interactions with Saudis, it does not become clear where all these stories take place. The 'Middle East', 'India', 'Saudi Arabia' – the words Omar uses to locate his story – are geographical descriptors, but all they convey are the impression of a vast, disembodied space. This is not to suggest that his story is placeless, but while Omar's story is clearly taking place, within the settings of that story there is no place for him to be or become a part of. With the impossibility of becoming part of a larger whole, of walking, talking, seeing and hearing the place in togetherness with others, the place refuses to be known by him in all its experiential dimensions. In short: while Omar's story *takes place*, this place refuses his emplacement.

Let me, for a moment, go back to the first of Omar's opening stories: 'I was born in Puntland in Somalia', he tells us there. In the next sentence he specifies: 'Particularly I was born in the north-east of Somalia, in a town called Gardo'. Omar then explains that Gardo was mainly inhabited by a specific group of people, the Majeerteen. So we come to understand the geographical location of the country, the area and the town where he was born. But we also begin to grasp that the social unit organizing the place is the clan. Thus, within a few sentences Omar has placed himself and his story, leaving us without any doubt about his being-part-of this specific place. As mentioned above, in all its political, social and historical specifications, the first part of Omar's story can be read as a way of positioning himself and the place he came from, as an emplacement of himself and his story in the world.

Omar's storying of his time in Saudi Arabia and India does not provide this specificity and meaningfulness of emplacement. The few locations he mentions – the nameless hospital in Saudi Arabia where he works, the tiny balcony within the immense largeness of poverty-struck India, where a baby was born, or the 'somewhere else' he is working towards – could be anywhere. While it did not strike me as important during the telling and I did not ask for more details, the lack of place, both for Omar to become a part of and for the story he told, began to preoccupy me. It led me to the question of what constitutes the *hereness* of a place.

From the Enclosed World to the Infinite Universe

In ancient philosophy, place was seen as essential to human existence. In the *Physics*, Aristotle (2007: 60) wrote that, 'everything is somewhere and in place'. Building on Archytas' treatise on place, he concluded that because no things are without place, and yet place itself does not stop to exist when the things in it disappear, place takes precedence over all other things. Place, then, is where a thing is. But place goes beyond the mere function of locating, it is also something surrounding, and it is coextensive with what it contains. The inner and the outer surface of the things contained are dependent upon each other, or, as Aristotle formulates it: 'the limits are together with what is limited' (quoted in Casey 1997b: 273).

Until the Renaissance, philosophers followed the Aristotelian axiom that 'to be is to be in place' and that hence 'to be without place is not to be'. In the seventeenth century, this was replaced by a new axiom, 'to be is to be in space'. Space took on the meaning of something non-local and non-particular, 'something having little to do with close containment and everything to do with an outright infinity' (Casey 1997b: 275). Alexandre Koyré described this radical transformation of thought from place to space as one 'from the closed world to the infinite universe' (Koyré 1979). Key thinkers on space, such as Johannes Kepler, Isaac Newton, René Descartes and Gottfried Leibniz, developed a new conception of the universe and humans' place within it, which eventually led to the replacement of the Aristotelian conception of space as a differentiated set of inner-worldly places, by a geometrization of space. Space came to be seen as an infinite and homogenous extension, as something that is only unified by the identity of its ultimate and basic components and laws (Koyré 1979: viii), and place was dissolved into space as the dominant term of Eurocentric discourse (Casey 1997b: 288). This shift from place to space, which has gone largely unrecognized within anthropological theory, has influenced debates on space, movement and displacement to such a large degree that it defines the settings of much of what is at stake within this book.

In modern thinking, time and space have come to take such dominant positions that there seems to be no room left for place. Paradoxically, the inflationary use of locational vocabulary in contemporary scholarly writing could suggest the opposite: terms such as 'position', 'location', 'mapping', 'centre / margin', 'inside-outside', 'displacement', 'liminal space', 'third space', 'threshold', 'interstices' and so on, have become the staple of academic writing in the humanities and social sciences. As Michael Keith and Steve Pile (1993: 1) argue in the introduction to their landmark collection of essays, *Place and the Politics of Identity*, these terms are commonly used to refer to complexity but are hardly ever directly explored or confronted.

While many modern thinkers champion space, place appears to be the neglected stepsister, made to hide behind space and time. Where space and time promise change and movement, place has come to stand for stagnation and boredom. Michel de Certeau's opposition between space and place can be read as paradigmatic for the way place has come to be connected with immobility. He sees place as determined by objects that are reducible to 'the being-there of something dead', likening it to the functions of a tomb. Space, on the other side, is determined by actions, as it is composed of 'intersections of mobile elements' (De Certeau 1984: 117). For de Certeau movement is always the condition for the production of space, while place is immovable, or just there.

The shift from place to space raises the question of where this leaves the human subject. Have we, with the beginning of modernity, become placeless beings? Is Omar, in his stories of the time he spent on the move, lost in the ever-expanding vastness of the universe? Edward Casey has suggested otherwise. He argues that we humans are so place-oriented that sheer placelessness is incomprehensible. The Greek word *atopos* – literally: 'no place' – also means 'bizarre' or 'strange' (Casey 1993: x).

While striving for a place to dwell, humans are at the same time amongst the most mobile animals. 'We are beings of the between,' Casey (1993: xii) writes, 'always on the move between places.' But despite the mobile character of human life, Casey (1993: xiii) argues that, 'where we are – the place we occupy however briefly – has everything to do with what and who we are (and finally, *that* we are)'. For Casey, place and body are inescapably linked. Modern Western philosophy, however, has rarely discussed the role of the body in the determination of place (Casey 1993: 45). Given the predominance of space and time in modern philosophy, this development is not surprising, because the more we consider space as unlimited, the less we will be concerned with the position of the human body within its vastness. Casey (1993: 46) suggests that the importance of place and its distinctiveness to space can be understood only by giving explicit attention to the lived body in relation to its whereabouts. According to Casey, knowledge of place begins with the 'bodily experience of being-in-place'. At once an agent and a vehicle, our body continually takes us into place. Without our bodies we would be disoriented and confused and there would not be a lived or sensed place. Indeed our bodies help us to structure and configure the hereness of place (Casey 1993: 48).

It is by my lived body that I am here. The body becomes the bearer of the here, or its *Träger*, as Husserl called it. Husserl (1981: 250) described the *hereness* of the body as the 'absolute here', meaning that it cannot be diminished or compromised. 'I cannot become not here and remain (myself),' Casey (1993: 52) writes. 'Part of the absoluteness of the here is that I cannot detach it from my body-self and thus from the place to which this body-self now gives access.' While Omar's story suggests the inescapability of bodily hereness, it also suggests that sometimes, people make use of other faculties in order to circumvent the absoluteness of the here. His decision to adopt a one-eyed view of the world indicates that memory, storytelling and imagination can work as a means of actively changing (or perhaps even manipulating) our bodily experience of place.

While I agree with Casey that it is through our bodies that we are always in place, I believe that imagination and memory need to be regarded as essential to people's experience of place, too. Casey does not neglect the importance of the imagination or memory,[1] but he portrays them as secondary to the body, which he sees as the primary site of place-experience. In doing so, he overemphasizes the importance of place-experience as directly lived through *(Erlebnis)* and overlooks the powerful ways in which the imaginary can also form and transform the ways we experience and make sense of our being-here. Omar's story of adopting a one-eyed view of the world suggests that while the lived body carries us into a here, this very body cannot be separated from the thoughts, hopes and imaginations that propel its movements between places.

Omar, who begins his life story by placing himself, does so by referring to explicit spatial functions that determine his bodily position (or the hereness). He tells us that the Majeerteen, who constituted the place where he grew up, were literally on the right side, in front, behind and on the left side of himself. He creates the impression that he was surrounded or enclosed by the people who, together with him, determined and inhabited the place called Gardo. His description can be read in terms of the immediate and lived bodily experience of being-in-place in Gardo. But it can also be understood in a wider sense as creating imaginary social room in which he could move about with ease and make sense of the place by walking, talking and testing it in togetherness with others.

Pondering on the links between place, space and experience, geographer Yi-Fu Tuan (2005: 136) writes that while we experience space and place with our bodies, space is transformed into place 'as it acquires definition and meaning'. It might be exactly the lack of definition and meaning Tuan refers to that explains the sense of placelessness marking Omar's story of his time in Saudi Arabia. If space is transformed into place by acquiring definition and meaning, then Omar's story clearly indicates that this meaning can only be written, spoken or performed into a place *together*. Places are thus made meaningful by the presence of others. Yet, as Omar's story shows, the opposite is also possible: places can quickly lose their meaning if there are no people to share this experience with (Tuan 2005: 140).

Thinking about Hansje's displacements and his (and my own) anger over it, I came to see that Omar's decision to temporarily adopt a one-eyed view of the world should not be understood as a 'lack of', for he used it as a tool to deal with a disempowering situation. While he might have been forced to live one-eyed, the other eye, the covered one, surely was not lazy. Perhaps the closed eye took on the role of the inward-looking eye, which enabled him to see the things that were surrounding him critically but to keep his thoughts and expressions about them inside the boundaries of his self. John Berger (1984: 50–51) stresses that the ability to see the world around us with an outward-looking eye is matched by the development of an inward-looking 'inner eye'. While the experience of seeing brings humans together, it also excludes them, because they are continuously confronted with disappearances. As a result, people develop an inner eye that keeps the visible inside the boundaries of the self and retains, assembles and arranges it according to their own means: 'With his inner eye man experiences the space of his own imagination and reflection. Normally it is within the protection of this inner space that he places, retains, cultivates, lets run wild or constructs Meaning' (Berger 1984: 51).

Omar's experience of living one-eyed can be read exactly within the realms of such an inner eye that orders, reflects and creates meaning. Deprived of becoming a meaningful part of the place he was living in, he closed himself off from experiencing it in all its dimensions. Letting the place and its habits become part of his being-here would have also meant letting its harshness and remorselessness enter his inner self. At the same time, living one-eyed did not mean that he was living in a placeless void. Rather it was the place itself that forced him to retreat and keep everything he saw, heard and felt locked up inside himself. Living one-eyed shielded him from the risk of getting lost in these painful dynamics. While it allowed him to see the place, it also allowed him to take what he had seen inwards in order to assemble, arrange and retain – and in doing so to make sense of his surroundings on his own terms.

Thinking about Omar's story with Hansje's story in the back of my mind opened a door for me to understand the dynamics of place that can make emplacement difficult or indeed impossible. Omar's metaphor of living one-eyed allows us to begin to grasp the complexity of place: the struggles over power and resistance that play into its production; the social and intimate forces that mould it into something like home; and the movement that keeps us always between the here and the there.

Note

1. In his earlier work, Casey focused on the phenomenological study of memory and the imagination (Casey 1976, 1987a). While in the foreword to *Getting Back into Place* Casey (1993: xvi) stresses that imagination, memory and place are complementary in character, the book mainly looks at our embodied experience of place.

4

An Accidental Move

Dundeeing Australia

Before I left Vienna to move to Melbourne, I imagined Australia as a postcard depicting the deep redness of the Uluru rock formation against a sharp blue sky. I did not have very clear images of Australia's inhabitants. Perhaps half because of my background as an anthropologist and half influenced by films I had watched during my childhood, my blurry imaginary Australian was almost more aboriginal than anything else. These films I grew up with were cheaply produced educational documentaries that showed indigenous people from around the world like animals, edited to amaze and to be gazed at, pitied or laughed at by Western audiences.

Later, as a student of social anthropology, I understood the stories and images these films created in another, more critical way. Then, I saw these films more as leftovers of the colonial fantasies of the Western world, than a portrait of 'lost tribes' on the other side of the world. But these images still lay in my unconsciousness, for while I had some (albeit stereotypical) ideas about its indigenous inhabitants, I had no picture of multicultural Australia.

Omar's image of Australia had been similarly stereotypical. As we were sitting in his small office one winter afternoon, huddled around the small radiator, eating the biscuits Omar had brought, he told me about the pictures he had had in his mind before he arrived here. 'Back in Somalia I didn't know anything about Australia at all,' he said. He explained that mainly because of the distance and because Australia had no presence in Africa at that time, very few people knew about it. At some point in the 1980s, however, with the release of a popular movie, images of Australia began to take shape in Omar's consciousness. 'I started to know more about Australia when I watched *Crocodile Dundee*,' he said. Laughing, he added: 'But it gave me the wrong impression.'

The source of his imaginary Australia was the hugely successful 1986 Australian comedy *Crocodile Dundee*. The film's plot revolves around Mick 'Crocodile' Dundee, an Australian crocodile hunter who lives in the outback in a place called Walkabout Creek. Mick, who has never been to a city, and has never been exposed to features of modern life, accepts the invitation of an American journalist, Sue, to visit New York. The film accentuates the comicality of his perplexed reactions to modern life and the way he uses his archaic outback knowledge to survive in the urban jungle of super-modern New York and finally to win Sue's heart.

'In the movie you watch someone who is struggling to live, someone who cannot adapt to American life, who cannot even understand or answer the phone,' Omar explained to me. 'So it gave me the sense that Australia was a more backward society.' I was struck by the irony of the reversed images of Australians we both had in our minds before we moved here: influenced by television documentaries, my imaginary Australian was indigenous and removed from the modern way of life; influenced by a similar source, Omar's imaginary Australian was also backward and removed from the rest of the world, but white.[1]

Omar even told me that it took him a long time to convince his friends who had stayed behind that he was not living a Crocodile Dundee-lifestyle here in Australia: 'I remember when I came here I sent a few postcards back to friends in Saudi Arabia and India, and they couldn't believe it. They said: "You're lying to us!" And I had to actually struggle to convince them that Australia was more modern than Saudi Arabia. They didn't believe me.'

In our own ways, we both had 'Crocodile Dundeed' our imaginary Australia, and for neither of us these first images had endured against the reality we found. Omar was surprised to see how diverse and multicultural Australia was. He was even more surprised, he told me, to find that he felt much more comfortable living in Melbourne than in Saudi Arabia, although he had always believed the latter to be much closer to his own religious and cultural background as a Somali. 'Saudi Arabia is a Muslim country and right next door to

Somalia,' Omar said. 'We call them brothers but the place didn't offer me the kind of freedom that I found in Australia. Probably the only common ground that we had was that we all prayed towards one direction.' In all other aspects that mattered to him, Omar explained, Australia had offered him more. That it had turned out this way, he said, was remarkable. After all, he laughed, his migration to Australia had been entirely 'accidental'.

I actually never went to New Zealand, because I broke my journey at Sydney airport. I didn't even visit New Zealand once. Maybe someday, Insha'Allah, I could go there and say: 'Look, this is the country where I was planning to go.'

That I came to Australia was accidental, and I tell you how it happened: when I was booking my flight from India to New Zealand the travel agency failed to find a route that could take me directly to New Zealand. Either I had to go through Thailand, or I had to go through Indonesia, or I had to go through Singapore and stay there for one or two days, and I did not want that. The more I had to break my journey the more money I would have had to spend and I didn't want to waste the money that I had initially set aside for studying. So I said that I wanted the minimum stopover time. The travel agency said, 'Fine, we will get you a flight that will take you from Bombay to Singapore, and from Singapore to Sydney. You will stay in Sydney for twelve hours and then early the next day you will be able to catch a plane from Sydney to Auckland.' And I said: 'Fine.'

When I arrived at Sydney airport I was really tired and I tried to find somewhere to lie down because I hadn't slept all the way from Bombay to Sydney. So I asked the staff at the airport to give me somewhere to sleep for a couple of hours until my flight was coming in. She said: 'Why don't you go to Sydney and sleep there and come back?' And I said: 'I don't have a visa.' And she said, 'Hang on, I will talk to that gentleman to give it to you.' She called him and said: 'Can you give him a visa? He would like to stay in Sydney for a couple of hours and sleep and come back.'

I went to him and gave him the passport, he filled in the form, and when he handed the passport back to me he realized that it was a Somali passport. Maybe he initially thought that I was Indian. And he said: 'Can I have the passport back?' And I handed over the passport to him. I understood that something suspicious was going on. He said: 'Are you Somali?' I said: 'Yes I am.' – 'Hmmm. Where are you going?' I said: 'I'm going to New Zealand.' – 'To do what?' And I lied to him, I said: 'Look, I'm studying in India, there are particular plants that are not available in India because I am doing agriculture, and I want to go to New Zealand to do more exploration on that particular kind of trees.' And he shook the passport like this, he looked into my eyes and said: 'Have a nice trip.' It seemed that he understood or at least he was suspicious that I was actually lying to him but he gave me what they call 'the benefit of the doubt'. He said: 'Good luck!' Then I left the airport. I went to the city and called my brother. I said: 'I'm in Sydney.' And he replied: 'Just wait for me.' He joined me in Sydney and we took a flight from Sydney to Melbourne in the night-time instead of going to Auckland. And I'm still here.

Spatial Tactics

When Omar told me about the chain of events that led to his move to Australia we laughed at the comicality of the remarkable coincidences, which, as if scripted, decided his future in just a few minutes. We laughed at the flash of wit that allowed Omar to quickly assess his possibilities and come up with a story that convinced the suspicious immigration officer. We laughed at the fact that he has never been to the place where he was intending to go to first, not even for a holiday. We laughed at the 'I'm still here' with which he ends his migration story; *here* despite the odds that seemed to be against him, and here instead of *there* in New Zealand or wherever luck would have taken him.

My own arrival in Australia in 2009 could not have been more different. Before I arrived I had received my visa, a mere formality that involved filling in an application form online. I arrived with a three-year scholarship to write my PhD, financed with money from an Australian institution. After all the excitement of months of organizing and preparing myself for my departure, with all my beloved books packed in boxes, my furniture sold, my apartment in Vienna empty, the goodbye party with friends celebrated, I vividly remember the sudden feeling of excitement that overcame me when I landed at Melbourne's Tullamarine Airport. When I handed my passport to the immigration officer, a quick glance at my country of origin and the visa was enough to wave me through. I cannot even remember him looking into my eyes.

After Omar finished his story we talked about the different rules and regulations that had determined our experiences of arriving in Australia. Telling him about my own smooth entry into the country, he laughed, saying that the European passport opens many doors that remain firmly closed to Somali citizens. For while Australia likes to pride itself as a multicultural nation, white Australians still have a privileged capacity to decide who does or does not have the right to lay claim to the place and who is allowed in or must stay out (Hage 1998; Noble 2009). Thinking about Australia's politics of exclusion, we wondered how many other people were denied entry at Tullamarine Airport the very same day I so easily gained entrance. I told Omar about a Somali man I had met while I was waiting for my connecting flight at Dubai airport. When I was restlessly walking around in the strange, almost worldless universe of shops, never-ending daytime and endless passageways, trying to find a place to sit down, he offered me a chair next to him. It was then that he told me that he had been wandering around the ever-busy airport for weeks, having lost any feeling for space and time. His hopes of escaping the harsh life in a refugee camp in Kenya and migrating to Malaysia on a student visa were shattered in Dubai, where the authorities did not allow him to board the plane. Because there was no place to send him back to, the Emirates officers simply kept him on hold within the airport, neither allowing him to go out nor in. After my plane to Melbourne took off, I realized that I did not even know his name. I told Omar that I often wonder what happened to this nameless man caught in a placeless universe.

The role of the airport in Omar's arrival story is an interesting point of departure for thinking through the ambiguous interplay of agency and control that determine our engagement with places. Marc Augé defines the airport as one of the most outstanding examples of the non-places that the dynamics of super-modernity produced. While 'anthropological place' is formed by individual identities, local references, and unspoken know-how about living in a specific place, a non-place at the most shares the identity of passengers, customers or other drivers (Augé 1995: 101). From the non-place Sydney airport in Omar's story represents, we can begin to anticipate the role of the state in the struggle over the places that make up the imagined community of a nation (Anderson 1983). Places are not only experienced on an intimate level, they are also highly contested constructions. Omar's assurance that he is 'still here' cheekily points towards the political inscriptions of place that determine who is allowed in and who is supposed to stay out. According to these politics of place, Omar was marked as 'undesirable', someone who was to be kept from entering Australian territory. Yet, his story also emphasizes his capacity to outwit and subvert these spatial power dynamics.

Setha Low and Denise Lawrence-Zúñiga (2003: 30) describe the use of space as a strategy and technique of power or social control as 'spatial tactics'. In Omar's case these spatial tactics are visible in the denial of a visa to enter Australia because of his brother's refugee status and the difficulty of finding another place in the world that would allow him in. But it also shows in the social isolation he experienced during his time in Saudi Arabia, where interactions with migrants were not encouraged. How deeply the ordering grip of the state can reach into our everyday experience of places and our capacity for placemaking has been famously demonstrated in Michel Foucault's work. In focusing on spatial arrangements he showed the role of architecture as a political technology to create a 'docile body' through an omniscient panoptic view (Foucault 1975). When, in his 1967 Berlin lectures, Foucault suggested that the 'anxiety of our era has to do fundamentally with space, no doubt a great deal more than with time', he hinted at the neglected importance of spatial tactics (Foucault 1986: 23). His emphasis on the power relations that delineate specific 'sites' (not to be confused with 'places') played a crucial role in the regenerated interest in space I mentioned earlier. But Foucault's use of 'space' and 'sites' remained vague and undefined, relying on a taken-for-granted understanding of the two categories without questioning their meanings (Lefebvre 1991: 3–4). His work could nevertheless offer an entry point for a new look into the lived experience of place – one that also takes the spatial tactics that constitute it into account. As Omar's account of his accidental arrival in Australia shows, his relationship to this place was regulated through a set of complex ordering principles that attempted to keep people like him from settling down there. At the same time, he refused to be determined by this ordering grip and found his own ways of challenging it. In doing so his story shows something important about the interplay of structure and agency that shapes our engagements with places. It brings me back to the importance of a balanced perspective on place that switches between an Icarus and Daedalus perspective, thereby taking into account both the larger structures that attempt to regulate places and the small, seemingly banal daily interactions, which, as Omar's successful tricking of the immigration official shows, have the power to constantly challenge the status quo.

Phenomenologists have often been accused of focusing too much on the intuitive and irrational and ignoring the social and historical determinants of life (e.g. Foucault 1975: 165–97; Eagleton 2008 [1983]: 47–78). Phenomenologists preoccupied with place, on the other hand, have argued that too many scholars have focused on the politics of place, without asking how place could assume a role of such strategic importance in the first place (Feld and Basso 1996: 4–5; Casey 1997a: 185–86; Malpas 1999: 10). Omar's stories suggest that places are intrinsic to humans; that we are who we are only because of where we are. At the same time they also draw attention to the spatial tactics that attempt to regulate places, thereby creating a dichotomy between insiders and outsiders. I agree with John Agnew and James Duncan, who suggest that place needs to be looked at from all the different aspects that play into it. They stress that the marginalization of place in modern social sciences as well as in history has much to do with the way scholars have come to look at it in an isolated way. Instead of seeing place as complemented by political, social, histori- cal and sensory elements, scholars have tended to focus only on one singular aspect (Agnew and Duncan 1989: 2). In order to understand the lived experience of place, however, we need to see all the different elements as complimentary, as related and as dependent upon each other. When Omar, in telling about his life, thinks back to the places he passed, left or arrived at, the political and historical struggles that form and transform a community or a place play such an essential role that it would be impossible to ignore them. The power dynamics that make up a place are, as I suggested before, an intrinsic part of the lived experience of place.

As Omar's account of the time he spent in Saudi Arabia demon- strates, the feeling of being part of a place is closely linked to political realities. As the story of his accidental arrival in Australia shows, immigration regulations, integration policies, work permits, and the bureaucratic labelling of different categories of people (such as 'migrant', 'refugee', 'asylum seeker', 'citizen') have profound effects on the ways people experience or identify with place. Who is to be seen as part of Australia's imagined community, and who is not, is part of an ever-changing pattern of discourses. From the White Australia policy, which attempted to keep (this initially 'black') con- tinent as white as possible, to the changing face of the country as a result of the admission of a large number of Indo-Chinese refugees in the late 1970s and early 1980s, to the current practices of othering directed at Muslims and boat refugees, these spatial tactics are con- tinuously changing. In order for Omar to be allowed 'in', he needed to become a refugee first, someone in need of protection for his being outside of a 'national order of things' (Malkki 1995b).

When Omar arrived in Melbourne in 1988, there were only a handful of Somalis in Australia, including his brother, who had been amongst the first Somalis to apply for asylum. Only eleven years before, in 1977, the then Minister for Immigration and Ethnic Affairs, Michael Mackellar had announced Australia's first compre- hensive refugee policy. As a result of that policy, the immigration department, which had already been in charge of Australia's offshore programme of identifying refugees for resettlement in Australia, also took control of the determination of refugee status for people who were already in Australia and had applied for asylum. The question of who is admitted to Australia, be it as a refugee or as an ordinary immigrant, has always been highly contested, with the government attempting to regulate the size and composition of the intake (Neumann 2015). From the mid 1990s, the government made a clear distinction between the treatment of offshore and onshore applicants for asylum – a distinction that was to lead to the creation of the discursive figure of the 'deserving' refugee, whose presence is the result of a formal resettlement process, and its counterpart, the 'undeserving' asylum seeker, who poses a threat to national security and cultural sovereignty (Neumann et al. 2014).

Omar arrived in Australia shortly before the eruption of the civil war in Somalia, before the introduction of offshore detention, and just before the Australian government decided to resettle significant numbers of Somalis, Eritreans and Sudanese. This shift enhanced Omar's case when he applied for asylum shortly after his arrival in Australia. Until then, not many African refugees had been resettled in Australia. This was partly due to 'a legacy of racially biased preferences', as Peter Browne (2006: 21) puts it, and partly because with the Balkan Wars Europe had once again become a source of a large number of refugees, a legacy that persisted until 2002, when people from the Horn of Africa came to dominate the resettlement programme for several years.

Looking at all the policies of inclusion and exclusion that are part of Australia's spatial tactics, the outcome on an individual level can be, as in Omar's story, indeed ironic. While he had left Somalia out of a mixture of a fear of an upcoming war, a spirit of adventure and the hope for economic advancement, here he was in Australia, accepted as part of the national community, but under the label of 'refugee'. For Omar, who, as I have pointed out before, never felt like a refugee, this bureaucratic label enabled him to stay, just as it enabled the Australian state to give retrospective meaning to his being-here. As much as spatial tactics attempt to regulate spaces and places, people will find ways to outwit them. It is exactly at this intersection of the state's attempt to control and define its space and people's ability to circumvent or contest these inscriptions that the ambiguity and movability of place comes to the fore.

Although place is so often described as lasting and unmoving, as the effect of politically driven spatial tactics rather than as a constitutive element of politics, places are indeed everything but static. As Omar's struggle to explain the continuously changing character of place in the Somali context shows, places' boundaries, meanings and habits change continuously – just like their inhabitants they are always on the move. Movement itself, Casey (1993: 280) suggests, is in fact intrinsic to place. Completely static places without movement or change do not exist, for the mere fact of being there implies the possibility of journeying to another place. However, we do not necessarily need to cross borders or oceans like Omar to get a sense of the ever-shifting meanings of places. Even in their everyday lives, individuals move between different places, changing the hereness with every return.

If place is intrinsically tied to movement and change then we also need to look at all the different elements that constitute it – from its sensed intimacy to the political interplays of power that make themselves felt in places. In a world where the movement of some people becomes highly regulated and restricted, where detention camps are built on remote islands and the term 'boat people' comes to stand for an outsiderness so extreme that it needs to be contained at all costs, I believe that we cannot even begin to understand the lived experience of place without also looking at the politics of space. In her book *Migrare*, the Italian philosopher Federica Sossi writes about how Europe's spatial tactics of fortressing itself against undesired people has created a situation where migrants and refugees *feel* national borders, and the spaces they are not meant to enter, long before they ever set foot on European (or, in this case, Australian) territory (Sossi 2006). They feel it queuing up in endless, hopeless lines at embassies, they feel it when, like Omar, they are denied a visa because of the risk that they might not leave again, and they feel it when they cannot, like I could, go through customs with no more than a bored look from the immigration officer.

Note

1. For Omar, Crocodile Dundee's story was interesting because it is about a white person taking on features that are otherwise attributed by white people to 'others'. This 'whiteness', however, is ambiguous, as Dundee's character draws on stereotypes about Aboriginal Australians. He takes on a role similar to Tarzan in the African context: while he is white, everything about him, the way he speaks, walks and interacts with the

world, embodies stereotypical images of a 'primitiveness' that clashes with modernity. The film ends with Dundee proposing to 'go walkabout' – a clear reference to Aboriginal culture and placing him in an ambiguous, quasi-indigenous position.

5

Home-Building

Abraham's Sausage Pot

I still remember some advice my father gave us kids shortly after we had moved from the Netherlands to Austria. We lived in Riegersdorf, a small village in the southernmost state of Carinthia, close to the Slovenian border for a few years, before we moved to my father's home village Millstatt. When we were walking to school or playing with other kids, curious villagers often asked us '*Von wem bistn du?*' – 'Whom are you from?' People in this part of Austria usually do not ask *where* an unknown person is from, but to whom she belongs. In getting to know the family the person belongs to, by reciting the uncles, aunties, cousins, nephews and nieces living in adjacent villages or towns, they can place her on the larger social map of the area. If the family one belongs to happens to come from another region, however, or, as in our case, from another country, people often react with an awkward silence. This embarrassment over our proper place within the village made us detest the constant questioning. My father instructed us that the next time they asked us again we should just tell them that we came from our parents. And laughing, he added: 'In the end we all just come from *Abrahams Wurstkessel*.'[1] We are all made of the same stuff.

Despite the five years I spent in Melbourne speaking, reading and living with the English language, the word 'home' still puzzles me. Part of it might have to do with the fact that in German, there is no sufficient translation for the many connotations the English term carries. Although the origin of the word home, the Old English hām, is related to the German *Heim*, the German term mainly depicts a physical shelter. The English home, however, does not just relate to a house or dwelling, but also to a much deeper, existential sense of belonging. Another word often used by translators to transfer the existential meaning of home into German, *Heimat*, rather hints at a sense of rooted or territorialized belonging; to the village where one is born, to the 'homeland' or the 'native soil'. Heimat is deeply embedded in place, and, as Eric Hobsbawm argues, it is, by definition, collective. 'It cannot belong to us as individuals. We belong to it because we don't want to be alone', he writes. But Heimat has a darker side: while we want to be part of it, it does not need us. 'It goes on quite well without us', Hobsbawm writes, 'which is the tragedy of political exile' (Hobsbawm 1991: 68).

The violent histories behind Heim and Heimat have always made me keep my distance from them. The suffocating closeness of the bourgeois ideal of the Heim, its tyranny and control over women and children, made me look at it as a prison rather than as a romantic shelter. And the weight of Heimat's blood-soaked abuse by the Nazis still weighs too heavily, and the consequences of its exclusionary tendencies have gone too deep, that I'd rather remain homeless, or *heimatlos*, than connect myself with a stained Heimat.

From the very first day I met Omar, he told me that, to him, Australia felt like home. 'They allowed me to stay in Australia, they gave me the opportunity to become one of their own, they helped me to bring my mother and some of my immediate family members,' he said, 'and I sometimes feel that I cannot even give that back to Australia.' In Omar's stories Australia takes on the form of a place and a community of people at the same time. Unlike in Saudi Arabia, where there was a well-functioning place but no community of people to share it with, Australia could become home to Omar because it allowed him to become 'one of their own'. At the same time, feeling at home in Australia is a loyalty he owes the country for all the possibilities it opened up to him. 'I am indebted to Australia,' Omar once said to me.

As I got to know him better, the ease with which Omar was able to speak of Melbourne and Australia as his home struck me, for in many of our conversations we also spoke about the prejudices and misconceptions he was fighting against day in and day out being black, African and Muslim. While he had told me that Australia was his home from the first time we met, he also told me about the pain of exclusion, which to him was particularly embodied in the difficulty of finding employment, despite having completed his university education in Melbourne. He repeatedly told me that the events surrounding 9/11 and the worldwide 'war on terror' had changed the Australian public perception of Muslims, turning them into threatening 'others'. This had greatly affected the lives of Somalis living in Australia, who were suddenly treated with suspicion or downright contempt. Scott Poynting, Greg Noble, Paul Tabar and Jock Collins (2004: 3) describe the deep-seated national anxieties and moral panics erupting in post 9/11 Australia around the discursive figure of the racialized Muslim 'other', who has since come to embody the 'pre-eminent "folk-devil" of our time'. By stylising Muslims into 'dangerous others' whose cultural and religious habits are perceived to be so radically different that they cannot be incorporated in an Australian norm, they are removed from a shared project of national belonging. Yet, as the authors point out, the creation of 'mythic Others' has very little to do with the lived experiences of those being labelled this way. Such narratives of exclusion work as a means to 'prop up the national project of belonging', of assuaging deep-seated anxieties of people from a white settler colonial background experiencing a sense of loss of control (Hage 1998). Omar often spoke about how much such policies of exclusion affect the Somali community, as they are intended to keep them from ever truly becoming attached to this place, or even more important, from participating in its political life. He told me about his five children and how they were often struggling to understand where they belonged. Omar said: 'When my kids were very young they believed that they were Australian. When they were young they didn't believe that they were others, or African.'

Listening to his explanation I was struck by the tragic depth of this comment. When they were young his children believed they were Australian, his comment suggested, but as they were growing older they were made to believe they were 'others'. Were his kids, as a consequence, not at home in the country they were born in? I was trying to imagine the pain Omar, as a father, must have felt over this refusal by others to see his children as part and parcel of the very community they were born into. He told me how, as his kids grew up and started going to high school, they were constantly told by their classmates and their parents that they were not Australian, but Somali. 'All my five kids were born here. But people continuously ask them: "Where do you come from?" "Do you like it here?" So the children begin to question: Who am I?'

And yet, although these spatial tactics of exclusion have such force, Omar refuses to give up the claim of being-at-home in Australia. Immediately after he told me about his children's struggles to find acceptance, he set himself above the diminishing effects of stories like these by having a laugh at them. He emphasized the humorous side of the situation by throwing the question of belonging back to those who ask it, troubling the assumption that their own position of belonging is safe and secure: 'Now, when I'm interacting with [Australian] people and they say: "Where do you come from?" I say: "I come from Somalia". But then I ask them: "What about you?" And they will say: "I was born here". I say: "Yes, you were born here, but where does your father come from? Where do your grandparents come from?"'

In Australia, where being white almost invariably means having ancestors who, at some point in time, came to the country as immigrants, the dominant narrative of belonging suggests the opposite (Hage 1998). When the first white settlers came to live in Australia, they colonized the country under the premise that the land belonged to no one. And, as Aileen Moreton-Robinson (2003: 25) argues, within this rationale of Australia as a terra nullius, the white body became the norm and measure of identifying who could belong to this place. Omar's reversal of the question of belonging refers the questioners back towards the complexity of asking who belongs where. His joke also perfectly illustrates how being-at-home is intimately linked to the politics of placemaking.

When I was asked whether I felt at home in Australia, I usually did not know how to answer the question. Even when I asked myself where my home was, the question evoked a feeling I can only describe as confused density. It resembled the feeling of staring at a blank page, waiting for it to fill up with words, which, although they are there, racing around in your head, refuse to be written down. I could talk about images of places I strongly connected with, like the old graveyard at the Kalvarienberg above Millstatt, on the way up towards the mountain villages. I could talk about the tranquillity of the view from the graveyard's chapel over the village, the lake and the mountains. But to call it my home or to conclude from this place of connection that Millstatt in general was my home was not how I felt. How I felt, however, was hard to grasp. Bachelard (1994: xxxviii) writes: 'At times when we believe we are studying something, we are only being receptive to a kind of day-dreaming.' It was within the vein of the daydream, somewhere in between the unconscious dreamlike imagination of the world and its conscious and reflected contemplation, that my experiences of home refused categorization.

Deep inside me, I might have thought that escaping to Australia would spare me the question of where my home was and make me feel part of a more cosmopolitan ideal of belonging. But becoming so deeply involved in the lives of Omar, Halima and Mohamed had quite the opposite effect on me. It made me question why, although I did not experience any of the disadvantages my Somali friends had struggled against, although I had always been welcomed with the kindest words by Australians, although I had found many friends and fallen in love with an Australian, I was so much more reluctant to describe Australia as my home. It made me question how far Omar's insistence of Australia as his home had to do with the fact that since the outbreak of the civil war a return to his physical home in Somalia was not possible. Beyond all the luxury of my chosen homelessness, I did not, like Omar, have to learn that the places of importance where I grew up were destroyed, the knowledge over their inner functioning forever displaced. Collaborating with Omar on his life story made me ask what it is that turns a place into a home. How do we actively *make* place into something outstripping the cold emptiness of space? Omar's stories shifted my focus to placemaking as a crucial existential parameter for being-in-the-world.

At the time when I arrived in Australia, in 1988, the Somali issue was hot and new – so many people in other countries were sympathetic to the Somalis' plight. Not like now, where everybody got used to it and it has become what is called a déjà vu. Even if they are talking about a hundred people killed in Somalia now, they seem to only be mentioning that. Like, 'oh, a couple of hundred people died there', as if they don't even deserve to live. But at that time it was easy to get a visa in Australia, it was easy to get approval from the immigration department to live here, and I think it took me less than a year to get the permanent residency, and two years after I became Australian citizen.

Immediately after I arrived in Australia I started working in a factory where they put signs on t-shirts. It was a very tough job, especially when it came to the speed, because you're using a machine and you had to get the garment and put it on the right place. And then as soon as the machine put the print on it you had to take it out, get the next one and put it. You had less than ten seconds to do that. And if you didn't do it in time you made a mess because the machine was not waiting for you, it was just stamping. So you had to be very precise: put it, take it off, put it, take it out, and so on. So it was a very hectic job. But that was good, it was training me, I didn't have a problem and I really enjoyed working there.

It was in the factory that I encountered my culture and how different it was from the Australian culture. I remember when I was working there I had a friend who was actually much younger than me, about eighteen or nineteen years old. One afternoon he told me that he was going to leave early that day because he was going to pick up his mum's boyfriend from another suburb. And I said: 'You mean your mother's husband?' And he said: 'No, no, he is her partner.' And I said: 'Is he married to her?' And he said: 'No.' And for me, because of my culture, someone who was going to get someone from another suburb so he could sleep with his mum was something beyond my understanding. You know, up till now I'm still struggling to understand how someone is supporting that kind of activity where you get someone to stay with your mum even though he's not married to her. But that's the way it is and that's where the issue of closing one eye comes in again.

Soon after my arrival I tried to study journalism but I realized that it was not easy for me to do it – or at least, I was discouraged by my teacher saying to me that my English was not good enough to play that role. Now I think he could have encouraged me to improve and empower my English capacity instead of telling me: 'You are hopeless, you can't go there.' He didn't really use the word hopeless but he painted a picture where he argued that it wasn't going to be easy for me to become a journalist. And he said: 'You're just wasting your time so you're better off doing something else.' So then I left journalism behind and went to study international trade at RMIT.

When I was in the middle of that programme, Somalia started to collapse and we got the news that all the people were leaving the capital, that they were displaced by the war, that they were living in different places. And my family was among those people, my mother, my sisters and my brothers. I decided to go back to Kenya to monitor the situation and to see if it was possible to get my mother out of Somalia – first and foremost. I could get the brothers and sisters out later on but at least I had to manage to get my mother out of Somalia. So I went to Kenya and I stopped my education at that stage. I started to financially support the people that I had left behind, so I couldn't go back to university. Only after I had managed bringing my mother, my brother's kids and my sister to Australia, I went back to university.

After my mum had arrived in Australia in 1991, other family members started coming. That's why I kept working to make sure that I could pay for their expenses wherever they were and also to help them to come here. My wife arrived in Australia a few months after my mother had come here. So she was the second one to arrive. We started to know each other when I was in Kenya to get my mother out. She was one of those people who left the country and came to Kenya. My wife was born and grew up in Mogadishu but originally she is from the same area where I come from. Our first child was born in 1992.

Back in Melbourne I started driving a taxi, but I didn't like the taxi industry and I didn't want to be a taxi driver. It wasn't the kind of profession my father had expected me to have. My understanding was that it was a failure to me and to my father, to my family, to be a taxi driver. I understand that it's an industry that supports many people. Many people working there are qualified people, much more qualified than I am, but I didn't want to make it my permanent work. So I left it once and for all and I went back to university in 1998. I was living from the social security benefit and I was also working as a freelance translator to earn extra money to support the family.

In the daytime I was studying, in the night-time I was either translating or preparing my essays. Sometimes I used to sleep only three hours a day. Sometimes I used to find myself sleeping in the class. The teacher said: 'What happened to you?' They probably thought that I was a drug user or something like that. Given the fact that there is such a media hype about black men taking drugs, they probably thought that this guy sleeping in the class was under the influence of something like that. But that was life. I went through it, I finished my BA and my Masters. I also became father again and father again and father again in that process – so it's just life. It's something that you just need to live with and accept it as it comes.

I recognize and fully accept that what my father was saying to me was right, that you cannot study and work and raise kids at the same time. He said that it was impossible. It was impossible but I did it. But it's not easy to be a husband, father, student and worker at the same time.

Brick by Brick

Sometimes when we are removed from our familiar environment we best understand the place we have left behind. By looking at the place we have left behind in another light, we also come to see ourselves in new ways. Omar says that it was by becoming friends with Australians and by being confronted with their different ideas and values that he began to encounter his own culture. And looking back to where he came from also initiated the slow process of finding his place within Australian society.

The feeling of being-at-home did not, as Omar's settlement story illustrates, come straight away. There were many hurdles to overcome. First there was the setback of his dream to become a journalist; the outbreak of the war in Somalia, which forced all of Omar's thoughts and attention towards *there*; and the many years he spent working as hard as he could in a job he did not like in order to support family members, in Melbourne and back in Somalia. But slowly, step by step, he was able to overcome the hurdles and build his life around a *here* in Melbourne. With other family members settling, with the formation of his own family and with the achievement of his educational aspirations, the here turned from a place of alienation to one of shared meaning.

In one of our meetings, Omar told me how dangerous he found the attitude of some of his Somali friends in Melbourne, who kept dreaming about going back to Somalia. 'Their bags are left unpacked, ready to go somewhere near the door, but nobody is actually taking them and going out,' he said. 'That keeps them in a situation where they are not here and not there; neither in Australia nor in Somalia.' Omar deliberately became part of Australia; he said: 'One has to sit down and say: "This is where I want to live, this is where I want my children to be raised and this is the life that I want to adapt to".' For Melbourne to become Omar's home, it required more than a shelter or a house to live in. It involved many years of place-making, of actively laying brick upon brick towards the feeling of being-at-home.

In his studies of Lebanese immigrants in Sydney, Ghassan Hage (1997: 100–8) uses the term 'home building' to describe the way the feeling of being at home is assembled. He sees the home as an emotive construct, which is built out of 'affective building blocks'. These building blocks, he argues, are 'blocks of homely feeling' (Hage 1997: 102). They relate to four key feelings: security, familiarity, community and a sense of possibility. Particularly the fourth of Hage's affective building blocks opens the door towards an understanding of Omar's placemaking practice. The feeling Hage describes as 'sense of possibility' challenges the notion of home as merely a physical and social shelter. Instead, it becomes attached with opportunities for change and improvement. 'Most theorisations of home emphasize it as a shelter but, like a mother's lap it is only a shelter that we use to rest and then spring into action, and then return to spring into action again,' Ghassan Hage (1997: 103) writes. 'A space which is only a shelter becomes, like the lap of a possessive mother, a claustrophobic space and loses its homely character.' Thus, in order to feel at home, a place needs to be open enough to perceive opportunities to move forward in one's life. In Omar's case it was the possibility of education, of taking control of his own life, of deciding that this was where he was going to live and raise his children that laid the foundations to his emplacement in Melbourne.

To arrive at a feeling of home, Omar's story seems to suggest, we first need to come to feel at home within the feeling of being-at-home. But, as Omar's story shows, just as it takes time to build a house, it also takes time to build a home. This reminds me of the distinction between *bauen* (building) and *wohnen* (dwelling) Martin Heidegger makes in his famous 1954 essay *Building Dwelling Thinking*. He argues that while dwellings are produced through the act of building, not all buildings are dwellings. For Heidegger, dwelling is a mode of being-in-the-world, which precedes building. 'Only if we are capable of dwelling,' he writes, 'only then can we build' (Heidegger 1975: 160). While Omar was capable of laying bricks, plastering and doing the things necessary to build a house, it was only when the bricks became invested with meaning and moved beyond mere bricks and walls that the simple shelter turned into a home.

That my reading of Omar's placemaking practices is so heavily saturated with constructional terms such as 'building', 'brick', or 'plastering' is not to suggest that home is mainly a physical shelter. Just like the English word, the experience goes far beyond it. For this reason, Alison Blunt and Robyn Dowling (2006: 2) define home as twofold – as a place and site in which we live and as an imaginary that is imbued with feelings. As opposed to Heimat or Heim, home allows for movement to be an intrinsic part of it – spatially and imaginary. A home, however much we are building towards it, always remains in the making. 'People always live in an approximation of the ideal home,' Ghassan Hage (1997: 104) writes.

The imaginary strength of home, this feeling we are building towards and that seems to always slip under our fingers as we are trying to grip it, embeds the word with an aura of mystery. Omar, with whom I share a deep interest in the stories behind words, once told me that in the Somali language, just like in German, there is no sufficient translation for 'home'. 'There are two words that people use to differentiate between where they live and where they belong,' Omar explained. 'Where they live is the house, which is *guri* in Somali, and where they belong is *wadan*, which means my country.' 'So when people are not in Somalia anymore but somewhere else, like here in Australia, which of the two words would they use?' I asked Omar. He told me that the answer was difficult, as the whole concept of home was not translatable. 'I think they use home, where home stands for where you live,' he said. 'That's what they use for the actual place of habitation. There are young people who say "Oh, that guy is feeling homesick", and they refer to the English language rather than to Somali. So the Somali language doesn't explain or refer to your country. The only word that they use for this is wadan, "my country".'

As Omar explained, the outbreak of the war and the sudden importance of the clan complicated the translation of the idea of home into the Somali context even further. The continuous violence between different clans forced people to move back to the regions associated with their own clans. For it is only on your ancestor's land, Omar said, that you could find a secure and safe environment. For many years, Somalis from different clans moved around the country freely, settling in areas associated with other clans, but the war changed these dynamics dramatically. Many people were forced to flee to places associated with their clans to seek their protection. As a result, Omar explained, Somalis now often refer to their home as the place where their clan has a stronghold. In fact, when in his story he talks about his wife, he says that she was born and raised in Mogadishu, but that 'originally she is from the same area where I come from'. So although before she was forced to flee she had spent all her life in Mogadishu, she is again associated with the place her clan is believed to originate from. It took me a long time to understand that when I asked the Somali people I met in Melbourne where in Somalia they came from, they very often referred to a place they had actually never been to.

While Omar stressed that Australia was his home, this did not erase Somalia from the feeling of being-at-home. In fact, many of Omar's stories suggest the opposite. When he begins to talk about his settlement in Melbourne, for example, his thoughts quickly wander back to Somalia, where so many people have been killed over the last decades that Australians often react to reports of the violence with indifference. That people *here*, where his home is placed, react so indifferently towards the well-being of the people *there*, where he is at home as well, is a painful experience, signalling a feeling Hage (1997: 108) poignantly describes as 'being there *here*'.

On the same day that Omar told me how he had decided that Australia was to become his new home, he also told me that the Somali community in Melbourne, which had grown much bigger since his arrival here in 1989, was deeply affected by what was happening back in Somalia. I asked him how it feels to constantly receive terrible news from his home country.

You like to hear from your country, regardless of how far away you are,' Omar responded. 'You're born there; you have relatives there and friends.

You feel sorry to see Somalia dying almost everywhere. The Somalian name demeaned and demolished on a daily basis. Somalia is equated to almost any bad thing now: death, destruction, poverty, lawlessness, anarchy, piracy – anything that you can think of. And surely that has an enormous impact on those of us who left the country. Additionally, we always have people seeking our support. And that's another burden on us. You cannot stay silent and you cannot satisfy everyone who needs your help, so you sometimes feel guilty by not supporting them. You feel guilty by giving money away where actually your children might need it. And it's a dilemma, it's a dilemma where you don't know whether you should do this or do that. So we wake up with that anger and unhappiness, we walk with that, we work with that, we sleep with that. It's very unfortunate.

I cannot even begin to imagine what it must feel to see, as Omar describes it, your home country 'dying almost everywhere', to live with this pain and burden day in, day out – and to still be able to build a new home. But, as Sara Ahmed (1999: 331) writes, home and away are not necessarily opposites. Home, she argues, is 'elsewhere', it 'becomes the impossibility and necessity of the subject's future', where one never gets but is always going to, rather than a 'past which binds the self to a given place'. Thus, it is exactly within the movement and journeying of people that we can begin to grasp the meaning of places and our connections to them. And because, as I mentioned before, we often learn most about ourselves when we are the furthest away from our familiar environment, in the next chapter I discuss these themes by focusing on the story of a return journey.

Note

1. The literal translation for 'Abrahams Wurstkessel' is 'Abraham's sausage pot'. It is a saying, commonly used in Austria to jokingly describe to children where babies come from. It refers to the biblical story of Abraham, the father of the people of Israel.

6

Homewards

Restless Minds

Many Australians I met over the five years I lived there gave me the impression that they were 'homeless minds' (Berger, Berger and Kellner 1973). Here I am not only referring to the enforced homelessness of indigenous Australians, whose displacement from the country that connects them to their Dreaming leaves them as trespassers on their own land. I am also (and even more so) speaking of the Anglo-Australians, whose ancestors came to this country and who, in many ways, seem to be at a loss as to how to feel towards this continent. I am speaking of moments when people who meet each other for the first time start to recite their ancestry up to the generation that first came to Australia. 'I'm half Scottish, half English,' you might hear from a person whose ancestors came to Australia as part of the first fleet more than two centuries ago. And very often, people even proudly announce the exact village or town in England, Scotland or Ireland, whence their ancestors originated.

In moments like these I often wondered why, generations later, it was of such importance to relate back to a home-place on the other side of the world. As if the here and now did not offer enough (of what exactly is not all that clear) to feel at home in. As if generations after their family's move to Australia, their minds had not settled here yet. Consider, for example, a conversation I had with an Australian academic. When he heard that I was Dutch-Austrian, he immediately asked me what on earth I was doing in Australia then, which, he said, was 'culturally empty'. And without giving me the chance to reply he began telling me about the marvellous time he had spent in Germany studying art. He told me a story about something that had occurred many years ago and had changed his way of thinking about Australia: he had just arrived in Germany and took the train from the airport to his final destination. He shared the compartment with an old man and a young girl whom he thought to be the man's granddaughter. Overhearing their conversation, he realized that the old man was reciting poems by Goethe to the little girl, discussing their meaning with her. 'At that moment I so deeply felt all that I had missed growing up in Australia,' he said, 'this level of cultural depth that I was always left on my own with here.' While the academic said that socially Germany did not feel like his home – and, in fact, nowhere did, as he told me later on – culturally he felt that in that moment he had arrived. Similarly, my friend David told me that years after his return from a year abroad in the Netherlands he still had vivid dreams of cycling through Amsterdam: 'I am cycling through the streets I used to cycle through when I lived there, and it feels so much like home. I feel more at home there than when I think about my hometown Wollongong.'

Is it not ironic that Omar, who wholeheartedly declares Australia to be his home, is so often put in the refugee box by the same people who seem to be much more at odds with their own feelings of belonging? The words 'migrant' or 'refugee' have come to be spoken in one breath with homelessness and nonbelonging – accompanied by the assumption that to lose one's home-place is to also lose one's identity and place in the world. In many ways, the homelessness I encountered in many Australians and that marks my refusal to identify with a stained Heimat is a chosen homelessness, one that sits perfectly within the restless nature of modernity. It is a homelessness chosen by people who do not want to feel at home in a world that continues to be defined by borders, exclusions and injustices. It is a chosen homelessness that stems from a feeling of uprootedness that John Berger described to be the 'quintessential experience' of our age. And it is a homelessness that, in various ways, desires the state of nomadic belonging embodied in the figure of the migrant or the refugee. Or, as Nigel Rapport and Andrew Dawson (1998: 23) write: 'Exile, emigration, banishment, labour migrancy, tourism, urbanization and counter-urbanization are the central motifs of modern culture, while being rootless, displaced between worlds, living between a lost past and a fluid present, are perhaps the most fitting metaphors for the journeying, modern consciousness ...'

Within this world of restless movement, some Western thinkers have begun to champion migration, exile and nomadism not only as forms of dislocation from home, but as metaphors to think *without* home (Deleuze and Guattari 1986; Braidotti 1994; Chambers 1994). Yet it is somewhat paradoxical that while a certain type of Western intellectual has come to wilfully choose a migratory sense of belonging, people like Omar feel they have become incarcerated within the same migratory metaphor. Maybe Gaston Bachelard is right when he questions the use of metaphors. He suggests that a metaphor 'should be no more than an accident of expression', and that it is dangerous to make a thought of it, as it is no more than a 'false image' (Bachelard 1994: 77).

The placelessness of the infinite universe, it seems, has brought with it the homelessness of our minds – because when there is no place to attach itself to, where, then, can home be? For Casey it is emblematic that Kant, who, as he argues, brought modernity to its most rigorous point, had no room for place in his conception of the human subject. 'By this I mean not just that the very term "place" drops out of his discourse regarding the subject ... but that the phenomenal self, the only self we can know, is radically unemplaced' (Casey 1997b: 292). In Kant's philosophy, the only unity of self becomes consciousness. 'Beyond this frail and formal unity there is nothing more lasting to grasp – nothing substantial, nothing simple, nothing of the nature of an abiding self.' Casey argues that with Kant we reach in extremis what was already prepared by Descartes: the modern subject as a placeless subject. 'This subject, living only in the flattened-out sites it itself projects or constructs, cannot count on any abiding place in the world.'

In this strange world, where some people choose not to belong, where the intimacy of place is vanishing against the sheer endlessness of space, it is perhaps more suitable to speak of 'restless minds' rather than 'homeless minds'. For much of the estrangement from the notion of place could only come about through the restless travelling so typical of our age of movement. With the heightened importance of journeying, people have come to see the places they left behind in radically different ways. And although chosen homelessness and placelessness might be an ideal upheld by many Western intellectuals, the estrangement felt upon returning back home in fact highlights the continuing importance of place. It is the act of homecoming that enables us to see the places we left behind in a new light. And it is through the changed look at these home-places that, through journeying, we also come to see ourself in new ways.

It is in this light that the last part of Omar's life story, a story of his journey back home, can be looked at. That I happened to hear this story was almost an accident. After many meetings in his office in Carlton and the many hours he spent telling me stories about his life, we decided that our work on his life story had come to an end. After that we did not hear from each other for a couple of months. I had been evicted from my share-house with only a month's notice, and having to look for a new place in the midst of a housing shortage was a task that took up most of my energy. I spent hours every day going through the housing offers, I queued up for inspections amongst dozens of other desperate house-hunters, wrote letters and tried to convince real estate agents that despite my low student income I was the best suitable candidate. With all the fuss about my chosen homelessness, how much effort I made when there was the slightest chance of really becoming homeless.

I met Omar again when I went to the wedding of one of Halima's nephews. Much to my surprise, he told me that he had just returned from Puntland, his first trip back to Somalia since 1983. I had so many questions: How was it to see the place he had left behind after so many years? How much had it changed? And how much had he changed? 'Let's meet again soon, and I will tell you the story,' Omar said, laughing. And thus the story continued …

In July 2011 I went back to visit Puntland for three weeks. It was mainly to see the people that I left behind thirty-five years ago. While I was away some of my family had passed away, so I was really concerned that many more would go before I could see them again. So I decided to visit them, to see their lives and to spend time with them. I was also interested to see how much Somalia had changed.

The Somalia I visited wasn't the country that I had left anymore; the people weren't the people that I had left anymore; their lifestyle wasn't the lifestyle that I knew anymore. That was very, very interesting. That is actually also how it is addressed by many academics, when they say that there is always a cultural shock when you go back and you have this cultural baggage behind your brain and you think that the people are still the way you left them behind. In fact that is not the case.

I visited my brothers and sisters, as well as the distant relatives, the cousins, in-laws, people who are either from my father's side or from my mother's side or even from my wife's side. When I say in-laws I mean anyone who came through marriage related links. They call me, even when I'm in Melbourne. They call me or they call my brother or my sister and ask for some kind of support. So there has always been a connection. But to see them and to sit with them and talk to them is a different matter. It was really emotional.

We had four different houses in Gardo, and now they are all occupied by my sisters and brothers. One thing really moved me. I went into my father's special room. It used to be always locked and nobody could get in except for the cleaners and my mother, who was supervising that the job was done properly. And now it has become a house for my sister. That means that my brother-in-law actually lives in that room now. His bed is where my father's bed used to be. Really, that moves me. I didn't cry, but … My father's position to be taken by another junior, unknown man and enjoying the luxury that he had made for himself, is something that really moves me.

But that's the way it is. He was brought there by my sister, she lives in our house, and she has got the right to say where her husband lives. But this was one of the things that really moved me and showed to me how the structural changes are memorable.

When I went there, I was advised to have a security guard and I was provided with two men who were absolutely fully armed to go with me wherever I went. Sometimes I found that very uncomfortable. Because in Gardo, the town where I was born, I don't want to have a bodyguard. In Gardo, where I grew up! And the people I was talking to were people that I knew. But they said: 'You never know. Your brother is in a higher position in the government, you are elite …'

What really put me off was that I came back from a country that has no issues with me. In Australia I can go wherever I want, I can sleep whenever I want, I can walk wherever I want, without anyone even knowing me. But coming back to where I was born and where I grew up, I needed a security guard to protect me. That was something that made me question: 'Ok, where is your country? Where do I really belong? Do I belong to Australia? Or do I belong to Somalia? Or am I half and half?' Surely, I'm not even 5 per cent Somali if I am given a highly armed man to protect my life, whereas in Melbourne no one even knows whether I'm here or not. But the issue of recognition and understanding and knowing you and feeling that there is ownership, that they own you, that you are their son, is also a different matter.

Near my house in Melbourne there is a coffee shop where I go almost every day, either in the afternoon or in the morning. Just to get a cup of coffee. I missed that place when I was in Somalia. But when I came back, nobody had even felt that I had been away. That again really makes me ask: 'Oh, nobody even knew that you were not in Melbourne. So what is going on?' Back home, everyone knows my family, where I live, how many children I have, my situation, my education, my position in the community and so on. Getting that recognition tells you that you really belong to them. But then, when there is a bodyguard protecting you from them, that is another issue.

When I came back to Melbourne, I was interviewed by the ABC and the journalist asked me a question which was very interesting: 'Where did you actually spend most of your time in your life?' I realized that the city that I spent most of my life in is Melbourne. The country where I spent most of my life is Australia. I left Somalia when I was twenty-two, I went to the Middle East, left from there, went to India, I left from there and came here. So the country where I spent that many years is Australia, and not Somalia. The city where I spent most of my life is Melbourne. So I belong more to Melbourne than anywhere else.

I was telling that reporter: 'Look, regardless [of] what Andrew Bolt[1] says – if you asked him about me he would probably give you a totally different version – but I see Australia to be my country. I've got five kids, they are all born here, and they all belong here. I've got one house in the world, and that is in Melbourne. Ok? I graduated from different universities, they are all in Melbourne. If you look at all these facts, I'm more from Melbourne than from anywhere else, including the country where I was born and raised.'

Figure 6.1 *'This is what happens: As soon as the car stops, the soldiers jump out and they have to go in all directions to make sure that the place is safe.' Image courtesy of Mohamed Ibrahim*

World Inner Space

Against the idea that journeying and continuous movement are romantic and rebellious acts in a world that tries to restrict home to an unmovable locale stand the pains and efforts connected with homecoming – of coming home to an estranged place and as a changed person.

When, after years of restless travelling, Odysseus finally finds his way back to Ithaca, he is struck by the fact that Penelope has not changed at all. But he is also deeply shocked by the profound changes he observes in the political and social life of the place. In fact, Odysseus is unwilling to live with these disturbing differences and leaps into action to turn Ithaca back into what it had been before he left. The same feeling of estrangement and change can occur when we return to our hometowns, which appear 'at once recognizably the same and yet disarmingly different' every time we go back (Casey 1993: 274). For Omar, going back home confronted him with an entirely different place from the one he had left behind. The country was not the country he had left, he says, and the people were not the people he had left.

On my first visit back to Austria after only one-and-a-half years in Australia, walking through the streets of Vienna, which I still knew by heart, made me feel like a stranger. It was as if I was dreaming of myself walking through these streets, as if everything around me was so familiar and yet not real. The way people walked, the jokes they made, the stories they found interesting, appeared so strange to me, that I felt like somebody who had to learn how to walk and talk all over again. Edward Casey describes the feeling of place-alienation people often feel upon returning home:

> Given this reciprocity of person and place, place-alienation is itself two-way: I from it, it from me. When caught up in this double-sided other-ness, I feel, almost literally, 'beside myself'. I feel myself to be other than myself and not just somewhere other than where I am in world-space (e.g., my exact address, my cartographic location, etc.). (Casey 1993: 307)

In Omar's story of his return journey, the painfulness of this double alienation comes to the fore in the opening of the once forbidden door to what used to be his father's room. Throughout his stories Omar narrates the separation from his father as one of the most powerful symbolizations of his feelings of loss and displacement. That upon his return home he found the door of his father's room not only wide open, but also his childhood home's inner life entirely changed, touched him deeply.

In *The Poetics of Space*, Bachelard writes extensively about the meaning of childhood homes. He argues that the house we were born in is physically inscribed in us (Bachelard 1994: 14). Images provoked by memories of our past prove that 'the houses that were lost forever continue to live on in us'. Even more, 'they insist in us in order to live again, as though they expected us to give them a supplement of living' (Bachelard 1994: 56). The memories of Omar's childhood home in Gardo, the inner working of each room that had inscribed itself so deep into his sense of self, were thrown into doubt by the opening of the forbidden door – an opening to changes that he describes as 'memorable'.

Trying to make sense of the feeling of alienation both Omar and I had upon returning home, I am again turning towards Edward Casey's philosophy. Homecoming can, he points out, lead to the paradoxical situation where I return to a place that I can be said to know for the first time, although I have in fact been there before (Casey 1993: 293). While the place itself is still the same place, returning to it after having been away can make us see it differently and yet more clearly than ever before. Exactly this feeling of alien- ation, which Omar describes in his story, highlights the importance journeying and homecoming can play for a new understanding of home. 'It is as if I had to leave my home to become acquainted with a more capacious world, which in turn allows me to grasp more of the home to which I return,' Casey (1993: 294) writes. He points out that the movement of such a journey of departure and homecoming is one from part to whole and back to part. However, the second part directly reflects the whole, 'for I now know my home in the light of the larger place-world through which I have traveled'.

Throughout his life Rainer Maria Rilke – a poet whose writings have accompanied me for many years – was preoccupied with the experience of the vastness of space. In the fourth stanza of his poem 'Es winkt zu Fühlung fast aus allen Dingen' from 1914, he refers to the seemingly paradoxical situation of gaining intimacy from the world's immensity:

Durch alle Wesen reicht der *eine* Raum:
Weltinnenraum. Die Vögel fliegen still
durch uns hindurch. O, der ich wachsen will,
ich seh hinaus, und *in* mir wächst der Baum.

Through every being stretches *one* space
World inner space. Silently the birds fly
through us. O, I who wishes to grow,
I look outside, and *in* me the tree grows.[2]

Commenting on this poem, Bachelard (1994: 203) writes that it is through their immensity that the space of intimacy and the world-space begin to blend: 'When human solitude deepens, then the two immensities touch and become identical.' While all beings are shot through with the immensity of this world inner space – what Rilke calls a *Weltinnenraum* – this shared immensity also enables us to reach outwards and attach intimacy to all other beings that inhabit this space ('the birds fly silently through us').

This meeting point between the intimacy of place and the infinite-ness of the universe may allow us to reconcile the modernist home-less mind with an understanding of home as *in movement* between the two. It is only by experiencing the vastness of space through journeying that we come to an understanding of the felt intimacy of places. Although Omar described Australia as his home, the story of his journey back shows that there are many homes within his feeling of being-at-home – and as many questions about these very homes. We are thrown back upon exactly these questions in the journeys we undertake in our everyday lives; such questions keep the idea of home in continuous movement. Just like home is, as Robert Ginsburg writes, 'less about where you are from, but more about where you are going' (Ginsburg quoted in Mallett 2004: 77), belonging is not so much about a state of being but about ways of becoming. The very condition of being is to be continuously on the move and directed towards something or somewhere – or *unterwegs* (underway), as Heidegger (1962: 110) puts it. However much we are striving to reach a standstill, moments of pause and frozenness in place are, in fact, the exception and not the norm.

Travelling Minds

It comforts me to think of home as something that does not force me to decide whether it is here or there. As Omar's story shows, he has home-like and estranged feelings for both Gardo and Melbourne. While his hometown is where he feels that he is best known or 'owned' by other people, the fact that he could only move about there with heavily armed bodyguards made him question whether this was really his home. Upon his arrival back in Melbourne, Omar was again alienated, this time by the lack of ownership by others, but he also felt that this was the city where he and his children belong.

It is as if the feeling of home attaches itself to places – but in sync with our own to and fro journeys that change our look upon them over and over again. With the highlighted importance of move-ment in the constitution of place, can we thus use James Clifford's (1992: 103) often-applied metaphor of 'dwelling-in-travel' to describe Omar's experience of home? I once discussed this question with Omar. I confronted him with an article I had just read, which touched upon the importance travelling has in Somalia in new and (for me) compelling ways. While many authors have written about the historical importance of nomadic movement, trading expeditions, and seafaring for Somali culture, this text related to the expression of an inner, spiritual urge for movement. The article's authors write about a common belief in Somalia that people who desperately want to leave the country are possessed by the *saar* (spirit) of travel. To cure persons possessed by it, the healers ask the saars to reveal the causes for the misfortune. In return, the saar expresses his wishes and promises to leave once they have been fulfilled. The authors write that very often, to help a person possessed by the travel saar, the community has the responsibility to mobilize the affected person to go on a journey in order to satisfy the spirit's desires (Rousseau, Said and Bibeau 1998).

When I had finished my summary of the article, Omar laughed. He had never heard about any such thing as a travel saar before. 'Look,' he said, still chuckling, 'nowadays we've got so many writers who just come up with something and write it, to amaze, surprise, and make the reader laugh. Many of them are not accountable to what they're doing.' Then he told me a story – another travel story – that had made him see the reasons behind people's desire to move in new ways:

In 2001, I was in Malaysia. One day I was talking to an old Malay man. I asked him: 'Have you ever travelled from one place in the country to another?' He said: 'Why should I?' And I said: 'Why not?' He replied: 'Look, what I can get in my particular space is what I can also get in a far distant area.' He said: 'I don't need to travel to somewhere else. Because I have what I need here.' And really, that impacts me strongly. Because I realized that why people move from place to place is to change their life, to enhance their lifestyle, to achieve more, to learn more, maybe to get peace and stability. This guy has peace, he's got a little space where he can plant vegetables and harvest them whenever he wants to. He's got a river he can go to and get fish out of. So why should he travel from place to place?

Again, Omar's story reveals how far away metaphors can be from people's lived experience. While it is appealing to think of belonging in terms of 'dwelling-in-travel', Omar reminds us that the very meaning of travelling itself is not all that unproblematic. He was convinced that 'apart from those who started to go out just to have an experience, people don't travel for the sake of luxury. They travel for the sake of changing something in their lives. In most of the cases they are not happy with where, how and what they have in a particular place. So to achieve more, they have to go somewhere else, where they can get a better life.' Omar felt very uncomfortable describing his own situation in terms of 'dwelling-in-travel'. For him, travel does not stand for borderless belonging, but quite the opposite: the need to travel only arises from a feeling of discontent with oneself or the place one is currently at. To be at home in travelling would thus accept a never-ending repetition of the very discomfort that has led Omar to leave Somalia in the first place. It would constantly reinforce a feeling of restless commotion, of losing hope to ever arrive anywhere. But although the move away from Puntland has, at times, been painful, although settling in Australia involved many hurdles, and although his home in Australia is anything but perfect, what counts for Omar is what he actively makes out of these situations to overcome them.

While Omar attaches feelings of being-at-home to different places, and while the meanings of these places are continuously on the move, the act of travelling itself does not constitute his home. Yet the importance of travelling should not be dismissed entirely. Sara Ahmed's work offers an explanation that highlights the importance of change and yet does not lose sight of the importance of the intimacy of place. She suggests that the lived experience of being-at-home engages subjects in a space, which is not simply outside of them. Instead, subject and space leak into each other; they inhabit each other (Ahmed 1999: 341). She relates the lived experience of home to the image of inhabiting a second skin. Similar to Rilke's *Weltinnenraum*, this skin does not only 'house' the subject, but also allows him or her to touch and be touched by the world. 'The home as skin suggests the boundary between self and home is permeable, but also that the boundary between home and away is permeable as well. Here, movement away is also movement within the constitution of home as such' (Ahmed 1999: 341).

If we look at home as a second skin that allows us to simultaneously touch and be touched, then being-at-home is an imagination, in that it is always in the making, and in that the ideal home is what we are always striving for but never arrive at. It is also a sentiment, in that being-at-home is so close to our innermost feelings that it becomes hard to theorize. Within this tension between the imagined and the lived, we can read Omar's story of his journey homewards – a homewards that is familiar and alienating, here and there, now and then, inwards and outwards.

I am ending Omar's story with his own words. They relate to both home as a sentiment and home as an imagination, and for him they encapsulate the experience of being-at-home. They came about as a response to my question of whether he could explain to me what home was to him as opposed to where it was.

I think home is where you are happy. I think home is where you are satisfied. I think home is where you are respected. I think your home is where you get what you are entitled to. I think home is where you are seen as another human being. There's a Somalian proverb that says: 'Waad taqaan qofka kuu sokeeya laakiin ma taqaanid qofka kuu roon' – 'you know who is closer to you in terms of bloodline, but you don't know who will help you more when you need them.' Yes, I'm Somali and I'm born Somali from one of the Somali families; however, I didn't choose to be born Somali, it just happened that way. But I believe Australia offered me more than what Somalia offered me in terms of the past and in the present.

When the time passes your needs differ. I always sleep with my wife side by side, sometimes holding her and sleeping in that situation. There was an era when I couldn't sleep without my mother's lap. The things have changed. So within that change – what will control you and decide and shape your life is where you feel more comfortable. Whether it is sleeping next to your wife by holding her, or whether it is sleeping and lying in your mother's lap. It's the comfortability, and that's where it goes back to. If I go back to Somalia but Somalia cannot provide me at least the minimum of what I need, the security, forget about anything else, then surely Somalia is not my country, is not my home. My home is where I'm happy.

Notes

1. Omar refers to the right-wing Australian journalist Andrew Bolt, who in a series of provocative blog posts in the *Herald Sun* newspaper

had maintained that African immigrants were refusing to integrate and were more likely to commit crimes than the wider (white) Australian community. Omar was interviewed by an ABC journalist about Bolt's provocations.

2. Translation by the author.

PART III

Displacement

When Mohamed and I first looked through the photos he had taken in Mogadishu, I almost skipped this image. Somehow the emptiness, the greyness, the absence of liveliness it depicted, made me believe that the image had no story to tell: as if it had been taken by accident; as if its very existence was displaced. Yet, Mohamed asked me to have

Figure PIII.1 *National Somali television studio in Mogadishu. Image courtesy of Mohamed Ibrahim*

a closer look. 'What do you think this is?' I had no idea. To me, the photo gave no sense of the place it depicted. 'This was a TV studio and that's what's left,' Mohamed explained. 'The rest is gone.'

Mohamed said that he had been shocked when he entered this room. It used to be the studio of Somalia's national news. The presenter used to sit at that desk. During the war, people looted the studio, leaving nothing but the old, rusty desk and a broken air conditioner, its wires and hose spreading over the empty floor. Mohamed found it unbelievable that simply nothing had been left behind that reminded of what the room had once embodied: the pride of Somalia's national television station. Founded after independence, it had become the nation's voice, eye and ear. Mohamed found it hard to describe a place like this: ravaged, empty, stripped of its meaning and life. Looking at the photo a feeling of compassion engulfed both of us for this naked, abandoned room – as if it was not a room but a person. What hurt Mohamed more than the ravaged place, however, was the loss of memory it represented. He told me that when he had walked through the building, he had found the former archive, a room full of old cassettes containing historical video footage of Somalia. The tapes were in a terrible state. Many of them had been taken out of their casings, strips of film hung down from the rusty old shelves. Exposed to the weather in a room without proper windows,

Figure PIII.2 *Broadcasting archive in Mogadishu. Image courtesy of Mohamed Ibrahim*

Mohamed feared that most of the film tapes had been ruined. 'It's very sad,' he remarked. 'I found it interesting that obviously there used to be a system with index cards, but all this got mixed up. Now people are using the index box, the box itself, as storage, they're putting the cassettes inside. It's very sad, but anyway.'

Rather than displacement, the images of the former broadcasting building embody de-placement – this is a place that has been emptied of itself and its inner workings. It has not just lost its present function, but also the memories of its very past. Could this be the end, the death of a place? Can there be such a thing as naked, unbounded space? In other words, can there be a *placeless* place? The question arises whether this does not overlook the role of Mohamed's imagination, where the studio with its former pride and beauty still lives on and plays into his present ways of being-here. Maybe the image captures displacement, but not as an end in itself or as something that deteriorates into unbounded nothingness. Rather, this unboundedness could be read as a clearing, as an opening towards the imaginary, which, in turn, contains the boundless. For, as Friedrich Hölderlin (2008: 254) so beautifully puts it in his drama *Death of Empedocles*, 'always into the unbounded a languorous longing goes'.

7

At Home in the Universe

Meeting Halima

I was born in the central part of Somalia, in Buuloburde, which is in the Hiiraan region. I was born in Buuloburde but I didn't grow up there. After I was born, we moved north to the town of Galcayo because my father was a policeman, and he was transferred to different places all the time.

My mother was a very helpful mum, a very beautiful mum – as they told me, because I can't remember much. But I heard her history from my sister and my father. She used to do small business. She got stoves from Hiiraan, stone stoves, and she sold them around Galcayo. She died when I was six years old. My mum was pregnant and when she was giving birth, she got a bleeding and her child died. Thirty minutes afterwards she also died. When we lost my mum, my father was not with us. He was sick and that's why he had gone to Mogadishu to see a doctor. So people told him: 'Your wife died,' and he came back. When he returned, he called all of us kids together and he told us that our mother had died.

My mother had left nine kids behind, three boys and six girls. One of the boys didn't live with us. He used to live with our grandparents. But even that boy came when my mum died. When we came together, every person was crying for us and saying: 'How can they survive?' I remember my sister telling me that my father had answered: 'God has taken my wife, but he also created these kids, so I'm sure they will survive.'

My oldest sister Zeinab was thirteen years old then, and she took over the responsibility for the family. She lives in Dubai now. She looked after us and she always said: 'Go to school. Go to learn the Qur'an!' And if we were disappointed or sad she reminded us: 'Our mother died, but do you want to show all the people that we don't have a family, you want to show them that you are weak? They will not respect you if you do that.' This is how she helped us to build our self-esteem.

When mum died, my father asked for his job to be moved to Mogadishu. But the government said: 'No, you will be transferred to Hargeisa.' But Hargeisa is far away in Somaliland, so he said: 'No, I'm not going there.' And they responded: 'Then you have to leave the police. We will dismiss you.' And he decided, and he said: 'Dismiss me, but I don't want to go to that place, because my children are little kids and they need people that they know or an area that they can understand. That is too far for me and I have never been there. In Mogadishu I have some family, I have my brothers there, so they can look after my kids, they can help me.' When they dismissed him, he talked to his brother and asked him: 'Can you help me if I move to Mogadishu?' He said: 'I will give my life for your kids and you.' So that's how we came to Mogadishu. When we came to Mogadishu my uncle took the responsibility over us kids. He said: 'Until you get a proper job I will look after your kids.' We grew up in a very big family, we loved each other.

My brother who had never lived with us came to stay with us too. It was hard for him to get used to the new environment in the beginning, because he had grown up in the countryside with my grandparents and we had grown up in the cities with my parents. When my father got his first child, my grandmother had said to him: 'When you get your second child I need that one to keep it for my heart, because you are moving so far away, and I want to have someone around me.' She loved her son. So that's why my brother stayed with my grandparents in Xaafun, which is a coastal area in Puntland.

My uncle gave us the opportunity to go back to school, to go to the religious schools from morning to evening and we were taught to nurture each other, to help each other, and we never allowed people to hurt us. My sisters were very, very brave. My sisters Sahra and Zeinab and my two older brothers were connected, they said: 'We have to look after these kids.' They were kids too, but they didn't feel that way. They felt like parents, they took that position.

Sometimes a first encounter with someone leaves an immediate imprint. It is as if this stranger, by mere presence, touches on something so deep, so difficult to grasp and yet so palpable that there is an instantaneous connection, turning strangeness into something familiar. Meeting Halima for the first time was such an encounter.

For weeks I had carried her phone number around with me, postponing that very first call. Although Omar, who had given me her number, had encouraged me to talk to her, saying he believed she could be interested in participating in my research, a phobia of talking to strangers on the phone had kept me paralysed. When I finally convinced myself to pick up the phone, however, Halima's response was so welcoming, that all my nervousness immediately vanished. 'Oh, it's you, darling,' she said after I had introduced myself, 'I have been waiting for your call.' She invited me to come and meet her at Federation Square in the city centre the next day. She told me that she would spend the whole day there, painting a container for an initiative called the Peace Project.

On the phone Halima told me what the project was about. She told me how Ahmed, a young social worker from Melbourne's northern suburb of Flemington, had returned from a visit to his hometown in central Somalia recently, shocked to see how children were trapped in a vicious cycle of poverty and conflict. He had found his town's children gathered under a large tree, patiently awaiting the arrival of a man who volunteered to teach them in the shade of that very tree with what little means he had. Ahmed had taken photos back to Melbourne, showing children so eager to learn that they used the barks of trees on which to scratch the letters of the Arabic alphabet they were learning. There were no books, no pens, no chairs, no blackboards – let alone a house that could shelter them from wind or rain.

Back in Melbourne, Halima had been so touched by these photos that she and Ahmed, together with Halima's friend Pauline who ran a small NGO in Melbourne, began to think about what they could do to help. As a result, the Peace Project came into being. Their idea was to motivate the Somali community in Melbourne to work together, and regularly send containers with furniture, schoolbooks, pens and clothes, as well as money, to different regions in Somalia to help set up basic schools and employ teachers. In order for the idea to work, Halima had to establish links with schools in Melbourne that were willing to donate the items that were needed. She also had to organize fundraisers and get Somalis living in Melbourne to contribute to the project financially. From the beginning of the initiative, Halima knew that the step of bringing Somalis in Melbourne to support it would be the most difficult part of the Peace Project. Their reluctance was a direct reflection of how unsettled the idea of place had become in the Somali context: because of the abuse of clanism during much of Somalia's brief history as a nation state and the decades of violence between members of different clans and sub-clans, the idea of a unified community of Somalis has become out of reach. For many it has become replaced by an idea of belonging that is deeply linked to clan affiliation rooted in very specific places. Although Somalis in Melbourne generally showed a readiness to donate money to aid projects in their home country, they were reluctant to do so if the project was not located in the area where their clans had the stronghold so that their own people would benefit. Halima's main motivation for setting up the Peace Project was to work against these dynamics and to create a more open and inclusive notion of community – both in Melbourne and Somalia. In order to reach this goal, she had to be inventive and find means of accommodating all these splintered groups and affiliations. As a result, Halima came up with the idea of shifting the Peace Project's focus between different regions in Somalia. So while the first container was sent to a town in central Somalia, the following projects were to be located in other places. Halima's hope was that conflicting clans living in Melbourne working together would send a signal of reconciliation to the communities receiving help in Somalia. At the same time, she also hoped it would be the beginning of a process of rapprochement within the community in Melbourne. The container that was about to be sent to Ahmed's hometown, painted with colourful messages of hope and reconciliation, was the beginning of the Peace Project.

When I went to Federation Square the next morning, I found the container Halima had told me about on the boulevard next to the Yarra River. Three women were busy painting colourful motifs onto it. When I approached them, Halima immediately recognized me. A tall and self-confident woman in her mid fifties, dressed in an apron and swaying a tin of paint, she waved me over. Within no time I, too, held a paintbrush, and I was to spend many hours painting with Halima, her youngest daughter Sagal and their friend Pauline.

Sitting under the burning sun, the brush moving monotonously up and down, and colour patterns ever changing, created a somewhat meditative atmosphere. It opened us all up to sharing stories and jokes, but it also created a space where it was acceptable to withdraw into oneself, lulled by the rhythm of the paintbrushes and the sounds of the surrounding city. Throughout the day, curious passers-by would come and ask about the project, some of them picking up a brush and joining us for a while. And so brush stroke by brush stroke, layer upon layer, we slowly got to know each other.

By the end of the afternoon Halima took me aside: 'Let's go and have a glass of orange juice together.' As we sat down in the shade, she told me how she had arrived in Australia as a refugee and how, soon after her arrival, she was diagnosed with a serious illness. She told me how the doctors had only given her a 15 per cent chance of surviving and how she had spent a long time in hospital, her children devastated by their mother's deteriorating state. 'But I'm still alive.' she said. 'In the hospital I believed that it wasn't time to go yet. I believed that I needed to help my community and go back to university.' She told me how, soon after she had left the hospital, she began studying community development and welfare and how straight away she had started to work on her own ideas to support Somali women in Melbourne. 'Helping my community has helped me survive,' she said. For Halima, 'helping my community' was about much more than supporting her people. It was about combating the feelings of estrangement that had accompanied her first steps through Melbourne and it was about befriending this new place and its people by actively carving out her own paths. In doing so, she was literally placing herself back into the world: 'To not exclude myself, I decided to be in the people's world,' Halima said. 'What I found out was that my medication is to work with the community.'

Sitting under the shade of a large gumtree, we observed a group of children inspecting the giant African animals Halima and Pauline had painted. 'Just imagine how the children in Somalia will love the stories we painted onto this container.' Halima said. We both smiled at the idea of the native Australian bush flowers we had just drawn flowering somewhere in Somalia.

I had already told Halima about my research during our phone conversation the day before, and I had also told her that I was looking for people who would be interested in working with me on their life stories. But I had not raised the topic again. Having spent the whole day in the burning hot sun painting and seeing the exhaustion on her face, I thought it best not to bother her with the details of my project. But while we were enjoying our rest, Halima brought it up herself. 'Look,' she said, 'I am very happy to tell you about my life so that you can use it for your book. I want people in Australia to understand our stories.' I told her that I would be keen to listen to her stories. 'But you have to understand,' she said, 'there are things I cannot speak about. I had a devastating time fleeing Somalia, and for many years I didn't know where my husband was.' I promised that I would never pressure her to speak of things she didn't want to speak of. 'You will decide where your story goes,' I said. 'That's good, darling,' she replied.

Figure 7.1 *Halima painting the container. Image by Annika Lems*

That day, when Halima and Sagal hugged me goodbye, I sensed that I had not just found a research participant. I had found a family that, over the months to come, I would feel part of – a feeling that I so often missed in Melbourne, because I did not have my own brothers and sisters around me. I had found a family ready to take me in as one of theirs, as a daughter, sister, loved one. In Halima I had found the unconditional, calm, protecting warmness of motherly friendship. Her concerned phone calls when we had not heard from each other for a few weeks became an intimate part of the texture of my own emplacement in Melbourne. In Halima I had also found someone to whom my stories mattered as much as the stories she came to share mattered to me. And having one's story valued by others, I have come to understand, is a key building block towards the feeling of being-at-home.

In 1968 my father got a job with the airport security. There had been an advertisement in the newspaper: 'We are looking for officers who know how to protect people'. So he applied for it and was one of the successful people who got the job. He got a good salary; at that time the airport was different than nowadays. My father always talked to us, he never ever beat anyone. He would call for us and say: 'Look, if you want to help yourself, I will help you.'

On Fridays he took all of us to the sea and we swam there. He took a ball with him to play basketball or football or whatever we kids wanted. And when we came back he said: 'The person who got the best mark at school last week will order what he likes, and all of us will eat that food today.' That was the punishment for the person who didn't do well at school.

We loved Fridays. He would say: 'It's Friday-time, you have to prepare yourselves, we will go swimming from the morning until the afternoon.' We walked a very long distance because we didn't have a car. So we walked a very long distance to swim in the sea and then we would walk back. And when we came back everyone was happy. Then we would have a storytelling time with my father. He always talked about the ability of God, how he created this world. We went outside and lay down on a very beautiful mat, we took our pillows and we all had to look up into the sky and see the stars and the moon. And my father told us: 'Do you know who created all this?' And we said: 'Yes, father, God created it.' When he finished whatever he wanted to tell us, whether it was fiction or a true story, he said: 'Okay, this is the time to pray now.' But we were kids and I said: 'Father, it is very cold, I cannot go to the water now and wash myself.' And he said: 'Oh, you are not a good believer. Why are you saying that? God who created this world, who created this sun, the moon, the stars, is looking after us, and you don't want to pray!' – 'Father, I will pray.' – 'Good girl.'

Most of the stories my father told us were religious, but there were also others. There was one story my father used to tell us when we were very little: there was a man who was brave amongst people, but a coward when it came to animals. He was very afraid of wild animals, and the other villagers laughed at him because of this. One day he went for a walk and climbed into a tree to have a rest. Soon a very big lion sat down underneath it. The lion didn't see that someone was there, because he didn't look up. The man was scared; he was shaking all over his body and fell down, on top of the lion. Panicked, he caught the lion's ears. The lion ran and ran, it wanted to throw off what was on its back. So the lion ran and ran, until finally it ran into the village. When the people saw the man on top of the lion they called out: 'He is a very brave man!' In reality he didn't know what he was doing, he was so afraid that he was going to die, and the lion kept on running. Only one wise man understood that it wasn't bravery that had put him on the back of that lion, but fear. He went to the sharp shooter and said: 'Please kill the lion.' So he took the gun and shot the lion into his heart. He killed the lion and the man crawled off the lion's back and said: 'I am a very brave person! Did you see that?' So the people who had laughed at him before stopped doing that because they thought that he was very brave. Only the wise man knew that what he had done was very dangerous and that the lion could have eaten him alive. So we as children asked: 'How could the wise man understand the situation?' My father said: 'The wise man is a person who has lived for a very long time and through different histories. He listens to people, and when he listens, he learns.' That's the story he used to tell us. I never forgot that story because that night when my father was telling us that story, he was not just talking, he was playing the lion, he was crawling like the lion, he showed us how the lion was sitting there, peacefully, but how the tree began to shake and the lion saw the tree shaking. My father was a very good storyteller. And especially when he was telling this story, he was laughing a lot. So I had to laugh with him. May god help him.

I never forgot this. I passed the stories to my kids. Even my daughter in America says to me now: 'Mum, I always have your storytelling in my mind and I give it to my children.' So it was good, we were a very well-connected family, and my sisters helped us to keep in touch with our study, with our culture, looking after each other. So what I'm always thankful for to my father is how he created this environment.

I remember when we first started to have a home in Mogadishu – we built it by ourselves. No one built it for us. Only for the toilet-hole we got workers. Other than that we built our home with our own hands. And we created a four-bedroom house. My father married another woman. She lived in one room – my uncle lived in one, the boys in one and the girls in one.

It was very good to have that connection, and I am still holding that happiness in my family. Me and my sister here, Sahra, we were so close then and we are still so close. When we are talking about our past and we remember, we sometimes hold each other and we cry because what we feel is that these were fantastic days. When she hasn't seen me for a week, she calls me and says: 'What happened to you? Don't you remember that you never used to sleep without hugging me – and now you are sleeping seven days without even talking to me?'

I like to look after people, I like to help create good families, and that was the thing that my father always guided us in. He was saying: 'Look, if you want something good to happen to you, you have to make something good happen to others.' You know? I feel that this kind of connection stays in my own and my sister Sahra's home now. She has lots of children and for instance, last Saturday her son prepared a beautiful picnic. We were cooking and everyone came together and we were eating together. All the members of the family were together, so the house was full. Me and my sister were sitting in the corner of the house and were looking at what was going on. She said: 'Halima, does this remind you of your past?' I said: 'Yes.'

It's beautiful to have family and the family is the best thing to have, all your future happens with them. If you missed that kindness, if you missed that nurturing, if you missed that helping each other in the first stage of your life, you would never get it back. It would be gone. Sometimes I feel really sorry when I look back at my country and see the kids that are born and grow up in these fights, and they don't have any other idea about life. It makes my heart hopeless. This is the generation with whom we wanted to change the future and they already don't have any idea about life.

Memory Places

While Halima had warned me that there were things in her life that resisted storying, she recalled memories of her childhood in Mogadishu with ease. Sharing cups of tea in the small Iraqi kebab café in Footscray that had become our regular place for the recorded storytelling sessions, the lightness and homeliness of these 'fantastic days' of her life felt ghostly present. The warmth and protection of her sisters, shielding her against any harm from the outside world; her father's guiding stories, told under starlit skies; and the joy of 'Friday-times' – all these were elements of a storied past, but they felt so close, so *here*, that in the end we were both infected by a weight-less cheerfulness. When the storytelling came to its end, we were both surprised to see that the initially empty café was now crowded with people eating lunch. We had both been so *in* the story, that we had not noticed what was happening around us.

'It felt good telling you these stories,' Halima sighed. 'I also felt good listening to your story,' I said. 'I felt as if I was there with you, on the beach in Mogadishu.' She smiled. 'It always makes me feel happy when I remember these times and especially when I can speak of my father. He was a fantastic father. Masha'Allah – may God reward him with paradise.'

I chose the two story snippets for the opening of this chapter as they are exemplary for the way Halima storied her Mogadishu childhood. It is part of a larger body of stories that could be entitled 'fantastic days', in which she recounted her upbringing, the relation-ship with her father and siblings and the beauty of past Mogadishu. While these narratives do not reveal many details of the physical features of the place where she grew up, they still carry a deep sense of emplacement, of being-part-of. The recollection of the intimate and idyllic – or in Halima's words, 'fantastic' – days of her childhood in Mogadishu point towards the importance of the interplay between memory and place. They suggest that just as memories stick to us, we are connected to the places in which the events occurred, creating a mutual dependency between place and memory (Trigg 2012: xvi).

In his tremendously detailed phenomenological work *Memory, History, Forgetting*, Paul Ricoeur thinks through the interplay between memory and place. He argues that memory and place are so closely tied together that it is impossible to think about the one without the other. The things remembered, he stresses, are intrinsically associated with places. When we speak of something that happened, it is therefore not coincidental that we say that it 'took place' (Ricoeur 2004: 41). For Ricoeur, inhabited places form the strongest ties between memory and place – so much so that he speaks of 'memory places' – places that remain as inscriptions inside of us. While memories that are transmitted orally 'fly away as do the words themselves', memory places remain inside of us and create a link between past and present. These memory places form a crucial ingredient for our ability to navigate present landscapes. For it is through the memory of the places of our past, of the having been *there*, that all the elsewheres take shape (Ricoeur 2004: 40).

I find Ricoeur's notion of the memory place a helpful metaphor for understanding the role of memory in Halima's placemaking efforts in Melbourne. While her life was decidedly located in the here and now, and Halima put all her energy into actively making Melbourne a place she could call her own, she often returned to the memory place that was formed by the 'fantastic days' of her childhood. This memory place was made up of stories of social cohesion and mutual solidarity – stories she enjoyed telling again and again, not just in the recorded storytelling setting, but also in everyday life. Indeed, the memory place of her childhood days has inscribed itself so deeply into her self-understanding that she stories it as the very condition for her re-emplacement in Melbourne. As such, this memory place does not form a temporal incision that is entirely disconnected from the present. Rather, it sheds light on the lived messiness of life's temporal flows; how in everyday life present, past and future often are not experienced as separate entities, but continuously push and shove into each other. Amidst this pushing and shoving, people attempt to create a sense of temporal coherence in the stories they tell about their lives. Shedding more light on these dynamics is crucial for understanding the role of Halima's stories of idyllic childhood days as a means of creating a sense of temporal and spatial continuity.

The Past, a Foreign Country?

In *Yesterday, Tomorrow,* novelist Nuruddin Farah describes the impact of the events of one day in 1976. He was planning his return to Somalia from a visit in Europe, but in a telephone conversation his brother advised him to stay away because he risked arrest. The sudden realization of being displaced, of having no place to return to or call his own, provoked a unique reaction in him. 'A few minutes later, still clutching the dead telephone receiver, I felt as though something live was surging up from inside of me,' Farah (2000: 49) writes, 'in that moment another country was fired into existence, a new country with its own logic and realities' (ibid.).

In the years to come, through decades of drifting between countries, Farah would rely on his imaginative country to dwell in and carry him through difficult times. Memory and imagination played a quintessential role in his process of creating another, a new home. So powerful was the role of the imagination in actively overcoming the sense of displacement that threatened to drag him down, that Farah (2000: 49) asks what happens to people who cannot access it. What happens 'to a people who cannot go back to the hypothetical reality of their homes, nor to their actual residences? Is this the clay out of which refugees are moulded?' People who cannot find shelter within the realms of their imagination, Farah says, become the true embodiment of the helplessness and hopelessness that the figure of the refugee has come to stand for.

While for Farah it was through his imaginative country that he was able to create a place to feel at home in, for Halima, her memory place takes over this enlivening role. As shown in the previous chapter, when I asked Omar to tell me about his childhood place, the stories he told me were saturated by the harsh reality of present-day Somalia. He could not revel in the beauty of a past place without having the horrors of its present state trumping. Asked the same question, Halima told me a very different story, one that encapsulated all that has happened to her home-place of Mogadishu ever since, and one that returned to the fantastic days that constituted her childhood memory place. Although clearly situated in the past, the story was so powerful, that both, Halima and I felt strangely vivacious and happy at the end of it – as if a little piece of the there and then had come to touch us in the here and now. The fact that both Halima and I had felt the story's intensity in our bodies raises the question of whether the story's beauty had somehow made us both long to be *there*, in that memory place, instead of *here*, in the café in Footscray. It raises questions about the kind of temporality her memory place encapsulates. Does Halima's nostalgic look back into the past prevent her from accepting the reality of being-here, now, in Melbourne?

Nostalgia has not had a very honourable reputation in modern Western thought. Associated with invention and a certain sense of manipulation of the past, it is often despised for its failure to acknowledge the complexity of the past and for its tendency to be instrumentalized by political forces (e.g. Nietzsche 1957; Davis 1979; Shaw and Chase 1989). Derived from the Greek words *nostos*, which means 'to return home' and *algos*, which means 'pain', nostalgia depicts the painful yearning for the past. In the late seventeenth century, Swiss physician Johannes Hofer coined the term to describe an illness that had not been catalogued yet and that had so far only been described in colloquial terms such as *Heimweh*, homesickness or *mal du pays*.

Nostalgia's all-encompassing grip has been a recurring theme in modern Western literature, philosophy and art. In L.P. Hartley's novel *The Go-Between*, for example, an old man named Leo Colston finds the diary he wrote as a thirteen year old. This unexpected discovery brings back long-forgotten childhood memories. Reminiscing about the innocence and beauty of his childhood days, Leo feels a painful yearning for times that appear forever lost. 'The past is a foreign country,' Hartley (1971: 7) writes, 'they do things differently there.' The nostalgic mourning for an irretrievable past expressed in Hartley's novel can be read within the lines of a wider modern Western fascination with loss and time. While Hofer had initially read nostalgia as a pathological yearning for place, modern thinkers have come to treat it as a metaphysical longing for a lost time. Displacement came to be read in metaphorical terms, while place itself was deliteralized and turned into a metaphysical landscape (Casey 1987b: 370). Hartley's suggestion that the past is so removed from the here and now that it literally forms a foreign country corresponds with the sense of fragmentation in terms of which modern thinkers often interpret our experience of temporality. While these readings of nostalgia paint a picture of the metaphysical pains that leave modern man in constant temptation to exchange the struggles of a rapidly changing world for the comfort of a past that is long gone, in her stories of the 'fantastic days' Halima does not appear to be yearning in vain for a displaced yesterday. To stay with Hartley's words, in her stories people do not appear to do things differently in the past from the way they do them now.

In recounting her childhood in Mogadishu as 'fantastic days' without sorrows and devoid of the conflicts that were to lead to Mogadishu's collapse and eventually to Halima's own displacement, the quality of nostalgia as a lived experience comes to the fore (Lems 2016b). Halima's enjoyment in taking a look back in time shows nostalgia as an essentially positive experience, as something that can be intentionally sought out. Importantly, the two opening stories shed light on the kind of past Halima's memory place relates to. The 'fantastic days' that constitute her memory place are not part of a remote and romanticized past. In the moment of the telling it is experienced as something real and here, as something present and absent at the same time. Through the act of storying, the temporal reach of Halima's childhood Mogadishu leaks into the present, and in doing so becomes constitutive of the possibility of becoming-at-home in Melbourne. Linking back to the discussion on the links between narrative, experience and time, this speaks for David Carr's (1986: 95) insistence that we should not simplify the experience of temporality as a form of being in the present whilst remembering a long gone past. Leaning on the work of Heidegger he speaks of human reality as a temporal 'reach' or 'stretch' (*Erstreckung*), as a way of encompassing or 'taking in' time. Thus, being-here can never be fully disconnected from being-there or being-then. Rather, it hinges on a continuously shifting temporal horizon, thereby literally replacing our current relationships to places.

> Like the Here in relation to the space we perceive, the Now is a vantage point from which we survey the past and the future. To exist humanly is not merely to be in time but to encompass it or 'take it in' as our gaze takes in our surroundings. (Carr 1986: 95)

When Halima and her sister Sahra observe their children at the end of her story, they feel the past almost physically present. 'Halima, does this remind you of your past?' Sahra asks; Halima affirms – yes, she remembers. And it is through this shared memory that the lost place of their childhood home in Mogadishu can be re-emplaced *here*, *now*, in Melbourne, and with (and perhaps through) their own children. Despite the painful displacement from the intimate places where her childhood memories are located, the act of remembering embeds the far away there in the here and now. Halima's memory of the past, it seems, is the old acquaintance that helps guide her through foreign countries – and in doing so turns foreignness into something familiar and inhabitable. 'We need the past, in any case,' writes David Lowenthal (1975: 5), 'to cope with present landscapes.'

While Halima often expressed a longing for an idyllic past, this was not an experience that was dissociated from the present. Instead, her stories of the past as 'golden' were a way for her to deal with a disrupted and difficult present. While most of Halima's narratives lacked detailed recollections of the landscape or other physical features of home-places, this haziness was counterbalanced by her recollection of social worlds. Close to Farah's imaginative country, Halima's memory place thus functions as a kind of moral guideline for her placemaking efforts in Melbourne. Instead of reading her nostalgic look back to her childhood as an escape or a refusal to deal with the present, it can be understood as a direct and active engagement with the world she is confronted with here, now, in Melbourne.

If we think of home in terms of the act of inhabiting a place, the closeness of the word *inhabiting* to the word *habit* might not be coincidental. It is through habits, through repeated practices so close to our inner workings, that they become almost one with place, that inhabiting becomes possible. In Halima's story two elements are quintessential to the carving out of the habits that lead towards emplacement – faith and the family. Both elements are of such importance that they weave their way through Halima's entire life story. For their close links to the interplay of storytelling, memory and place, and for their strong presence in Halima's childhood stories, I now have a closer look at these two key elements.

Under the Panoply of Stars

Nothing can create as deep an understanding for the immensity of the universe, and for the miniature of our own place within it, as looking up to a starlit sky. It is against this felt infinity of the universe that the intimacy of our place in the world begins to take shape.

I vividly remember walking home after school through the fields on cold winter afternoons, when, by the time the school bus had arrived, it was already entirely dark. After my father had been forced to sell his childhood home in Millstatt, we had moved into a house in one of the nearby mountain villages, and the bus stop was a good twenty-minute walk away. Except for the icy snow crunching under my feet, the rattling of the milking machine or the mooing of a cow from a distant stable every now and then, there was an all-encompassing silence. Nature's winter-sleep was all around me. On clear nights, the darkness made the stars shine so bright, made them sparkle so splendidly, that I was overwhelmed by a feeling of immensity. If all these faraway stars were part of something as unimaginably bound-less as the universe, then how miniscule did they render me and my everyday worries, walking in that snowfield, located on a planet so tiny and insignificant?

Sometimes I stopped and tried to identify the constellations my father so often pointed out to us kids from the balcony on nights like these. I looked for the sharpest one of them all, the polar star, and from there I followed along the imaginary axis to the Little and the Great Bear and further along the Milky Way to the majestical Cassiopeia. By identifying the stars, by giving them names and stories, the immensity of the universe and my own insignificance within it seemed less intimidating. By telling a story about them, every planet, every star, every stone, house or country and every living being received its own place within the universe of my imagination.

At another time and from another corner of the earth, Halima, lying on a mat, facing the starlit sky, listened to her father's stories of their creation. His were stories of the beauty and ability of Allah, who first created everything and then put it into its proper place within the universe. Sitting in the kebab restaurant in Melbourne, Halima vividly remembered these stories. 'My father often asked us questions,' Halima said. 'He asked: "Who do you think created the world? Who created the sky, the stars, the sun, the moon? Who moves them? – The angels are moving them. God sent the angels to create these movements".' While the stories taught Halima to be humbled by the magnificence of God's creation, she also began to understand how everything had its own story, its own reason for being-in-the-world and how, in the end, everything was linked through Allah. Against the ordering line of a story's plot, the immen-sity of the universe transforms into something more understandable and close, into something of direct importance to our own lives.

Halima, listening to her father's creation stories under starlit skies, and my own search for the constellations my father had taught me, once more draws attention to the close links between place and sto-rytelling. In *And Our Faces, My Heart, Brief as Photos*, John Berger writes of the power of the story in making sense of the unimaginable immensity of the universe.

> Lying on our backs, we look up at the night sky. This is where stories began, under the aegis of that multitude of stars which at night filch cer-titudes and sometimes return them as faith. Those who first invented and then named the constellations were storytellers. Tracing an imaginary line between a cluster of stars gave them an image and an identity. The stars threaded on that line were like events threaded on a narrative. Imagining

the constellations did not of course change the stars, nor did it change the black emptiness that surrounds them. What it changed was the way people read the night sky. (Berger 1984: 8)

Under the protective panoply of stars, Halima learned how to read the sky, and how Allah, who had created them all so splendidly, had also created her. Through her father's stories, Halima's emplacement is thus not within an isolated, immovable or eternal home-place. Rather, it is a sense of being-at-home within Allah's universe, where everything and everyone has been created for a reason, and where everything links back to Allah, who has the power to call in and out of life. And because God created everything and is everywhere, being-at-home in faith opens up the possibility to a feeling of being-part-of the universe and to carrying this feeling with her everywhere she goes.

Halima's becoming-at-home within Allah's universe through her father's stories is a way of being-at-home in a place that appears to be stabilized and centred and still reaches out to the wider world. It is a way of being-at-home that centres her within the protective grid of the family, but also under the all-encompassing reach of God. Close to Rilke's 'world inner space', it is a form of emplacement that allows her to be inward and outward-bound at the same time. Halima's being-at-home in the universe thus once more reveals the closeness between intimacy and vastness – between the deep attachment to certain places and the insignificance of these places against the vastness of the universe – a vastness we, in turn, story back to something placeable and dear.

This condition bears many resemblances to what Michael Jackson describes as being 'at home in the world'. In his book of that title, he embarks upon a journey to find the meaning of home in our restless age of continuous movement. He approaches this search from the perspective of people for whom dwelling is not synonymous with being settled in a house. Over a period of three years he lived among the nomadic Warlpiri in Central Australia's Tanami Desert. The experience of living in the desert and observing the way his Warlpiri friends place themselves in the world enabled Jackson to come to a new understanding of home and belonging. It is an understanding of being-at-home that is deeply attached to place but does not require the claustrophobic privacy of the modern house or the narrow-mindedness of the nationalistic imagination of the nation state. Camping in the desert with a few of his Warlpiri friends, surrounded by nothing but the endlessness of the desert, Jackson describes a moment when he felt deeply what it means to be at home in the world:

> At that moment, sitting there with Zack and Nugget, Pincher and Francine, I think I knew what it means to be at home in the world. It is to experience a complete consonance between one's own body and the body of the earth. Between self and other. It little matters whether the other is a landscape, a loved one, a house, or an action. Things flow. There seems to be no resistance between oneself and the world. The *relationship* is all. (Jackson 1995: 110–11)

Moments of lived intimacy, of being-at-home in the world, when *things flow* and self and other become one, do not necessarily always need an exact physical location. These experiences can be placed in a locale, like a house or a landscape, but they can also be located in people or actions. Just like Halima emplacing herself under the panoply of stars, it suggests a wider understanding of place, one that allows place to not freeze within itself but to touch and reach out to the wider world – if not to the entire universe.

People as Places

When I was trying to describe the place I came from to my Australian friends, I often found myself talking about people. Like Halima in her story, I would not speak of the landscape, the lakes, rivers, plants or trees that lend the place its specific character. Instead, I found myself speaking of my family, my neighbours, my friends, my enemies – in short, of the characteristics of the people whom I shared the place with. And although I intimately knew the way certain places felt, sounded, or tasted, it was incredibly hard to convey these layers of being-in-place in words. For that reason, I usually did not speak of the feeling of the water on my skin when swimming in the lake in Millstatt on a warm summer night, or of the soothing warmth derived from looking at the soft, white, round tops of the Nockberge mountain range in winter. And yet, when thinking of all the people who made up the places of my stories, it is as if people and places merged into each other. Sometimes, places and people become one to the extent that it is as if people themselves become places.

When Halima speaks of her childhood in Somalia, some physical features of certain places find their way into the story, like their house in Mogadishu – a house they built with their own hands – or the beauty of the ocean they walked to every Friday. But these features seem to be no more than arenas for a much stronger force of emplacement: within the family. The house is primarily storied as a means to order and keep the family together, and the ocean as a place for the family to have a joyful time. Whilst at home in Allah's universe, the family forms the centre of that very universe. In her stories the family is of such importance that home, place and family seem to almost become one.

Consider, for example, the story of her father's second-born son, who grew up with his grandparents in the countryside. Halima's father, who was born in the rural coastal area of Xaafun in the Puntland region, became the first person in his family to begin working for the newly founded Somali nation. He was so tall and strong, Halima once told me, that her grandfather, a trader, thought he would make a good policeman. So he took him to town and presented him to the police officer. The officer agreed that Halima's father was of an imposing physique and that he could become a good policeman. And thus, Halima's father was sent to school and went on to join the police force.

While the position of the police officer was highly respectable, it also brought with it the necessity for Halima's father to leave his family and clan and to move to other places within Somalia. In her story Halima tells us how upon moving to Galcayo, he leaves his second born son with his mother – who needed someone to replace her absent son, 'someone for the heart' – as a means of retaining the ties to his ancestral home. This boy forms a human bridge to overcome the gap between his family who live in the faraway south of the country, and the grandparents who remain in the place where their families' and clans' history is rooted. He literally *re-places* his father and forms the human tie to keep the connection alive between the home-place and the people who inhabit it. When the boy joins the rest of the family in Mogadishu after their mother's death, he appears to have become so one with the place he grew up that he has difficulties getting used to the new environment he finds himself in.

The importance of place for the constitution of people also becomes apparent when Halima's father refuses to take on a job in Hargeisa in Somaliland. It is not just the distance that makes him refuse to go there and give up his position, it is the fact that his children are still small and that they need to be surrounded by an 'area that they can understand'. When I asked Halima what made Hargeisa so difficult to understand for her father, she told me that it had been a British protectorate and had developed very differently from other parts of Somalia. Mainly inhabited by members of the independently minded Isaaq clan, this region was marked by a very distinct politics of place – a politics Halima's father could not affiliate with. An 'area they understand', it seems, is a place where the meaning of its inner working is shared by others – and not by any others, but by others who are close to the family's heart.

Keith Basso's book *Wisdom Sits in Places* is one of the most powerful ethnographic contributions towards the revalidation of place in anthropology. Looking at the way four Western Apaches story their experience of place and landscape, he suggests that people shape places, but that people are also shaped by places. Although this sense of place is of such quintessential importance, it is a process that is usually so deeply rooted within our unconscious that we are not aware of it. It is only when we are (like Halima's brother, for example) removed from the environment we have become so familiar with, that our attachment to place is exposed.

> On these unnerving occasions, sense of place may assert itself in pressing and powerful ways, and its often subtle components – as subtle, perhaps, as absent smells in the air or not enough visible sky – come surging into awareness. It is then we come to see that attachments to places may be nothing less than profound, and that when these attachments are threatened, we may feel threatened as well. (Basso 1996: xiii–xiv)

When Halima speaks of the protective bond of the family, of her father's guidance, or of the love and care of her sisters Sahra and Zeinab, a sense of emplacement finds its way into the story. Again, it is as if these people become places themselves. Archaeologist Leslie van Gelder (2008: 85) suggests that we can only understand places through webs of relationships, and through looking into the emotional connections we create with them. 'In the home environment, like no other place, person and place merge,' she writes. 'We are both *of* a people and *from* them. Impossible to separate, we dwell in each other.' This being of and from, or, in Merleau-Ponty's words again, being 'born of and into the world', is quintessential to an understanding of the way people constitute their places and are at the same time constituted by them. In Halima's story, being from and of a place is equivalent to being of and from a certain people. In her story, place is thus so closely linked to the people who make it meaningful, that it is hard to separate family and place. It is, in other words, as if Halima's feeling of being-at-home derives from a place that is located within other humans – her family.

Van Gelder speaks of a 'sensuous landscape of home', a feeling of home we learn from the people closest to us. It is impossible to separate our sense of home from a sense of family because they were one from the very beginning of our self. Like double-woven baskets, people are both – inner and outer, they are *of* and *in* at the same time. 'Like places we visit over and over again,' Van Gelder (2008: 88) writes, 'we ourselves are storied landscapes, where each scar holds a story and each moment hangs pregnant with possibility.' Emplacement has a strong connection to the degree we are recognized by others. It can only develop in a place where our voices are heard. If we are not heard, we can feel as if we do not exist (Van Gelder 2008: 92). Storytelling and place are therefore intimately linked through the meaning of creating an environment where one's voice is recognized. Without an audience and without a place to tell the stories, people can begin to feel a deep sense of displacement.

Not every family holds the ideal balance between openness and protection that is required for emplacement. Halima ends her story with a deeply felt sadness over the disruption in the lives of many young Somalis, who, growing up in fear and violence, never receive this nurturing feeling of being-at-home within others. Not having this kind of home, Halima explains, means being lost and deeply and utterly homeless. In her story the destruction of the family is thus inextricably linked to the destruction of the country – and with it of her childhood Mogadishu.

8

Gendered Dis/Emplacements

Becoming a Daughter and Sister

Soon after I had met Halima for the first muddled recorded life story-telling session in the Iraqi restaurant, I became a frequent guest in her house in Maidstone in Melbourne's western suburbs. While sharing some sweet baklavas after the interview, she had told me that writing assignments in English was at times very challenging and that Sagal often had to help her. Sagal, however, who studied medical sciences, also had much learning to do, which made exam periods extremely stressful times for both of them. Before we left, I suggested to Halima that I could assist her with her next assignments, which were due soon. 'That way you help me with my studies and I help you with yours,' I said. Halima liked the idea. 'That's a good deal,' she said. This 'deal' proved not just enriching for both our learning processes; working together and getting to know each other's routines and interests also created the common ground for the storytelling to take place.

Only a short while after we had first met, Halima called me for help with an assignment on research methodologies. 'You can come over here and we work for a little, and then I will make sure that you get enough to eat,' Halima said. She joked that, as my parents were so far away, she had to make sure that I was well-fed and not leading a sloppy student lifestyle.

And thus, on an intensely hot Saturday afternoon in February, when the sun's strength was so overpowering that everything appeared to be dressed in a transparent white coat, I cycled my way through the parklands on the northern side of Melbourne. From there I went across the Maribyrnong River, the natural border that seems to draw a sharp line between the luxuries and social order of the inner city and the forgotten outskirts in the West, which are so close to the city's centre and yet appear to be so far away from it. Leaving behind the colourful and lively heart of the West, Footscray, where Vietnamese grocery stores and Pho-soup bars are lined side by side with Ethiopian eateries and Pakistani spice-shops, I cycled through kilometres of suburban streets until I arrived in Halima's street. I found her house nestled between an old milk-bar cornershop that looked like it had long closed its doors and a row of 1960s-style brick houses that are so typical in suburban Melbourne – complete with small front gardens and large windows that open towards the living rooms, but with the thick curtains or blinds always closed, leaving the passer-by deeply and utterly outside.

From the very first time I took off my shoes and entered Halima's house, I felt comfortable. The small, three-bedroom house was filled with life. Her daughters Sahra and Sagal were busy in the kitchen, chatting and laughing. As I arrived, Halima's son Said, just back from his factory job, was retreating into his bedroom to have a rest. Except for Halima's husband Mohamed, who had gone, as he does every day, to the neighbouring suburb of Sunshine to help out as an accountant with a Somali money transfer business, all were at home. The television, ignored by everyone in the room, was blaring to itself at full blast, while Halima was sitting next to it, patiently working on her assignment. 'Sagal, Sahra, look who is here!' Halima announced, and directed me to a seat while ordering her daughters to bring me something to drink. 'Come on, take off these clothes,' Sagal laughed, eyeing the scarf I had put on upon arrival, eager not to offend anyone by keeping my arms uncovered. 'Look, we're all dressed lightly. It's only us girls here today, and it's hot.' The moment I sat down with them for the first time, I began growing towards these three women who made me feel so at home.

Before they first spelled it out to me, I could sense the deep bond that existed between Halima and her daughters. And listening to their stories and to the constant jokes thrown back and forth, I could also sense that, far from confirming the stereotype of Somali women being subservient, silenced by or dependent on their husbands, the three of them knew very well how to stand up for themselves. Later that afternoon Halima told me that educating and empowering her three daughters had always been her strongest priority. Even under the most difficult circumstances, suddenly on her own with five kids, deeply shaken by the war they just had escaped, without money and without the prospect of receiving a visa to legalize their stay in the United Arab Emirates, she had somehow managed to send her children to school. 'Yes, I lost everything I ever had,' she said, 'but I couldn't just give up. I needed to go on for my kids.' Listening to Halima's story, Sagal commented: 'It is only now that I understand what my mother has done for us.' She explained that when they were children she and her siblings took their mother's strength for granted. She said that they were never fearful of their future, even under the direst circumstances, because their mother carried them through these times, shielding them from the harshness of reality. 'So what do you think of it now that you are all in your mid or late-twenties?' I asked. 'I am amazed,' Sagal replied. 'How did she do it?'

Between all the stories, the cups of sweet Somali tea and the plates of food we shared, Halima and I also discussed the differences between qualitative and quantitative research methodologies she had to write about for her assignment. It was through my own project that we came to talk about the meaning of participant observation. I told her that in anthropology, the act of sharing people's everyday life, of becoming acquainted with their daily routines and struggles, is the most important research tool. I explained that the life stories in my research could only come to life if I got glimpses into the everyday lives of the people who shared them with me. Immediately Halima acknowledged the role she could play by letting me take part in her own life. 'You're right,' she said. 'You need to come with me and see my community's life so you can observe and learn to understand.'

By the end of the day, Halima had formulated the distinctions between the different research methods commonly used in social work. At the same time, my own reasons for choosing to focus on life stories had also become much clearer to her. 'Whatever it takes to write this book, I will support you,' Halima said. I felt relieved that in this roundabout way, we had been able to discuss and come to terms with the politics of research methodology. Instead of keeping us apart, it had become common ground for us in our shared interest in humans and their social lives.

Within a short time, after only a few more visits, I was given my own place within Halima's home. It was then that she told me that I was part of her family now. 'You remind me of my daughter who lives in America so far away from us,' she said, hinting at her second-born daughter Amal, who, like me, had left the protection of the family to build up her own life in the US, shortly before they were to be resettled to Australia. As is usual amongst people who share webs of deep meaning, we constantly told each other stories of our lives. But while getting to know each other so closely made Halima's stories flow with lightness, it also gave me an understanding for the stories that were shared with me as a friend and could not otherwise be retold. In pointing me at the taboos and limitations of storytelling, it gave me a deep understanding for the gendered nature of emplacement – how one and the same place can carry an entirely different set of rules, possibilities and meanings depending on the individual's gender and the spatial tactics that come with it.

I still remember the revolution in Somalia. I was fifteen or sixteen years old. At first it was very hard for us as a family, because the president whom they killed before Siyaad Barre came to power was from our tribe[1]. So it was hard for the people who came from that background. But what was different for us was that we didn't grow up with my father's family. I grew up in a different area and my father was a policeman, so we were sympathetic with the military taking over. When they killed the president we said: 'Nothing remains, so what are we waiting for? Just let the revolution happen.' So what we started to do was helping that to happen.

After the revolution in 1969, I became a youth activist. I was the first one in my family to get involved, and after that my sister Sahra, my brother, and two other sisters joined. In 1976 the Somali Socialist Party was created and we became members. My brother Said became a governor at one stage. My sister Sahra finished her nursing school and she became responsible for the district pharmacy.

I was very young at that time, but they sent me to Russia. From every school they chose one person to study in Russia, and when they came to my school they assessed me and asked whether I would like to go. To go outside, to go overseas, that was something big for me, so I said yes.

I went to the High Komsomol School[2] in Moscow. There were people from all over the world in that school. In that year more than three thousand students came from different countries. I studied political economy, philosophy and international communist movement. What I learned in Moscow is still guiding me in my studies in community development now.

I was worrying a lot. I was a little, beautiful kid and before I left Somalia my father had advised me not to mix with the wrong people. When I left, he said: 'I know my kids, I trust them.' I got that message in my mind, and while I was in Moscow it always guided me. My friends were from the school group, and from outside I wouldn't speak to anyone.

I met my husband in Moscow. He was in the Trade Union School. When they took him there he was a worker, while I was a student. He was working for the Somali Airlines. He used to be in the ticketing department and they promoted him as an accountant. Later they promoted him as a catering manager.

Both of us finished our course, and then he asked me to talk to him. But I said: 'No. I'm not ready to talk to you.' Then he tried something else and invited the whole group of Somali students to their place so that I would go there as well. One of his friends, who became a member of the parliament with me, and who is living here in Melbourne now as well, was responsible for that gathering. He invited all of us, because if he invited only me he knew that I would have never gone there. So they invited the whole group and I went.

When he left Russia, my husband straight away went to the airport in Somalia to where my father was working. He said: 'I have information about your daughter.' And my father hugged him and said: 'You have to come to see my family and tell how you saw my daughter.' My husband was very clever! So then he went to see the family, and they loved him. He said: 'You have a very clever girl, she's very tough, she never talks to men, and she's very active in her study.' My father said: 'Really?' And they invited him again and again and again. He arrived seven days before me and in these seven days, they invited him three times. They already saw that he was a good man and that he had a very good job. When I arrived, all the other people had to wait outside, but he brought my father in front of the plane, waiting there. I was surprised, I said: 'Hey, you know each other?' My father said: 'This is a very beautiful man. He's good.' The next day my husband came and said: 'I wanted to ask your father for your hand. Do you accept?' I said: 'No. I don't know you. I have to know you before.' So we were together for three years before we married. I married when I was nineteen.

But first I finished my school, because I hadn't finished it when I left. Then I studied political science. I also proceeded with my work with the youth; we created the Somali Youth Union. In that era there were lots of other activities, like the Women's Workers Union, but I always stuck with the youth because I believe that youth is the main future of the country.

When I had finished my education, we got our own home, we married and after one year I got my daughter Sahra. My first child was born in 1979, my second child was born in 1980. It was very close. First two girls and the third one was a boy, and the forth was a girl again. They were all born in Mogadishu, the capital city.

Like a Stick Burning from Two Sides

From the very first moment I met Halima, I was struck by her political demeanour. Her presence, her way of walking through this world, her readiness to take on any hurdle, created in me an impression of her as somebody who had learned how to lay claim to place. And my image of Halima was also the way she liked to see herself. 'I think I'm pretty strong,' she said, whilst discussing the ups and downs of her political career in Somalia. 'But you know, being a female politician in Somalia has taught me so.' She was convinced that the years she had worked as a member of parliament under Siyaad Barre while raising her children, and the struggles she had gone through to find acceptance as a woman in a men's domain, had helped her to develop a strong sense of independence. 'All people were criticising me: "Why are you doing this? This is a man's job",' Halima said. 'But I never gave up doing things, because what my father taught me was that I could do what every other person could do: if men can do it, you can do it as well.'

While she was telling me this, we were walking through the Somali mall. The tiny shop rooms were filled with rugs, teapots, pans, spices, Arabic perfumes and fashionable scarves. There were also hairdressers, dressmakers, international call shops and xawilaad businesses to send money overseas. Unlike in the shiny new big mall that had been built a few blocks away, in the Somali mall people did not seem to rush through like ghosts. They strolled through in a slow pace, stopping every now and then to greet someone. The shops were filled with men and women, sitting on plastic chairs and sharing cups of tea or coffee. Snippets of laughter and conversation echoed through the old, bleak building. An island apart from the buzz of Footscray, the mall felt like a calm street somewhere in a small town, where everyone knows everyone. It was this feeling of familiarity, of being surrounded by the melody of the Somali language, of smelling the cardamom scent of her Mogadishu home, of being known by others, that drew Halima to the mall.

That day, however, Halima had come on a mission. She wanted to show me how her own strength was mirrored by the strength of countless other Somali women who were the owners of shops in the Somali mall. She was worried by the way the Australian public portrayed the women of her community. The Somalia in which she had grown up and where, as her story shows, she became part of the revolutionary new order, was very liberal. While a small urban minority of middle- or upper-class Somalis practised the seclusion of women, the majority worked inside and outside the house (Abdi 2007: 187). It was only in the 1980s, when the Muslim Brotherhood began to penetrate Somalia's urban centres, that a small number of Somali women first began wearing the full chador with face covering. Yet, with the outbreak of the civil war in Somalia, many Somalis turned towards the certainties that the rules of an imagined 'pure' Islamic community could offer. As part of this shift, 'authentic' Islam came to be inscribed into women's bodies. This led not only to new dress habits for Somali women, but to their seclusion from public places.

While many scholars have commented on the fact that this new conservatism has crossed the bridge from war-torn Somalia into the diaspora (e.g. Berns-McGown 1999; De Voe 2002; Bryden 2003; Tiilikainen 2003), Halima found that the religious imagination did not have the power to overrule the lived reality of Somali refugees' everyday lives. Many of the women she was working with in Melbourne, and indeed her own daughters, were following this conservative trend, yet, she urged me to be cautious in my prejudgements about them. While these women might live a much more pious life than they used to in Somalia, a large proportion of them were, in fact, the main breadwinners. This new situation, Halima said, where men had to rely on their wives to feed the family, had changed the dynamics within many homes. 'Before, the woman was just called by her husband: "Hey, woman, do this or do that!"' Halima explained. 'But now she is "darling", because she has money in her pocket.'

We went from shop to shop, where women, old and young, welcomed us. 'This is my friend Annika,' Halima told the tradeswomen and curious onlookers. 'She came all the way from Austria to write about us.' Many women laughed in astonishment. Who would come that far to write about them? In one of the shops, however, a group of outspoken young women who were sitting on a pile of rugs, sharing a cup of Somali tea, thought otherwise. 'Someone should write about Halima', one of them said. 'Yes,' another girl in a colourful hijab with a broad Australian accent agreed. 'You found the right topic. Auntie Halima is awesome.' She told me how Halima helped young mothers like her to feel strong, to leave the house, to join her in one of her sewing groups and by doing so to break through their isolation. She said that it was only through Halima's encouragement that she had been able to complete a course in childcare and eventually make her living from it. Halima's strength, I thought to myself, was thus so all-encompassing that despite all the struggles she had to go through in her own life, she still had enough left to share it with others.

It was during her work in politics, she told me, that she had learned to be so strong. And, as her story of growing into adulthood during a time of revolutionary changes shows, it involved much bargaining, savvy and determination to find acceptance in a world that was dominated by men. 'Sometimes it was so tiring, I felt constantly exhausted,' she said. Especially towards the end of Barre's regime her position became complicated. Not only did she have to struggle for acceptance as a woman, but the regime had begun to turn against dissident clans. 'My position became harder and harder,' Halima explained. Like Omar, she was from the Majeerteen, a clan that slowly fell out of favour with Barre's ruling clan, the Mareexaan. This brought a large portion of distrust from other MPs and officials. At the same time, her family sometimes turned against her for working with the regime, accusing her of supporting the discrimination of her own people. 'In Somalia there is a proverb that describes how I felt in that situation: we say it is like a stick that starts burning from both sides,' she said. 'So I felt like the stick that was being eaten up from both sides.'

And yet, despite all these pressures, despite the growing dangers and despite the endless struggles that fatigued her to a large extent, Halima said that she never contemplated giving up her position. 'Why did you decide to go on under these circumstances?' I asked, thinking about the terrible last years of the regime when the country slowly began to dissolve. 'I always wanted to work for the community,' she said, 'and I believed that it was easier to do that from within the regime than from without.' Halima tried to stay in her position to help save as many of her people as possible. 'If I had left, they would have killed me too,' she said. 'By staying I could actually try and help my people from within the system.' It was the hope embodied in her socialist ideals as well as the possibility of actively working for change from within that helped Halima bear up against the odds. Having become close to Halima now, many years later and far away from the glamorous context of a political career, I see the same hopeful determination mirrored in her work with the Somali community in Melbourne. It is a determination that has survived years of war and insecurity, and it is a determination she now uses to actively carve out a place for herself and her community in Melbourne.

This strength and hopefulness, this urge to act and resist disempowering situations, speak through many of Halima's stories. This strength also comes to the fore in her account of growing up and of her marriage in a revolutionary Somalia. In her account, the

Figure 8.1 *'This guy used to be the president, Siyaad Barre. A very rare photo, very rare. The others are members of the Supreme Revolutionary Council. Some of them were killed by him later on.'* *Image courtesy of Mohamed Ibrahim*

groundbreaking events of the military coup and the society's shift to a radically new order are closely interwoven with groundbreaking events in her own life. In a poetic way, the major personal changes of growing up, of developing her own ideas and of establishing her own family become inseparably linked to the surrounding political changes. On yet another level, the strength in Halima's story also gives an insight into women's complex involvement in Somali politics and society. It is in light of the complex struggle between tradition and change, between the imagined and the lived, that I have come to read Halima's story. Like Omar's opening story, it sheds light on the complex interplay of the historical and political situatedness of her emplacement in Somalia. By bringing in a decidedly feminist perspective, Halima's story questions the often-repeated claim that in Somalia women are excluded from public space and have no say in the ways places are shaped.

Poetesses and Freedom Fighters

In the heart of Mogadishu, close to the popular monument of Sayid Maxamed Cabdille Xasan ('the Mad Mullah'), Somalia's most prominent national hero, there stands a concrete figure, a woman in a flowing dress, firmly holding a sword and a stone in her hands. It is a statue of Xaawo Cusmaan Taako, whose story has inscribed itself into the historical consciousness of many Somalis (Aidid 2011: 103). She was killed during an anti-colonial protest of the Somali Youth League in 1948, which was violently disrupted by pro-Italian groups the colonial power had organized against them. Like many other Somali women, she had been actively involved in the anti-colonial struggle, and had ultimately given her life for it.

I first heard of Xaawo's extraordinary story when Sagal posted a photo of the heroine's statue on her Facebook page, urging Somalis not to forget about the contribution of women like Xaawo to their country's history. After all the stories I had come across of great warriors, versatile poets and spirited freedom fighters, all of whom were male, it was the first time I had heard of the public celebration of a Somali woman. In most of the ethnographic and historical accounts I had read of Somalia, women were either described as the weakest links within the social hierarchy or did not appear as voices in their own right at all. This portrayal, however, did not mirror Halima, her daughters, or, in fact, any of the Somali women I have met over the last few years, even though many of them had turned towards a very pious lifestyle. Beyond the public Western imagination of Somali women as hidden behind their veiled, Muslim identities and as oppressed and silenced victims of a misogynistic culture, I found their presence and self-assertion striking. Many of the women I met in Melbourne had become the main breadwinners, and even those who were not were far from silently obeying their husbands. Just as Xaawo's contribution to the country's struggle for independence speaks for a role of Somali women that goes beyond their restriction to the household, so does Halima's story, a story that tells of the interplay between tradition and the renegotiation of women's right to lay claim to a place in Somali society.

That stories of women like Xaawo Taako are usually missing in historical or ethnographic discourses on Somalia has much to do with the way the Western imagination of Somali women has been coined. Historian Christine Choi Ahmed's essay on the representation of Somali women forms the first and most powerful critical evaluation of the discursive production of stereotypical and essentialized views of Somali women (Ahmed 1995). Ahmed specifically criticizes I.M. Lewis for his orientalist imagination of Somali women. In his work, the anthropologist creates a picture whereby Somali men represent the noble part of society, while women are likened to a person without any rights. In *Blood and Bone*, for example, he writes that women are expected to always obey, honour and respect their husbands or fathers (Lewis 1994 [1957]: 56). He stresses that Somali women have a subordinate status and that their main task is to 'provide for her husband's sexual needs, bear children, especially sons, and care properly for these, as well as adequately performing her herding tasks' (Lewis 1994: 57). In describing women in such generalized and static terms, without giving much space for movement and change (or indeed their own voice), Lewis has shaped the myth of *the* Somali woman as a chattel, a commodity, and as a creature with little power (Ahmed 1995: 159–64).

Lewis, who spent years amongst northern Somali nomads, was blind to the ways the women he was living amongst contradicted his patriarchal portrayal of them in their daily lives. Where Lewis (1994: 57–58) claims that women's subservient position is linked to the fact that they do not own anything and are always dependent on their husbands, Ahmed (1995: 163) argues that almost all Somali women gathered their own wealth through the jewellery they collected, sometimes over generations. Women often received a great deal of their wealth at their weddings, and jewellery formed an essential part of their assets. Because of its influence on the writing of Somali history and ethnography, Ahmed suggests that contemporary literature on Somalia needs to be entirely freed from the canon of Lewis so that we can begin to evaluate the historical data afresh. She stresses that it is evident that if women are not even interviewed, let alone being considered as a part of history, they will be absent from most accounts.

One afternoon, as we were eating lunch together in Halima's house, I told her about the way women were described in classical ethnographies of Somalia. I explained how Lewis had described Somali women as figures with little power, as silenced by their husbands and fathers. Listening to my account, Halima shook her head in disbelief. While she acknowledged that women were structurally disadvantaged, she did not agree with the picture of them silently obeying these circumstances. 'In my family, the women have always been the stronger ones,' Halima said. 'And I'm not just talking about myself, my sisters, my daughters. I am talking about generations back.' And then she told me the story of her great-grandmother, a woman who lived in the Puntland area during the times the poet, mystic and warrior Sayid Maxamed Cabdille Xasan led a war against British, Italian and Ethiopian forces and almost brought them to a standstill. During this anti-colonial struggle, which took place between 1900 and 1920, many men from the Darood clans became warriors.

It was during these times, Halima said, that her great-grandmother, who was known for her courage and outspokenness, supported Sayid's cause by cooking for the warriors that were in her area. But the fighting, the killing and the violence had changed some of these freedom fighters. Sometimes they would come into the village, mistreat the women and create mayhem. Halima's great-grandmother watched the situation for a while. But one day, when a group of warriors rode through the village on their horses, and, out of a pure desire to hurt someone, snatched her pot and stole it, she decided that she needed to take drastic steps. She was furious, Halima told me. This was not just her only pot; it was also the pot she had used to support the very people who had treated her so disrespectfully. And so Halima's great-grandmother travelled all the way to Sayid Maxamed Cabdille Xasan's fort, where she demanded to see the leader so insistently that, in the end, she was let in. The story goes that Sayid had little chance to say anything for a long time. And then, when he could finally respond, he apologized to her. He said that he felt embarrassed about how his warriors had treated her. When she left, the family saga goes, he showered her with praise – and with a new pot, a cooking pot made out of pure gold.

Rather than seeing herself and her fellow countrywomen as voiceless victims, Halima sees herself in the tradition of a larger history of female struggles. Far from being a powerless chattel, she found many ways to voice her opinions and thoughts. By actively engaging other Somali women to participate in her sewing groups, by organizing initiatives like the Peace Project, and by returning to university, she was anything but silent. Besides her activism, as I was to find out, she also voiced her thoughts through more creative forms of expression. In line with other Somali female poetesses, Halima expresses her hopes, sorrows and frustrations in poems.

Men dominate the higher forms of Somali poetry, the gabay. This is closely linked to the fact that the poet is often also a spokesperson for his group and acts within the public sphere, a role that is usually not seen as appropriate for women. But women developed their own poetic forms, the highest of it being the buraanbur. Some of the poems composed by women were traditionally sung to break the monotony of their work, but their more important function was to express daily problems, desires and aspirations, and also to protest against oppression and subjugation (Farah, Adan and Warsame 1995: 175). By focusing on poems, a number of fascinating oral history studies have revealed the hidden history of Somalia from women's perspectives (e.g. Aden 1981; Jama 1994; Kapteijns 1999; Aidid 2011). They unfold another picture of Somali women, one that is much closer to my image of Halima. The poems bring women's strong and critical views on their place in society to the fore; they show them as active participants in political life, as savvy mediators and, just like Xaawo or Halima's great-grandmother, as determined fighters against colonialism and injustice.

Consider, for example, a poem written by Hawa Jibril, who was actively involved in the fight for independence. When Somalia achieved independence in 1960, women like Hawa, who had committed themselves to the nationalist cause, suddenly found that they were left outside the very political institutions they had fought for. Far from silently accepting this act of disempowerment, the poem expresses the frustration and disappointment many women felt. She finishes her poem by asking: 'Sisters, was this what we struggled for?' (Aidid 2011: 117).

One summer afternoon, on a day when Halima's thoughts had wandered back to war-torn Somalia over and over again, she expressed her pain over all she had fought for and that seemed lost now by singing me her poem 'Somalia Window of the World Weeyo'. This poem, which she had written years earlier, expressed her longing and hope for a better Somalia. Halima began composing poems after the outbreak of the war, mainly as a means of finding relief. The soothing rhythm of the song allowed her to travel to painful landscapes of her past, but also to a future Somalia, which her poems hope and call out for. Over the years, these poems have come to accompany her and form an essential ingredient of her placemaking efforts in Australia. Her songs express the sense of community she is actively building towards through her engagement in projects like the Peace Project, but also throughout her career as a politician. This imaginary community is inextricably linked to the Pan-Somali ideas Halima had grown up with and that had propelled her to become involved in Somalia's socialist movement in 1969, shortly after Siyaad Barre came to power. Halima often told me how she had been deeply impressed by Barre's promise to establish a country that was built on the national unity of all Somalis, regardless of their clan affiliation. While the reality of building such a community soon proved to be far more complex than the regime's rhetoric, Halima had never given up hoping for it. Thus, the community she was actively building towards embodied an ideal, an aspiration after a group that would be unified through their Somaliness. This unity of the community in

Melbourne, she hoped, would in turn flow back into the politics of place in Somalia and allow for its inner workings to be rebuilt. For the Somalis living in Melbourne, she hoped that a restored sense of togetherness would work as a shield against the debilitating feelings of disorientation and liminality that had marked her own experience of displacement. For their persuasiveness and poetic strength, her songs have gained popularity amongst her friends and in the wider Somali community. Thus, Halima is not just a gifted storyteller, but her stories are also directed at allowing other Somalis to create a bridge between the places they have left behind and the reality of life in the suburbs of Melbourne. By reciting her songs in public spaces, she actively works against the voices dismissing her for claiming her right to participate in politics.

Somalia Window of the World Weeyo

Wareerka dhulkayga galay baan wadiiq u doonayaa
Waayeelkaan dumarikbaan walaalow oran hayaa
Wadaaka wanaagsan baan wariiksii tabinayaa
Dhalinta kala weecataan wanaaga u sheegayaa

I am trying to find a way out to save my country from the senseless confusion
I am inviting the elders, the women for advice
I am gathering the wise people
I am informing and guiding the fragmented youth

Wow, wow, wow, window of the world iyoo

Wareerka dhulkayga galay baan wadiiqo u doonayaa
Waayeelkiyo dumarki baan walaalow oran hayaa
Wadaaka wanaagsan baan wariisi tebinayaa
Caruurta la weeciyaan wanaagii barahayaa

I am trying to find a way out to save my country from the senseless confusion
I am asking all to reunite and hold hands
I am advancing and highlighting the sound advice of the good preacher
I am rehabilitating the misguided and wrongly indoctrinated children

Wow, wow, wow, window of the world iyoo

Wareerka dhulkayga galay baan wadiiqo u doonayaa
Waxaan leenahay dhul weyn
Batroolkiiyoo ku waran
Wabiga ku wadiidayoo badii weegaaran tahay
Tharwatul xayawaanka iyo xooluhu ay ku badanyihiin

I am trying to find a way out to save my country from the senseless
   confusion
We have vast land
Filled by mineral resources
And extraordinarily packed by all types of livestock

Wow, wow, wow, window of the world iyoo

Wareerka dhulkayga galay baan wadiiqo u doonayaa
Bal eeg waxan hasaniyo wareerkaan dul taagannahay
Waddanki waa uu burburay waxgaradkii waa la dilay
Haweenkii wanaagsanaa weerbay wada xiranyihiin
Carruurta warkooda daa weerbaa kula jirah wadada

I am trying to find a way out to save my country from the senseless
   confusion
Imagine and compare what we had and where we stand now
The country is destroyed and the intellectuals are massacred
All decent mothers and wives are widowed
Don't mention our children – they are at the mercy of the merciless
   along the road

Wow, wow, wow, window of the world iyoo

Wareerka dhulkayga galay baan wadiiqo u doonayaa
Wanaaga intii rabtoo dunida wada saaranahy
Waxyeelada taala ciidda intii ku wareersaney
Wanaaga intaad duntaan xumaha wada daadisaan
Walaalooba oo wadaaga
Waddanku wadyiin deeqayaaye

I am trying to find a way out to save my country from the senseless
   confusion
Those who are with us in this universe and crave for peace
Those who are sick and tired from the chaos in our land
Advocate for the good and discard the evil
Unite as brothers and sisters
This country can accommodate all of us comfortably

Waa Window of the World Weeyo[3]

Notes

1. Halima is referring to the military coup d'état on 15 October 1969, when
   president Cabdul-Rasheed Cali Sharmaarke was killed. Six days later,

members of the Somali military and police forces, led by general Siyaad Barre, called out the end of the civilian regime and the rise of a revolutionary order (A. Samatar 1988).

2. The Higher Komsomol School was a cadre training unit run by the youth division of the Soviet Communist Party.

3. The poem was translated into English by Omar with the assistance of Halima.

9

Displaced Stories

A Taste of the Past

It was a rainy day, foggy patches of wet greyness hanging like a thick, impermeable curtain from the sky. Gusts of cold and moist Antarctic wind swept through the deserted streets of Footscray, leaving me chilled to the bone, anticipating the beginning of the inevitable arrival of winter.

'Quickly, close that door,' Halima said as I entered the house, letting in a blast of cold air. 'Come, sit down next to the heater, darling, you must be frozen. Oh, how scared you always make me riding that bike everywhere. You're tiny and the wind today is so much stronger than you.' I laughed at the idea of the wind being so strong that it would lift me with my bike up into the air, carrying me away, spitting me out somewhere else. 'Look what I found at the Footscray market,' I said, trying to change the topic. I took a papaya out of my backpack and presented it to Halima. 'Maybe it helps us pretend that winter isn't coming yet.' 'What a good idea,' she said. 'You know, I love papayas and mangoes.'

Later on, when we had settled, huddled together on the dark wooden couch next to the heater that blew hot air into the living room, we shared the papaya I had brought. Biting into its soft, sweet flesh, Halima said: 'How I love the sweetness of papayas. But you know what? They just never taste the same like at home.' And suddenly, the taste of the papayas seemed to awake in her the texture of a feeling slumbering deep inside of her – the bittersweet feeling of being-at-home in Mogadishu.

The taste of papaya first took her back to the 'fantastic days' in Mogadishu again. 'So often do I think about the beautiful trees that I planted around my house,' Halima sighed. 'Papaya trees, mango trees, I had planted them all.' She told me how early in the mornings, soon after getting up, she would sit down on a chair in the garden and watch the birds picking the fruits from the trees. 'The birds loved my garden,' Halima said. 'And the flowers, they had such an amazing smell, I can't even describe it to you. Every morning I used to eat a papaya from my own garden, and they were so sweet – as if someone had added sugar to them.' Sharing the papaya, Halima's garden in Mogadishu suddenly felt so close, so here – and yet so sadly distant and far away. The garden with all the beautiful mango and papaya trees, the birds that inhabited them, and the flowers that were at home there, they all came to life in Halima's memory and conveyed a sense of the web of smells, sounds and other beings that weave a feeling of being-at-home. But unlike in the storying of her childhood days, when she could encapsulate all that had happened to Somalia ever since and draw strength from re-embedding the memories of a beautiful past into the here and now, this time the look back did not work as a source of strength. Instead, the papaya, in failing to bring a taste of the sweetness of the past, provoked the painful realization of all that was lost.

With the last pieces of fruit cleared from the plate – this fruit that did not carry the sweetness of home – the memory place vanished. A feeling of sadness hung in the air, a sadness for everything that had made up that place and that now seemed lost. Getting up to take away the empty plate, Halima said decidedly: 'Anyway, who knows if the trees are still alive? It's all lost. Everything is destroyed now.' On this note the story ended; there was nothing more to say. The violence of the war had not only destroyed or scarred people, it had also violated places. Her house and garden still existed in Mogadishu, but they were now inhabited by strangers who had taken posses-sion of it many years ago. For Halima it had become a lost place, a place emptied of itself and its inner meaning. War and violence had literally de-placed it. Like Omar's 'dust-state', the place Halima had looked back into resisted storying. While I felt like comforting Halima, telling her how much her story had given me a sense of all the sadness and suffering she had been through, its abrupt ending had also made it clear that the telling of this very story had reached its limits. Beyond its endnote, what else was left to tell that was sayable, shareable to anyone in the outside world?

Wounded Stories

Experiences of displacement can sometimes be felt as so removed from the everyday world of the here and now, as so extremely *other*, that people struggle to integrate them into a constituent flow of words that make sense, into a story that can be shared. What is left, then, are mutterings, stutters and silence.

Primo Levi, a survivor of Auschwitz, spent much of his life thinking about the role of retelling and bearing witness to the almost unspeakable experiences in the death camps. He came to believe that traumatic events are experiences of such singularity that only the person who lived through them can bear witness to them; the only true witnesses to the concentration camps were the 'drowned' ones – all those people who died there without being able to tell the world about the violence that was done to them (Levi 1988). Despite the years he spent telling his own story, bearing witness to all he had seen and lived through, Levi became deeply depressed by the lack of understanding and recognition that many of his listeners expressed. He felt as if the stories of trauma and injustice he was trying to share with the world hit a wall of numb deafness, catapulting the woundedness these stories carried back into himself. Stories of extreme suffering can only be told, it seems, if there are listeners sensitive enough to, if not fully understand, at least sense the untellable dimensions of some memories.

When Halima so abruptly moved from the beauty of the memory place of her Mogadishu-home to the utter sense of displacement that surrounds it now, I as the listener sensed the end of what was tellable and shareable. Even if she had told me all the violent details that had turned her former home into something lost, it would not have changed the insurmountable fact that I had not lived through it with her, that, while she was running for her life, this life-changing moment had gone unnoticed in my corner of the world. While her world was breaking down, I had probably spent a normal day.

In his poem 'Musée des Beaux Arts' W.H. Auden describes suffering as something we always witness removed, as something that happens in the midst of us and yet appears to be distant and unapproachable (Auden 1976; Morris 1997). Looking at Pieter Bruegel's masterpiece *Landscape with the Fall of Icarus*, Auden notices how, while the painting foregrounds a beautiful landscape and people peacefully pursuing their everyday activities, in the background is a scene of incomprehensible suffering – a drowning Icarus, fallen from the sky, his wings melted, his head already under water. He describes the paradoxical relationship between closeness and detachment inherent in human suffering, how the most unbearable anguish takes place in the midst of everyday life's flow, so that one person can be going through a horrific experience, 'while someone else is eating or opening a window or just walking dully along ...'.

In the face of such sadness and suffering, it seems, not just Icarus' life is shattered, but with it also the possibility of understanding the world in terms of the smooth wholeness that characterizes the Icarus-view onto the world I have described before. The people surrounding this cruel scene, the walkers of the everyday, find it impossible to integrate such an event into the unity of everyday experience. As a result, they look but they do not see; they know, but they do not understand. The Old Masters' real triumph, then, was to confront us with the sense of detachment marking our engagement with experiences of suffering (Morris 1997: 28–29). In Auden's view suffering contains at its heart an absolute and insurmountable otherness. According to David Morris (1997: 27), it is a counterview to the modern parable of the Good Samaritan and adds an irreducibly nonverbal dimension to suffering: 'The quality of such suffering remains as blank to thought as the void opened up by a scream.' Morris suggests that exactly because of its paradoxical status, the scream can serve as a fruitful image for the metaphorical silence that is at the heart of suffering.

> A scream is not speech but the most intense possible negation of language: sound and terror approaching the limits of absolute muteness. Like the ceremonial wailing of grief, it seems to come from a region where words fail. (Morris 1997: 27)

But while Morris' metaphor of the scream captures all the layers of the unspeakable that surround memories of suffering, it was not the language Halima used to share her experiences of war and destruction. Her silence was not absolute. It was not like a wall that would not let anyone through. Instead, there were many attempts to let me understand: beginnings of stories, never told to the end; snippets and glimpses of war and being on the run; and memories of violence and pain suddenly breaking into the here and now only to quickly disappear again, leaving behind a trace of unspoken words and feelings.

While telling a constitutive story of her displacement as a chronology of meaningful events was simply impossible to Halima, she also did not render these experiences fully untellable. Within the controllable realm of the fragment it was possible for her to speak of moments of extreme pain, while being able to quickly let go of them again, moving on and away from them, back to the here and now, to a worldliness we shared together. The fragment could be seen as a way of protecting herself against a sense of slipping out of the world. Hannah Arendt (1998: 50–51) suggests that pain can be experienced as a loss of the world, as a form of worldlessness; pain cannot 'transform into a shape fit for public appearance', for it is one of the most private of all human experiences, one that is at the borderline of 'life as "being among men" (*inter hominess esse*) and death'. Halima's attempts to turn her experiences of the outbreak of the war into a story formed such a borderline. What she struggled with the most throughout these stories was Mogadishu's disintegration – how a place she had loved so dearly (and had felt loved by) could so quickly turn into something hostile and ugly. 'The buildings, the schools, the universities, the museums – oh my god. All the libraries. It's all gone,' Halima said. 'But it was so beautiful. I remember when I was walking inside Mogadishu. When you see the places where we used to go to have fun – now the dogs live there, eating people. When they see you they run after you to eat, because they are used to eating the meat of the people, of the dead bodies. I'm hoping there will be an end.'

Halima found it difficult to make sense of a place and time that were marked by such violent ruptures – so hard indeed, that she struggled to integrate it into a story. This rupture, it seems, formed the most intensely felt pain of displacement. In contrast to the fluidity and lightness that marked the way Halima storied her childhood, her memories of war and displacement were disrupted and unconnected, almost like volcanoes, bubbling up pieces of memory every now and then, bringing them to the surface, just to quickly lapse again. Unlike the unity that made up her other stories, where different events and experiences were moulded into a coherent whole, the experiences of displacement represented such radical discontinuity from the here and now of the telling that they resisted the wholeness of a story plot. It was in the form of fragments and glimpses that she told me about the outbreak of the war, of the sound of the gunfire surrounding her house, making it feel like a trap, and of moments of utter fear she felt upon leaving Mogadishu to flee 500 kilometres southwards to the city of Kismaayo, the place where her husband's sub-clan had a stronghold, which they hoped could provide protection. It was in the realm of the breathlessness of someone on the run that Halima raced through the chain of events that rolled over her family: of the clan violence that broke out once they had reached Kismaayo; of her husband's arrest by a rival clan and the whispered murmurs that reached her that he had been killed, and the news that reached him that she had been killed, which led to years spent apart; of her decision to leave Somalia on an overcrowded ship to Yemen in an attempt to save her children's life; of the remarkable coincidence that led her to stumble across her sister Sahra's little son, who had been taken in by a group of refugees in Yemen after he had been separated from his mother on the run; of her decision to make her way from Yemen to Dubai, where her two sisters Zeinab and Amina were living; of the months she spent on the move, trying to reach the Emirates with her four children and her sister's son, whom Halima had taken with her.

So fragmented were these stories, and so painful, that Halima did not want to read them again. While she allowed me to, in my own words, recount some of the story-fragments, she made it clear that these displaced stories were not to be retold in her own voice. It was only around her point of arrival in Dubai, when all the running and hiding came to an end and when there was time to rest and take a deep breath, that Halima's storytelling could let go of the fragments' protective shelter, when the story itself could take breath again as well, and regain its sense of balance and order.

The hardest part of my life was in Dubai. If you didn't have legal documents to stay, your children could not go to school. So I worried about that. And my husband was not with me at that time, because we had lost each other during the war and I didn't know that he was still alive.

You had to work to get a visa, but you couldn't get work without legal documents. It was like running around in circles. One of my sisters was in France. She was working, so she said that she would always send me a little money. I also had my two sisters Zeinab and Amina there and their husbands were working, so they were all helping me to pay for my rent.

After some time I began looking for ways to create my own income. I started to connect myself to Somalis overseas, to people living in America, Canada and London. I contacted friends and they told me who owned Somali shops there. When they wanted to buy clothes for their shops, they always had to travel to the Emirates. So I negotiated with them. They knew who I was, and they trusted me, so I told them that I could help them and buy the things that they wanted from Dubai, send it to them and then get a percentage from the profit. They said: 'We will allow you ten per cent of whatever you buy, because if we had to take an airplane it would cost us thousands of dollars.' I knew the clothes, the styles and the things they were interested in, so they started sending me 5,000, 10,000, sometimes 30,000 dollars, and out of that money I was getting a percentage.

And then there was the problem that my children couldn't go to school, so I went to see Sheikh Saqr, the leader of the emirate Ras al-Khaimah, where I lived. I went to him and said: 'Initially we were three Somali families who fled here, but the others chose to go to Italy, London and America. Their children even have passports to live there now and I am here, and I don't have anything. If you don't want to help me, just let me know, I will try my best to go somewhere else. Otherwise, you are the ruler of this country, and God is looking at you and sees that we are struggling. So can you help me?' He immediately answered yes, and he gave me the permission that my children could go to school.

So that's when my children started going to school. I sent them to school, and when they were there I went to the other side of the city, collected clothes and put them into boxes and sent them with the post to the Somali shops overseas. I faxed the documents to the people and received my ten per cent. Those ten per cent I divided and bought all the food for two or three months, dry food, and got the books and pencils and what my children needed. Most of the time that helped me survive.

I spent twelve years in the Emirates, but I never felt at home there. They always see you as a stranger there. I was always running around in circles. If you are staying with them for so long you should receive proper documents, or a job, but I didn't get anything. I always remained a foreigner, a stranger.

So it was really, really hard for me. But I adapted to that life, because I didn't have anywhere to go, I couldn't go back to Somalia. If they had sent me back, I would have been killed. At that time they were searching for all the people who had worked with the government. So on the one side Dubai was heaven for me, but on the other side I felt that there were lots of gaps.

While I was living there, I was often thinking about what was happening in Somalia and that was very hard. When my children weren't there, I was crying. I write Somali poetry, so I began writing about my country. I wrote: 'Don't worry, my country, I will be back.' That was what I said. And I wrote a poem that said: 'I am far from you. Although I never wished to be out of your reach, God created these evil people who started this war. But, my country, I will be with you soon, don't worry, don't worry.' That was my poem.

I was all the time worrying. I felt hopeless, I felt like I was nowhere, like I was no one. I felt all this, but at the same time, what made my heart strong was believing in God. It helped me a lot. I prayed and worshipped God as much as I could, so I got a feeling of relief. I felt that there was help, that sooner or later I would get help.

Figure 9.1 *'I took that photo from a small window, I couldn't go outside, because there was a lot of fighting. For others it was business as usual.' Image courtesy of Mohamed Ibrahim*

If You're Alive, it's Better to Smile

For a long time I struggled to make sense of the way my Austrian grandmother, Oma Pepi, remembered the war years. While she did not build a thick wall of silence around those times like so many other people in the village, she told us kids wartime stories that were light, funny and beautiful – as if the entire war had been one big adventure.

She told us how her father, a conservative Catholic who used to be the village's mayor, was forced to flee when the Nazis occupied Millstatt, and hid in the mountains with a few other members of the resistance for the duration of the war. Sometimes she would take us to the war memorial behind the church, telling us to find the name of her beloved little brother Telesphor, who had died as a soldier in Russia and for whom we lit a candle. But instead of telling us about her emotions, about the fear I much later learned she had felt, a fear of everyone in the village and particularly of the group of people who had ganged up on her family and attempted to find and kill her father, she told us adventurous and funny stories of her father's years in the mountains. Her favourite stories highlighted her father's strong and heroic character, how he outwitted anyone pursuing him by using the creek that weaves its way from the mountains down to the lake in Millstatt as a secret way to smuggle food and messages to his hiding place, and how she was able to listen secretly to the Feindsender, the forbidden BBC German service. My grandmother's wartime stories always peaked in the time immediately after the end of the war, when she fell in love with my grandfather, a Dutch man who had come to the village as a forced labourer and who, on a cold spring night in the mountains, stole a first kiss from her.

As we grew older, a few years before my grandmother died, snippets of other stories came to the surface. She told us how during the war her neighbour, a fervent Nazi, who was now living three houses further up, had tried to shoot her from his window. She told us that her brother Telesphor's decision to join the Wehrmacht had not been voluntary at all, as she had pictured it before. Instead, the local Nazi officials, angry about her father's oppositional stance, made sure that, when the war started, he was the first one in the village to be conscripted to join the army. She told us that the old lady next door had a disabled child. She was trying to hide her child from the authorities but was turned in by one of the other villagers; the child was taken away to a 'children's home' and died in a medical experiment weeks later. I was shocked by these stories. This friendly old man, who always treated us with his homemade honey or jams, had tried to kill her. It was simply inconceivable to me how my grandmother could walk past his garden every day and have a chat with him about the weather, totally oblivious to what he had tried to do. And how could she go on telling us all these stories of the war that sounded like it had all just been a big laugh?

In his shockingly beautiful nine-hour documentary *Shoah* (1985), French filmmaker Claude Lanzmann asks this question. Within the film's human tapestry of horrifying, disheartening, but also beautiful and heartbreaking stories told by survivors of the Nazi concentration camps and by other eyewitnesses, there is one brief moment that struck me so strongly that it has not left me ever since. The sequence shows a conversation between the filmmaker and Michael Podchlebnik – in his mid fifties at the time – who survived the death camp in Chelmno near Łódź. While Lanzmann wants to know about Podchlebnik's feelings, his memories, his thoughts, the survivor tells him that he does not like speaking of those times; that he prefers to think that he is alive and that these bad times are over now. After a moment of silence, with the camera resting on the survivor's face, the filmmaker asks Podchlebnik whether he really is alive, or whether he is just that: a survivor. With a smile on his face, Podchlebnik insists that yes, he believes he is alive, and that he has to thank God for the ability to forget. There is a long silence; the camera piercing into the survivor's smiling face. Lanzmann, insisting that this cannot be all, asks: 'Why do you smile all the time?' 'What do you want me to do? Cry?' Michael Podchlebnik responds. 'Sometimes you smile, sometimes you cry. And if you're alive it's better to smile.'

I was struck by Lanzmann's insistent question, 'Why do you smile all the time?' Like my grandmother's wartime love and adventure stories, does not this smile, this silence over all the suffering, the violence and the atrocities, allow those who created the mayhem to escape the consequences of their deeds all too easily? But then, while watching the film, I was horrified by the consequences of thinking through the other option: What if Michael Podchlebnik did not smile all the time? What if he chose to speak of those memories that he just did not want to be part of his being-here anymore? What if smiling was his way of continuing the story he could not share with us in all its cruel details – continuing it in a way that allowed him to end a story of sheer suffering and trauma with the recuperation of control over his own life and his own story?

Instead of seeing Michael Podchlebnik's smile as an attempt to suppress, to neglect and to hide, it could be read as an attempt to regain a sense of empowerment. In the same way, my grandmother's emphasis on her father's heroism and on the sneaky kiss that began a love story could be read as a way to turn a loss into a win. As Michael Jackson suggests, survival is not just physical; it is also the ability to survive socially. And it is, he notes, *existential*, 'being able to make plans again, to choose, to outlive that time when one was reduced to nothingness, beaten like an animal, ordered to do the most shameful and terrible things in order to be allowed to live, defeated by one's abject powerlessness' (Jackson 2002: 104). Looked at from the perspective of the social and existential dimensions of survival, Halima's decision not to emphasize the disturbing and disempowering experiences of her life story, but rather to focus on the moments of hope and victory instead, appears in a new light. Perhaps the silences, the disjointed accounts of painful times of being on the run do not just stand for the impossibility to give suffering a voice and a language; perhaps the choice to highlight the positives and to downplay the negatives is a way to regain some sense of power and balance, a standing within a world that, not long ago, seemed to bereave her of any sense of choice.

Halima's story of the years she spent in Ras al-Khaimah is not one of glory and happiness, but what distinguished them from the fragmented and untellable period of flight was that they held out the possibility that she could become an actor within her own life again. Her story speaks of difficult times, of the hardships of being in a constant state of limbo in a country where she did not have legal status, of the financial instability and the feeling of being 'nowhere', like being 'no one'. But it does not get caught in a state of paralysis and liminality. Even her poem, despite all the sadness and loss it speaks of, is inherently one of hope and change, for, as she says, 'I will be with you soon, don't worry, don't worry'. Halima's account of that time does not fit with the public image of the refugee as helpless, hopeless and voiceless. In fact, Halima does not once use the word 'refugee' to describe her situation. It also does not fit with the idea that all that refugees have to share with the world are stories of suffering and hardship, or that they are forever lost in trauma stories that seem to cry out for help and intervention. The question Halima's story raises is the same question inherent in the troubles I encountered with my grandmother's stories or that Claude Lanzmann bumped into when interviewing Michael Podchlebnik: How can people speak, smile, live on after having experienced displacement and how can they integrate such experiences into a here and now, into this human world?

Social Suffering

In her story of the times she spent in Ras al-Khaimah, Halima highlights the importance of poems as a means of communicating with her lost country, of finding a form of relief from the desperation she felt for its loss. Directly addressing Somalia like a person, she almost seems to soothe her country like a crying child: 'Don't worry, my country,' she says, 'I will be back.' Comforting her country is also a way of comforting herself, of finding a way to dry the secret tears she is shedding while her children are at school. But while Halima's poem gives a glimpse of the sadness and suffering she experienced, her suffering does not stand by and for itself. Instead, her suffering becomes the suffering of a country, a nation, a community, and, only within these limits, of herself.

Lidwien Kapteijns (2010) writes about similar ways of addressing the state collapse in her analysis of poems of the destruction of Mogadishu. Many of the poems she analyses were written by Somalis in exile and disseminated through the internet amongst Somalis worldwide. Interestingly, a large number of poems she found dealt with the collapse of the Somali state without linking this wider social context of war and violence to personal suffering. While most of the poems, like Halima's, directly address Mogadishu and speak of its destruction as the destruction of a person, the poets never situate their individual pains and sorrows within it. Kapteijns relates this absence of personal emotions to the point that much of the Somali poetry about the impact of violence is written or performed with the purpose of effecting change and putting forward solutions that go beyond the individual (Kapteijns 2010: 30). As I have pointed out before, poems and songs written and performed in the realm of the Somali orature are sensual and poetic texts, but they are also made with the intention of persuading their audience.

On a similar note, Christine Zarowsky, in her work on Somali-Ethiopian refugees, found that the people she spoke to did not discuss refugee issues in terms of individual suffering. Instead, they tended to emphasize the sociopolitical dimensions of their experiences as refugees (Zarowsky 2004). She describes the way Somali Ethiopian refugees spoke about their war experiences as a 'politics of emotions', as a way of linking their personal experiences to wider political claims (Zarowsky 2004: 200). Zarowsky stresses that while people's everyday experiences included emotions, their principal concern was for justice, survival and a decent human life. Her informants wanted to tell her a master-narrative that revolved around dispossession, anger and injustice, but they did not convey their individual miseries, as they believed that this would not help them in resolving the underlying collective problems (Zarowsky 2004: 201).

The dominant Western idea of suffering is one that imagines it in a timeless and placeless void, free of local people and local worlds (Kleinman and Kleinman 1997: 7–8). In many parts of the world, however, people do not deal with suffering in terms of its individuality. Suffering, then, needs to be looked at beyond its representation as inherently individual and be mapped out as a social experience, as what Arthur Kleinman, Veena Das and Margaret Lock famously described as *social suffering* (Kleinman, Das and Lock 1997: ix, my emphasis). This way of emphasizing the collective suffering of a nation over personal emotions is also mirrored in Halima's means of situating herself within her life story. This suggests that in the Somali context, thinking of suffering and storytelling in individual terms is problematic. But it also leads me to think that even on a broader level thinking of suffering as something that is inevitably rooted within one lonely individual's life story needs to be questioned.

In many respects the image of the refugee as a figure who cannot be understood beyond the suffering she has experienced, as a pure victim thrown back to the barest bareness of life, is linked to the way public and academic discourses have come to deal with the phenomenon of flight and asylum in psychopathological terms. For example, over the last decade in Australia, the vast majority of academic publications dealing with refugees have written about them in terms of trauma and illness. Didier Fassin and Estelle D'Halluin have described a historic shift from a political to a medicalized discourse about refugees, and they argue that this has led to a paradigm in which refugees are seen in terms of their individual psychopathology, and their stories go unheard.

> The refugee's body, thus, becomes the place of an inscription, the meaning of which relates to a double temporality: an inscription of power, through the persecution they suffered in their home country, and an inscription of truth, insofar as it bears witness to it for the institutions of their host country. (Fassin and D'Halluin 2005: 598)

Having survived times of extreme hardship and suffering, refugees who manage to reach places of refuge and safety often become subject to another form of appropriation. It is here that their most intimate memories and images of violence are turned into what Arthur and Joan Kleinman call 'trauma stories'. 'These trauma stories then become the currency, the symbolic capital, with which they enter exchanges for physical resources and achieve the status of political refugee,' they write. 'Increasingly, those complicated stories, based in real events, yet reduced to a core cultural image of *victimization* (a postmodern hallmark), are used by health professionals to rewrite social experience in medical terms' (Kleinman and Kleinman 1997: 10).

The idea of linking 'refugeeness' to different levels of suffering plays an increasingly important role in the Australian context and influences decision-making processes over the regional focus of the resettlement of refugees as well as the foci of service providers dealing with the social and psychological wellbeing of newly arrived refugees. These developments can be seen as part of a larger shift towards a politics of suffering and compassion. With the entry of suffering into politics, Didier Fassin has argued convincingly that humanitarianism takes on a new language. Within this language, the biological life of the destitute and unfortunate is given preference over their biographical life, 'the life through which they could, independently, give a meaning to their own existence' (Fassin 2011: 254). The figure of the refugee becomes inescapably moulded into a problem in need of intervention, the shadow of trauma following it wherever it goes. The lack of a proper place for their stories to be heard engulfs the figure of the refugee, steeping it in a sense of placelessness and home-lessness, leaving it with nothing more than its bare survival. It is, then, not surprising that refugees are often portrayed as rootless, lost and utterly out of place.

The question arises whether these discursive dynamics make sense in Halima's lifeworld, where the pain and suffering felt in her own body stand side by side with the pain and suffering felt by an entire country. How does the public expectation that she will have a 'proper' trauma story as a humanitarian entrant relate to the strength and resilience her stories embody?

Who Does not Climb a Mountain Will End in a Well

On a winter afternoon in the Footscray kebab café, Halima made an attempt to explain to me the impact the war had on her life. She told me a story of how she had found the power and determination to keep moving on. It was a story of such strength that it flung open a window that helped me see why, after experiencing extreme forms of suffering and sadness, the sharing of stories of hope, of little victories and laughter, can be essential to the existential and social survival of human beings.

'When the civil war erupted,' Halima said, 'everything was destroyed, everything was taken, and we ran away. I remember one day we didn't have anything to eat that we could give to our children and we were nowhere, because we had run away from the city and we didn't have anywhere to go, because here's a bomb, there's a fire, there's another problem. At that time you only gave maize to the birds, you didn't give it to the people. But I took some maize and I had a little stick to grind it. And my husband, he sat down and sang to me: "Halima, the person who doesn't want to climb mountains, will end up living in a well".' 'What did he mean by singing those words to you?' I asked. 'It means that when you are in trouble, you have to try your best to climb out of the hole, the water well, and you will be safe, otherwise you will die in there,' she explained. 'He was trying to say that it's a hardship to grind maize, because he knew me, I used to be a very important person, I had my car, I had my servant doing this and that for me, so he was worried that when you have had that life and you lose it, that I would give up life. He didn't want me to give up, and he was saying: "Halima, this grinding-thing means that we are climbing. Please, be patient". He always said those words, he repeated and repeated and repeated them. I will never forget that.'

Like Michael Podchlebnik, who chose not to repeat the stories of the times when he was an object of other people's will and choices, in her stories, Halima chose to give her innermost strength to leaving behind the well, this hole that represented the lowest point possible. Her husband's song helped her to focus on moving forwards instead of backwards, on climbing mountains without looking back, on not giving up after all she had lost. And just as Mohamed's song had helped Halima to regain the strength she needed, so did the stories she told me about her life. Instead of losing herself in tales of deep loss and suffering, which would have risked throwing her back into the well, she told me stories that worked towards transporting her away from these limitations.

Halima's emphasis on strength and resilience, on climbing as opposed to free fall, calls into question the way refugees have come to be imagined as haunted by trauma and loss. In fact, her story calls into question the entire way we have come to deal with loss as something that requires medical intervention. I agree with Michael Jackson's (2005: 355–56) suggestion that we need to question the way we tend to describe the aftermath of war and destruction by indicating that 'nothing will ever be the same again'. Such statements hinge on the idea of history as a chronological succession of events and overlook the ways in which past events are continuously transmuted into myth. Importantly, such a view also ignores the ways in which the present appropriates the past and in doing so continuously revises how it appears to us in everyday life (Lems 2017). If, as suggested before, the past is not a foreign country but something that leaks into our being-here and has the power to constitute it, then it should not be looked at as rigidly severed from the present and the future. Halima's storytelling – whether it is travelling through the fantastic days of her childhood, revolutionary Somalia or the outbreak of war and destruction – suggests that we need to consider the past as a present concern, as a concern relevant to the way people live their lives in the present and to how they imagine them to be in the future (Hirsch 2008: 25). At the same time, her stories also suggest that the very act of storytelling can be a means of dealing with the hereness of that past, of reworking and reintegrating it into a here and now.

Keeping the details of war and violence fragmentary while emphasizing moments of strength and achievement was a means for Halima to, in the here and now, in the moment of the telling, move beyond those debilitating moments and reconstitute herself in new, powerful and active ways. As Jackson puts it, freedom is always exercised within limits. Human life thus can be described as a 'cybernetic' search for a balance between what can and cannot be done under given circumstances. At the same time, every human being likes to act as if she is in control of the situation, 'no matter how forcefully circumstance has obliged or compelled her to act in one way rather than another' (Jackson 2005: 374). The researcher therefore needs to listen carefully, to 'double listen' (Marlowe 2010: 192–93), to hear not just the harrowing and traumatic experiences they are expecting, but to also have an open ear for the stories of hope and resilience, of what helped them through these hard times in the first place.

That afternoon in the kebab house with Halima I realized why my grandmother had chosen to story the war beyond its destructive and terrifying forces. The need for her to move on and, like Halima, at least in her stories, climb mountains instead of risking getting stuck in the well the war had brought her so dangerously close to was her priority. If my grandmother was still alive, able to tell me her stories again, I would do what I did when Halima told me about those hard days in her life, when she was running around in circles and yet had the guts to approach the powerful sheikh of Ras al-Khaimah to remind him of his obligation before God to look after the weak: I would share a laugh with her.

10

Placeless Dreams

Nomadic Trajectories

In our age, so often described in terms of change and liquidity, of uprootedness and deterritorialization, many intellectuals have come to long for a means of replacing the rigid and suffocating narrowness of national belonging with the lightness and ease of the vagabond, the nomad, the traveller, who, owning nothing but her own life, continuously slips in and out of different worlds. As a child, I dreamt of becoming such a person, an adventurer and traveller, always on my way to somewhere else, at home everywhere. That I had such an early fascination with travelling and that I became an anthropologist, moving to the other end of the world to write about refugees, was perhaps no coincidence. In my family, leaving the suffocating narrowness of the village behind and throwing oneself into the openness of the wide world was always storied as the highest of all achievements. This urge to journey and move, to go beyond the protection of the known and to question oneself and one's point of departure, might be connected to my family's discontent with their role as outsiders within Millstatt's closely knit social web. Despite my grandmother's adventure stories, the war had destroyed many of the social relationships that were at the heart of the village. The villagers' deep-seated bitterness about the lost war, palpable behind the wall of silence that was built around everything that had happened during those years, became so unbearable to my father and his brothers that the idea of travelling came to stand for a sense of liberation. And it was this feeling of emancipation and freedom that led them, one by one, to move away from the village, 'to look further than the next mountain', as my father put it.

Beyond my family's history of emplacement, the idea of travelling, of roaming and self-estrangement, has far-reaching historical roots within the Western imagination. In many ways, stories of movement can even be seen as *the* central story told in European thought and literature (Peters 1999: 18). Many of the most famous figures in Western narratives are characterized by their mobility: Abraham, the sojourner and stranger who never returns to his home; Odysseus who only returns home to Penelope after a lifelong odyssey; Oedipus, the outcast within his own city. Even modern philosophy makes use of this trope: Nietzsche, the alpinist, stepping from mountaintop to mountaintop; Heidegger, wandering through the Black Forest; Benjamin, the flâneur, strolling through Paris; Michel de Certeau celebrating pedestrians and poachers as freedom fighters; and Deleuze, declaring the nomad as the embodiment of postmodernity. Many postmodern intellectuals like to think of themselves as always on the move, in transit, crossing frontiers, or in between worlds. But John Durham Peters points out that even this central motif of postmodern thinking, the idea that human identity is discontinuous with itself, can be traced back to old Jewish and Christian visions of the human. Both have the incompleteness of the self and estrangement from the home as key themes. 'Social categories of stranger, pilgrim, outcast, vagabond, tent dweller, and nomad all receive primordial formulation in the Hebrew Bible,' he writes (Peters 1999: 22).

It is exactly within these narrative lines of exile and eternal wandering, of estrangement and nonbelonging, that the figure of the refugee has come to be shaped in our minds and stories. For closely connected to the image of the refugee as the lonely sufferer and carrier of horrific trauma stories is the idea of the refugee as the ultimate embodiment of placelessness and homelessness. And, considering the emphasis on deterritorialization and boundlessness, on mobility and transnational social connections, which marks much contemporary writing in anthropology, it seems that this motif of the eternal wanderer has not lost any of its strength and fascination for Western academia. For it is within these lines that the refugee has come to be championed as the embodiment of the dream of a deterritorialized world, holding its rootless, creolized, rhizomatic identities against the narrow-mindedness of a world that likes to see people as irretrievably connected to specific places.

Much of the current urge to think nomadically was stimulated by a slim book published in 1986 by Gilles Deleuze and Félix Guattari. In *Nomadology: The War Machine* they celebrate nomads for their ability to move beyond the spatially controlled realm of the state. This mobility and evasion of authority, they suggest, turns them into postmodern warriors, ultimate outsiders who resist submitting themselves to the control and categorization of the nation state. Although nomads often follow customary routes, these routes do not fulfil the function of the sedentary road, which parcels out a closed space to people: 'The nomadic trajectory does the opposite: it *distributes people (or animals) in an open space*, one that is indefinite and noncommunicating' (Deleuze and Guattari 1986: 50–51).

It is through the infiltration of these mobile characters, these nonbelongers, who cannot be pinned down to a *place* but whose slippery movements in the vast *open space* pinch and provoke the state's authority, that the limits of state control are put radically into the spotlight. Deleuze and Guattari remain vague about who exactly these postmodern heroes actually are. But given the determination with which nations in the global north fortify their borders under the banner of migration control, it does not take much to think a step further and imagine the representatives of this nomadology within the boundlessness that refugees and migrants embody. Identifying the refugee as the embodiment of the postmodern nomad, whose mere presence destabilizes our supposed rootedness, is only a short step from longing for a figure of such strength to infiltrate our own lives. It is within this vein that Italian philosopher Giorgio Agamben's famous proposal that we are all refugees can be read. He suggests that the possibility of the refugee exists in all of us and within this possibility there rests a revolutionary potential for the future of humankind. 'In the context of the inexorable decline of the nation-state and the general corrosion of traditional legal-political categories the refugee is perhaps the only imaginable figure of the people in our day,' Agamben (1995: 114) writes.

The Love of Place

If the refugee has indeed turned into the only imaginable figure of our times, into a heroic fighter against the sadness of a world marked by territorial narrowness and exclusion, I wonder where this leaves Halima, who, against all the odds of such a world, keeps on climbing mountains. Does it turn her into another warrior, winding her way through steep paths and undefined roads, a mountaineer of *open space*, defying any attempt to stop and settle down somewhere? Has she then, in other words, become a postmodern nomad, at home nowhere except within movement, always looking for greener pastures, the personification of my nomadic childhood dream?

In the work of scholars writing on Somalis, the centrality of the nomadic feature of Somali identity is emphasized over and over. I.M. Lewis' ethnographic work on pastoralists in North Somalia had set the tone. In his classic monograph *A Pastoral Democracy*, he describes Somali pastoralists as proud, freedom-loving nomads, as poetic desert warriors, who, despite constant battles over scarce resources and waterholes, resisted settling down and developing any spatial ties (Lewis 1999). This idea that Somalis can be characterized in terms of their mobility, their constant readiness to pack up camp and leave for greener pastures, has found its way (via Lewis) into the work of many contemporary texts on Somalis. Many writers focusing on the Somali diaspora suggest that nomadism is still a striking feature of their identities, and point at their high level of mobility (e.g. Griffiths 2002; Horst 2006).

In her work on Somali refugees in the Dadaab refugee camp in Kenya, Cindy Horst uses the term 'transnational nomads' to point towards the continuing importance of nomadic heritage for Somalis in the diaspora, a heritage that has changed and become largely transnational (Horst 2006). 'As refugees, the Somalis have lost their homeland and the security of living in a place they can call their own,' Horst (2006: 35) writes. 'As "a nomadic people", mobility, including the mobility that crosses borders, is and has always been an essential part of their livelihoods and identities.' She suggests that this nomadic mobility enables Somali refugees to rapidly change their strategies for survival and livelihood. This includes the possibility that if there are better options across the border, they will, just like nomadic herdsmen, quickly pack up and move towards greener pastures. Coming close to Deleuze and Guattari's idea of nomadic warriors who do not fit within the spatial categorization of the state, she suggests that with their diaspora mentality, Somali refugees pose a challenge to existing ideas of the nation state (Horst 2006: 35). In Horst's sense, Somali refugees could thus be described in terms of their double movement: as refugees and as carriers of a nomadic heritage that urges them to keep criss-crossing the world.

Halima's stories create a more ambiguous picture of the links between movement, self and place. Observing the sense of activity,

of constant thinking and planning that characterized her everyday movements in Melbourne, I was struck by her tireless efforts
to work towards a feeling of stability. Halima was always on the
move, always planning or doing something. From the sewing group
where she gathered Somali women to encourage them to think
themselves beyond their duties as mothers and housewives, to the
multicultural children's playgroup in the community housing estates
near Flemington, where she spent a day a week; from the logistics
of the Peace Project, to the primary school where, together with a
group of five Somali women, she had taken over the school canteen,
to her studies, to her plans to found her own NGO – there was
always something that required her full attention. And yet, despite
the ceaseless amount of activities that marked her days, despite her
constant battle against clan rivalries that complicated her work, and
despite the fact that most of her projects did not bring any income,
Halima never complained. Instead, the sense of constant movement
and activity was at the heart of her entire family. 'This house feels like
a bee hive,' I once said to Halima jokingly, 'everyone's always flying
about.' Her husband, hearing my words, laughed. 'Sister, look,' he
said, 'I'm an old man. If I sit down once I will stop completely.' 'He's
right,' Halima agreed. 'If I sit down and rest I will get sick. Besides,
my heart never tells me to sit down. It tells me: "You know how you
can help, your people need you".'

Halima's urge to keep moving, to help 'her people', and to find
paths out of the isolation and loneliness many Somalis in Melbourne
suffer from was much more than just a career opportunity. Building
towards a greater sense of belonging in Australia within her community also allowed for her own attachment to grow and receive a place
within a wider whole. Walking with her through Footscray's Somali
mall often felt like walking through a village. Everyone knew her
and her family. And it was this feeling of familiarity, of knowing and
being known by others, that drove her. 'It is good to have them here,'
she told me when I asked her how she felt about being known by
everyone, which, at times, also made her an easy target for criticism
from those who were jealous or disapproved of a woman publicly
displaying such a strong and determined attitude. 'They helped me a
lot,' she said. 'I feel like I have lots of relatives here. I am creating my
own family around me.' As the stories of her childhood Mogadishu
have shown, for Halima the family is one of the key ingredients that
makes emplacement possible – so much so, that in her childhood
stories the people who form the heart of the family and the place they
inhabit seem to leak into each other and become one. In a similar

way, the act of creating her own family with 'her' people can be seen as a means of actively building a place and a people to dwell in.

Halima's climbing of mountains was not out of a joy for movement or an unwillingness to be pinned down; instead, it was a constant movement towards the top, a smooth place, where, after all these years of struggle, she could finally rest and truly arrive. Getting so close to Halima compelled me to look beyond the metaphorical and figurative treatment of the refugee in terms of eternal mobility and into the actual experience of movement instead. It made me realize that despite its mobile and unsettling character, travelling is not about going anywhere, about moving between meaningless points on a map swallowed by the *open space* of the world. Instead, journeys always take us through places and in doing so they engage us in them (Casey 1993: 289). It seems to me that in the nomadic dream of the world it is exactly this engagement with place, this love of and for places, which is ignored in favour of a space of vast endlessness that allows us to fly through the human world, birdlike, observing it from a safe distance, without ever having to land and arrive somewhere.

In Katrine Nielsen's research with Somalis in Denmark and the UK, one of her interviewees mentioned a Somali proverb that also speaks for Halima's urge to move forward: '*Dhul Xiiso Kuuma Oga* – "if you love a place, the place doesn't love you"' (Nielsen 2004: 12). The proverb emphasizes that place does not necessarily offer

Figure 10.1 *Driving through Mogadishu. Image courtesy of Mohamed Ibrahim*

an individual any opportunities but that the individual needs to leap into action to create these opportunities for herself. It is in exactly this way that Halima's urge to keep on climbing mountains can be read. And it was within this lived tension between the need for movement and the need for attachment and stability that I was confronted with the necessity to question the Icarus-view on boundlessness and displacement.

After twelve years in the Emirates they told me: 'Your time is up. You have to leave the country now.' My daughter Amal ran away when they said that they were going to deport us. That's when she met her husband and went to America with him. My other children decided to stay.

I sent the letters in which they were asking me to leave to my sister Sahra. She was already living in Melbourne. Her daughter had sponsored her to come from Kenya. When she arrived she tried to sponsor me to come as well, but they rejected it two times. When they said they would deport me, and when she saw that document she cried. She took all those documents to a local MP and said: 'She used to be a big person. She used to be a Member of Parliament. If we send this person back they will kill her. She's my sister, can you help me?' Immediately they sent me a sponsorship. She sponsored me, and that's how I got here.

Before I came to this country, the government had told my sister: 'We don't have a home for Halima now, what can you do?' She said: 'Don't worry.' She went to her two daughters and sons who are working and said: 'Everyone has to pay something for my sister's house.' And then she rented a house, put everything inside for us and when I arrived she said: 'This is your house, my sister.' Sahra helped me with every single step of my journey – until now.

And then, because of the tiredness, the years of worry inside me, and all the problems, I collapsed. I really, really collapsed. When I realized that I was settled, my body told me that I was so tired. That's when I became very sick. I got a very rare blood disease, and I ended up in hospital. While I was in St. Vincent's Hospital I prayed a lot and I said: 'God, if you give me another chance, I will go and help our women, people like me, who suffered a lot. So please God, don't make my time end today.'

While I was in the hospital, my sister Sahra was by my side, and she never left for a second. I remember when I was in the most critical state, I never heard one single word of what the doctors or other people said, but I used to hear my sister's voice. She came early in the morning, combed my hair and cleaned my face. While she was doing that she was talking to me. She said: 'Sister, you know what I am feeling? I feel that you will survive, you will wake up and you will help us – you always liked to help people, and I'm feeling that's coming soon. You are so beautiful, and I don't want you to die. I am here for you. If you understand my words, please, sister, squeeze my hand.' So I squeezed her hand, and she jumped up and said: 'My sister is ok!'

After I came out of hospital I started to cope and understand the system. I organized a sewing programme for Somali women. My community had asked me to run a programme and Centacare[1] said: 'We will give a little funding for that, so she can run it.' At the same time I was still feeling very weak, so I received help from the public welfare. Then they sent me to the Commonwealth Rehabilitation Centre.

The people there were beautiful. They helped me a lot. They gave me courses and they were working hard to build my self-esteem. They advised me: 'Halima, you can do more than you think. Don't give up, life is not easy.' They listened to me, and I talked, talked, talked. I felt very comfortable with them. I felt they were near to my inside feelings. So that's when I decided to go to university to study community development and welfare.

Around that time my husband joined us. He had found out where we were and contacted us. Immediately we decided to give him as much money as we had to bring him from Yemen to Kuala Lumpur. He stayed there for five years. He had been to lots of places. I wrote down our whole story, I sent it to the Immigration Department, they found out that it was true and let him come here.

I was at the airport when he arrived, and my family and all my kids and all my friends were with me. When I saw him I nearly collapsed, because I couldn't understand his face. I said: 'What happened to this world?' And then he came and he cried. He was praying a lot and he cried and cried.

I am a citizen of Australia now – like many other Somalis. But citizenship and settling in this country are two different things. Especially when people have gone through many hardships, they risk to always stay in transit. They say: 'This is not my country,' because they didn't get what they were expecting. But I want to cancel that word, 'transit'. In the end, no one is from here. Every person has migrated here, except for the Aborigines, so why should I not also fit in this country? That's what I'm fighting for. I don't want to be in transit. My heart is working hard to settle, to settle and to belong to this country. I have my country, but if this war is not ending, I cannot lose my time for nothing, so I have something to do here – with people who are Somali and who live in peace here, but who have other problems.

We still have to settle and teach ourselves how to belong to this country, how to be a member of this community. No one is born into it, everyone else had to learn it too, so why not you?

That's what I am exercising and doing my best for.

The Horrors of Boundlessness

In 2006, when her husband was granted a humanitarian visa to join his family in Australia and, after years spent apart, could finally hold his wife and grown-up children again, feelings of happiness, excitement and deep sadness overcame Halima all at once. During the times of struggle and hardship, neither of them had ever been willing to accept the idea that the other had died. The instability that came with being a refugee in countries that did not provide for their basic survival, the constant change of addresses and phone numbers and the immense strength that was needed to face the daily fear of deportation had foiled Halima's earlier attempts to find out what had become of Mohamed. The moment she saw him entering the arrivals hall at Melbourne's Tullamarine airport, she was shocked by the years of loneliness and hardship she could read from his face – a face that she felt she could not understand anymore.

But when Mohamed arrived in Melbourne, this place he had not really chosen, but that, due to an incredible range of twists and turns, had somehow chosen him, Halima made sure that he was not going to drown in an alienating new world. In the months before his arrival she had carefully thought of ways to create an environment for him that would make his transition to a life in Melbourne and into a changed family as painless as possible.

Just as her sister Sahra had gone to great lengths to make her arrival in Melbourne as comfortable as possible, Halima felt that now she needed to do all she could to minimize the feeling of exhaustion and alienation she feared could overcome her husband after his resettlement. For it had been the moment of arriving, of realization that the times of constant instability had come to an end, that had led Halima to 'really, really collapse' soon after her own move to Melbourne. 'I felt that if he came here and didn't have a task he would get depressed and very sick,' Halima told me. And because she was still recovering from her own illness, she knew that she would not have the strength to face such difficulties. With these thoughts troubling her, she borrowed money from her sister and nephew and bought a shop, the milkbar at the corner of the street. 'It was the first Somali milkbar Australia has ever seen,' Halima joked. 'When he arrived I gave him the keys. I said to him: "I created this for you, take it and I will help the community. Is that okay?" He said: "That's fantastic".'

While grappling with the new situation, with the feeling of not just being a stranger in an unknown country but also within his own family, the task of running the small store helped Mohamed to come to terms with his new life. It was against the possibility of staying in a limbo, of getting caught in a paralysing sense of transit, that Halima wanted to protect herself and her family – and, in the end, the entire Somali community. After the frightening experience of her total collapse, it was in recognition of what Mammad Aidani (2010: 133) so poignantly describes as the 'existential need of returning oneself to oneself', that developing a love for Melbourne as a home was of crucial importance. In the context of Iranian refugees in Australia and their yearning to return to their homeland, Aidani stresses that their longing was not just directed towards returning to a place but also to themselves – to restoring their sense of self and their own identities. In Halima's case, returning to a home in Somalia was not an option. While many of her hopes and dreams here in Melbourne were directed to a future Somalia where things will be better, she always told me that a return to Somalia seemed to be something so unrealistic and far away that she kept herself from hoping for it. Because of the ongoing clan conflicts in and around Mogadishu, and because of her former position in the Barre government, going back to Somalia was too dangerous. 'Somalia is my country. I would love to be there with my people and I would like to help them,' Halima explained. 'But after I saw how they were killing the educated people and how they were fighting about all this tribal stuff, my heart stopped encouraging me to go back.' Close to Omar, who kept himself from indulging in thoughts about a past Somalia, Halima did not allow herself to become immersed in daydreams about its future.

While the refugees Aidani worked with linked the existential need of restoring themselves to an imaginary *there* (a homeland in Iran), Halima, for whom a return was no option, did the opposite: She tried to bring the *there* into the *here*. 'Instead of risking myself by going back to Somalia I decided to help from here, to create the Peace Project and to help the orphans and little kids and their mothers from over here. That's the only way I can support them,' Halima said. 'The other thing is: My family is everywhere. Some are in Somalia, some are in Ethiopia, some are in Kenya – they are everywhere. So if Somalia settled down and became peaceful it would be good for my family to reunite again over there, but I think that needs a long time. It's not now and it's not near. Somalia needs time to settle down.'

Rather than longing for a return to Somalia, Halima was determined to invest her being-here with some of the thereness. When she was helping 'her' community here in Melbourne, it was also an attempt to heal their wounds. Halima's community did not just involve her own clan or sub-clan. Instead, her work was marked by ceaseless attempts to rebuild a sense of togetherness between the clans that the war had destroyed. Rebuilding this sense of togetherness here in Melbourne, removed from the immediate violence of Mogadishu and determined by the settings of a new place, was essentially also a way of restoring herself. Close to Omar's being-at-home within the ceaseless acts of building towards a home, Halima's placemaking process involved her entire community and it involved a constant back and forth between the here and there.

This existential need for stability that speaks out of Halima's story of her settlement in Australia, this urge of the heart to befriend Melbourne and to work against the threat of detachment, of 'cancelling the word transit', stand in stark contrast to the endless mobility and transition in terms of which Somalis are so often characterized. The idea of refugees as borderless nomadic beings might fit within my own fascination with boundlessness and nonbelonging. But while Halima's life story is marked by a high level of mobility, would describing her in terms of a deeply ingrained mentality of nomadic freedom not mean to reinscribe the exact state of uprootedness that the anti-sedentarist paradigm set out to fight against in the first place? For it is exactly against this feeling of being caught in limbo, against the panicked fear of losing hold within the open-endedness of space that Halima's heart is working hard to settle down – to settle down and to do so *in place*.

Perhaps it is time to rethink the current aversion to the idea of setting roots. While roots have come to stand for the postmodern 'horror of being bound and fixed' (Bauman 1995: 91), this horror does not seem to be shared by people like Halima, whose horror seems to be the exact opposite. Her horror is the horror of boundlessness; her fear is the fear to remain in transit and unfitting forever, to never arrive anywhere, to never be someone in relation to somewhere anymore. While Halima's quite exceptional story cannot, of course, speak for the stories of the hundreds of thousands of other people who have experienced displacement (from Somalia and from elsewhere in the world), the majority of whom live in protracted situations and are forced to be mobile, I believe that her story still opens up a window to new views on displacement. Without having to argue for or against boundlessness, storytelling offers a way of exploring a more nuanced perspective, one that moves beyond the metaphorical. It allows us to not just question the way Somalis have come to be portrayed in terms of their nomadic heritage, but to also link this portrayal to wider questions of the homelessness of our time.

Halima's insistence on the importance of place-bound stability and against a continuous state of limbo speaks for Nielsen's (2004: 14) position that many scholars working with the concept of Somali nomadism fail to take into account the context of what they perceive as nomadic movement. As Nielsen points out, the type of movement that drives Somali refugees from country to country takes place out of necessity and not for pure joy of movement (Nielsen 2004: 16). In fact, the context of such movement could not be more different from the idea of travelling light. For against the romantic dream of Somalis as boundless nomads, as world travellers who do not have the need to belong anywhere, stand the horrors and violence of an age that Somali intellectual Ahmed Samatar has described as *qaxootin*. It is an age of desperate exodus, the magnitude of which can only be described as a catastrophe. The rupture in the collective identity is so severe, Samatar writes, 'that Somalis have taken almost *any* road out of the country' (Samatar 2004: 10). Those who are leaving Somalia come from all different categories – 'men and women, old and young, poor and not so poor, statesmen and the ordinary, educated and uneducated, urban and rural'. And, as Samatar writes, although many Somalis hope and yearn for a better Somalia, many are so disheartened that they do not see hope for a return anytime soon.

While Halima does not have the hope to return to Somalia, this does not lead her to question Mogadishu as the home-place she so

Figure 10.2 *Celebrating Halima's graduation in community welfare in Melbourne, September 2012, with (from left to right) her daughter Sahra, her sister Sahra, Halima, her daughter Sagal and the author. Image courtesy of Paul Reade*

beautifully storied at the beginning of this chapter. Being displaced does not automatically lead to the feeling that any and no place in the world is home or that, in the end, being-on-the-move itself is home. Instead, as Halima put it in her story, her 'heart is working hard to belong' – it is working towards a stability and rootedness in place, towards a regrounding of the self and towards an end of the restlessness that accompanied the years on the move.

From Routes to Roots

Despite my fascination with travel and boundlessness, with movement and fluctuation, I have a terrible fear of flying. While I still force myself to take a plane whenever it is not avoidable, the state of detachedness and floatation through space and time evokes in me a feeling of panic. It is the moment when the plane takes off that terrifies me, when I literally lose ground and have to submit myself to the rules of this strange spatial machine and give in to a sensation of utter placelessness. When lived to its extreme, my dream of not having to set anchors anywhere within this free-floating human world thus turns into its vast opposite: a nightmare of losing grip on myself within the incomprehensibility of open space.

It is against this nightmare that Halima steels herself and that her heart keeps on working. And while Halima's everyday paths in Melbourne were marked by a remarkable level of mobility, this mobility was not, by any means, boundless. Instead, the movements in Melbourne that I shared with Halima took place within routes that were tied to the boundaries of the western suburbs, the boundaries within which she felt safe and homely. The occasional event that forced her to drive her car beyond the imagined border formed by her sister's house in Kensington, led her to feel insecure, to agonize over the unknown streets, places and people she would be confronted with. Halima often relied on the support of her son and nephews to drive her to places beyond the boundaries of where she felt at home.

This attachment to her suburb, neighbours and everyday trajectories had indeed become so strong that when after years of waiting for public housing Halima finally received an apartment, she turned down the offer because the allocated house was too far away from the neighbourhood she had grown so fond of. Her neighbours, many of whom were Italian, were happy to hear that she would not leave. Over the years the people in her street had become close to each other. That her refusal threw her back into a long waiting list for public housing and that it could take years for another offer to come up did not bother Halima. 'If I have to wait ten years I don't mind,' she said. 'I don't want to go to another place, I really like this area.'

Halima's desire to stay put and her eagerness to work towards a feeling of being-at-home in Australia again throws the romantic imagination of the world as boundless and the refugee as the embodiment of nomadic belonging into question. Rather, her desire turns the gaze from the figure of the refugee back to those who came to imagine them as emissaries of a homeless age of movement. Looking at refugees, migrants and other mobile peoples in terms of a placeless paradigm does not just neglect their actual experiences and lives. It also keeps us from having a serious look into the ways this paradigm has been formed and into the reason why movement has come to be a symbol of such strength. It keeps us from understanding what, in the end, all these metaphors, symbols and representations really stand for.

In an article laconically titled 'From Roots to Routes: Tropes for Trippers', Jonathan Friedman takes a critical look at a dominant stream of thinkers in anthropology such as Appadurai, Gupta and Ferguson, Malkki and Clifford, who, over the past three decades, have confronted ideas of boundedness and territoriality (Friedman 2002). Friedman points out how proponents of a placeless paradigm have sketched dwelling as something that was the premise of classical anthropology, where culture and bounded territoriality were seen as a given. The opposite of this view, the idea that displacement is at the heart of the human condition, has now become so accepted in anthropology that much of it has, in fact, turned into a cliché: '[I]deas of locality, of place, of community are miserably innocent of the realities of movement, of the transnational and transcultural.' But is there really a contradiction we can speak of? 'Is the assumption of locality in error merely because there has always been contact?' Friedman (2002: 23) asks.

Despite the fact that estrangement and nomadic roaming might so well capture a certain discontent with the state of the world and modernity, I agree with Friedman that the strong focus on fluidity and instability seems to overlook the way place continues to be of importance in people's everyday lives. While compared to one hundred or two hundred years ago, the world is more mobile than ever, the actual percentage of people on the move internationally is very low compared to those who stay put. And while our own experiences as anthropologists might be unbounded and unsettled this does not mean that place, roots and settlement have ceased to be of importance altogether. In fact, I question the proposition that they have ceased to be of importance to those who celebrate nonbelonging. The danger of using displacement as a trope through which late modernity can be understood is that it quickly disintegrates into a flirting with uncertainty and mobility. Again, there would be a necessity to look beyond the uncritical use of movement as a metaphor and into the actual experience of the phenomenon. As Dick Pels argues, construing the migrant, exile or nomad as alter ego of the modern intellectual can lead to an 'intellectualist domestication and appropriation of the experiences of "real-life" migrants and exiles, while it simultaneously euphemizes the comparatively settled, sedentary and privileged position of academics, who are invited to indulge in fictions of social "weightlessness" and dreams of perpetual transcendence in boundary-breaking journeys of the critical mind' (Pels 1999: 72). This is not to suggest that displacement is an experience unique to refugees or migrants. Rather, it is a call to take displacement seriously, to not overlook the *placement* in *dis*placement (Lems 2016a).

To look beyond the flimsy, the fluid and the unstable thus involves looking into the lived experience of being-in-place. In Halima's case, her movement away from Somalia and towards years of uncertainty was not a chosen step. It was an *existential* decision, one between life and death. Once on the move, however, she needed to keep going, for there was no place for her to rest and put down roots. This continuous mobility that marked her years of flight and asylum was not a desirable condition. It was, in fact, a condition that put such heavy strains upon her that it caused Halima to get seriously ill as soon as she found herself settled after her move to Australia. And it is against this debilitating state of liminality and instability that Halima's heart keeps on working hard and attaches itself to the place where, after years of climbing, her feet well and truly felt ground again.

This is not to suggest that the climbing has come to an end now or that it will ever come to an end – for Halima or for any other living being. But it suggests that the act of climbing itself does not mean that the paths she takes and the ground she touches are mere backdrops to an endless vastness of space. If place is so deeply ingrained in our bodies and minds, if there is no outside of place, its neglect does not just throw the existence of the world as we see and experience it into question but our entire sense of being. Although places change and the universe might stretch into endlessness, the fact remains that humans have to deal with the limits of being-in-the-world from the places their bodies are currently positioned at. While being-here, they can dream the rhythms of somewhere else – a somewhere else that is perhaps so far removed from the here that it appears to be lost in open space. In the end, not even the nomad travels routeless (or perhaps better: rootless) – quite the opposite, nomads need to be able to read and understand places better than anyone else. Without a deep knowledge for places, their characteristics and seasonal behaviour, the nomad would be truly lost. The idea that mobile people do not roam about unmarked open space is supported by accounts of anthropologists working with nomads who have pointed out that they are deeply enmeshed with the places they are moving through (see Khazanov 1984; Ingold 1986).

I suggest that movement has to be thought of as twofold: inwards and outwards. The inwards movement is the motion within an individual, experienced as the sense that one is existentially moving forwards, that one is not treading water, or that one is not, as in Halima's fears, caught in transit. It is the movement Omar described when he stressed that the need to travel does not usually arise out of a pure joy for movement. Rather, people travel in order to achieve more and to change something in their lives. It is a movement that also propels people like me, the student-anthropologist, to come to the other end of the world to learn and see new things and by doing so to create a movement inside of me. The outwards movement, then, is the physical movement, the movement that actually brings us to move about and go to other places. These two movements balance each other. If the need to existentially move forward is satisfied, then the need for a movement outwards is not of such importance. If, however, the need for inwards movement is marked by stagnation, then the need to move outwards grows.

It is close to what, in the context of Lebanese migrants, Ghassan Hage (2005: 470) has called 'existential mobility', a need to 'move physically so we can feel that we are existentially on the move again or at least moving better'. Looking at movement by taking the relationship between existential and physical movement into account could allow for a new anthropological take on the interplay of mobility and immobility (Lems and Moderbacher 2016). According to Hage, it would 'allow us to construct a whole social physics of socio-existential mobility, explaining different kinds of mobility rather than homogenizing them with one term that equates the travel of the totally-at-home-having-fun tourist to the travel of the fragile, dislocated and hesitant refugee' (Hage 2005: 471).

For Halima, the inwards movement is marked by her ceaseless placemaking efforts. It is marked by her continuous struggle to make Melbourne a home to her community – a community that, itself, is a form of dwelling. In the end, the very act of building, of working-towards, of actively engaging with one's surroundings, needs to be understood as a form of emplacement. As Heidegger notes, to build in itself is already to dwell, and even when we turn inwards we never abandon our stay among things (Heidegger 1975: 146, 157). Because being-in-the-world is essentially a staying with things, inwards movement can take us to imagined and storied places, and yet never make us lose ourselves in the vastness of open space. Rather, these imagined, storied places come to permeate the here and now. They come to enter our continuous acts of building and with it mould our stay with things and, in the end, our very emplacement.

Note

1. Centacare is an organization funded by the Catholic Church in Melbourne that offers family services to people from diverse socio-economic and cultural backgrounds.

Final Juncture
Concluding Words

This book ends as it began: with the image of a path and the stories it weaves into the viewer's imagination. This photograph depicts another crossroads. As a point where some things pause, rest or halt and others mingle, melt or begin, it can tell us stories about the meanings of endings, boundaries and horizons. It establishes an idea of the openness of place, and of people's continuous movements towards emplacement within it.

Figure 11.1 *'I think this is the police academy – or it used to be. It's near the Parliament in Mogadishu.' Image courtesy of Mohamed Ibrahim*

Mohamed and I never talked much about this image. Yet, like all his photographs – like any image, indeed – it did not require many words. Seeing, as John Berger (2008: 1) has observed, comes before words. It is through seeing that we establish our place in the world: '[W]e explain that world with words, but words can never undo the fact that we are surrounded by it', he writes.

The image depicts a deserted road in the centre of Mogadishu, leading towards the Parliament – a building that, as Mohamed told me, is crumbling under the weight of years of war. What once was the heart of Somalia as a modern nation state now looks deserted. 'Some time ago there probably used to be a guard at the gate,' Mohamed said. 'It's very sad, very sad.' This sense of sadness does not need to be verbalized in more detail. The image says it all. The sadness appears through the cracked road, the derelict building and the absence of any sign of living beings inhabiting this place – as if the photographer, following the many people who have already left the city, was about to go through the gate and take one last look at what he is leaving behind. Without people walking, talking or simply living – the place's being-here – the viewer's attention is drawn to boundaries: the endless row of white walls on the right; the sequence of windowless buildings on the left; the blueness of the sky over and above and across, criss-crossed by power lines in the distance; and in the midst of it all is the inescapable presence of the gate, the ultimate attempt to keep things within bounds.

As much as the image seems to depict an endpoint, it does not exclude new possibilities. Not all is lost; not all is drenched in sadness. After all, the gate is open, allowing the viewer of the photograph to imagine herself walking towards the openness of the blue sky. Rather than speaking of the boundary as a totality at which things stop, the photograph hints at the boundary – in Heidegger's sense – at which things begin their presencing. Such an understanding of bounding allows for place to be looked at in terms of its openness and potentialities, as 'that for which room has been made', rather than as something enclosed within itself (Heidegger 1975: 154). Despite all the sadness, the displacements and corrosion that speak through it, Mohamed's image also allows for hope: for imagining new paths to be walked, forgotten directions to be uncovered and unexpected clearings to open up. Literally and symbolically, the photo makes room for change and, perhaps, future emplacements.

When he first returned from his journey, I asked Mohamed whether he had felt relieved to leave the war-torn city and all its problems behind. 'You see, that's it,' he responded. 'I was not happy at all to leave that place.' His sense of attachment to the place blotted out memories of the dangers of walking through the streets of Mogadishu, and the feelings of estrangement and ambiguity it created. It was only by being there, Mohamed explained to me, that he began to understand that he had actually been homesick for Mogadishu all those years. Led by this strong sense of attachment that came to the fore during his first visit in 2011, Mohamed has since returned to Mogadishu and other parts of Somalia regularly.

With all its problems, its evidence of suffering and abandonment and his own journeys away from it, Mogadishu has not lost its presence in Mohamed's life. As all the photographs that have formed crossroads within this book show, the line between emplacement and displacement is, at times, so thin that they cannot easily be separated. While displacement, this stinging pain of being lost to or within a place, often seems to have the louder voice, Mohamed's photographs also speak of people's enduring relationships with places – even if at first glance these places might seem utterly lost to them. Notwithstanding the years of war and violence that have left their imprint on Mogadishu and its inhabitants, it is still home to many people. Be it through the persistence of memory places, imaginary past or future landscapes, or the transforming power of stories, as living, breathing, walking and seeing human beings we employ manifold ways to come to terms with the inescapable fact of our being-here.

Ways of Being-Here

This book has also been a dialogue that allowed me to begin to grasp my own being-here. Becoming so closely involved in Halima's, Mohamed's and Omar's lives and observing their movements towards emplacement confronted me with the necessity to look at my own refusal to be pinned down. It urged me to look into the places and people that moulded me and to understand the reasons behind my rejection of *Heimat* and my confusion over the idea of home. It led me to move beyond the metaphorical use of the figure of the refugee as a representative for an age of deterritorialization and pay attention to the roots of this perceived homelessness, which, in the end, is a chosen homelessness.

Listening to Omar's stories of home-building, and observing Halima's urge to keep climbing mountains in order to arrive and settle down, made me realize that the feeling of the restlessness of our

times needs to be read in the context of a wider narrative of placelessness that can be traced back to modern Western conceptualizations
of the world. The turn towards space has left the human subject
moving back and forth within the vastness of the universe without
any abiding place to rest and take root or dwell. My own romanti-
cization of travelling, non-belonging and movement, it seems, stems
from a muddled understanding of space as marked by a sheer infinity of possibilities and place as the embodiment of claustrophobic
closeness. Coming to Australia and listening to Omar's and Halima's
stories made me understand that while there are good reasons to
choose to be at home within a sense of movement and non-belonging,
there is an urgent need to look beyond the conceptual and the metaphorical and into the way being-at-home or being-without-home
are actually made sense of in people's everyday lives. Omar, Halima
and Mohamed urged me to see the paradoxical ways in which *Dasein*
(being-here) is always grounded and on the move at the same time.
For what is so baffling and somewhat mysterious about being is, as
John Berger (1984: 41) has suggested, 'that it represents both stillness
and movement'.

Omar's and Halima's stories have shown that this groundedness of Dasein as being-here cannot be circumvented by ignoring
place and reducing space to a purely mathematical essence. Omar's
numerous acts of home-building, and Halima's tireless climbing of
mountains in order to move actively towards emplacement, illustrate
the importance of place in people's lives. Even in the face of the
disorienting feeling of displacement, and despite years spent on the
move or caught in limbo, the intimacy and immediacy of place is not
swallowed by the endlessness of space. Halima's and Omar's stories
have opened up the possibility of understanding human emplacement as located at the crossroads between the closedness of place
and the infinity of the universe. 'The world is wholly inside and I
am wholly outside myself,' Merleau-Ponty (2003 [1945]: 474) says,
describing the inward and outward directions of our emplacement
in the world. Place, his comment suggests, is not just where we
are. It is something surrounding, yet not immovable, it is something imagined, yet material, and it something that gathers, yet also
disseminates.

The stories in this book say much about being emplaced as being
inward and outward bound at the same time. Through movement, by
arriving in Melbourne and befriending Australians, and by returning to the place he had left behind so many years ago, Omar began
to look at the places he had inhabited in a new light. By seeing

Melbourne and Gardo from the perspective of the larger world, he saw himself in new ways. In Halima's stories, her being-at-home in faith created a feeling of being-part-of the universe and allowed her to carry this sense of home with her wherever she went. In my own case, coming to Australia and being-here with Halima, Mohamed, Omar and all the other people I have met in Melbourne, made me look back at the place I had come from and see my homelessness in a new light. These stories suggest that emplacement, the acts of investing our surroundings with meaning, is of fundamental importance, because places are not mere backdrops against which life is written. Rather, it is in our (daily or not-so-daily) journeys through places that our lives take shape and that we make sense of the wider world – and perhaps even the universe at large.

Rather than thinking of emplacement as immovable, I suggest that it needs to be thought of as continuously changing and moving. We develop a deep attachment to certain places, but as Halima and my own experiences of looking up into a starlit sky suggest, against the infinity of the universe the groundedness of these places and our own emplacements within them become destabilized. At the same time, by telling stories, by making sense of the universe, by giving stars a name and identity, we story vastness back into something placeable and meaningful. Like Rilke's *Weltinnenraum*, where birds fly silently through us and all beings are shot through with immensity, emplacement as inward and outward bound allows us to reach outwards, to let the world touch us, and, at the same time, story this immensity into something intimate and dear.

The importance of the openness of emplacement is mirrored in Omar's and Halima's placemaking processes. Omar's stories suggest that in order to feel at home a place needs to be open enough to perceive opportunities to move forward in one's life. Halima's and Omar's efforts to invest their surroundings with meaning and their continuous processes of home-building also hint at the close relationship between place, building and dwelling. Omar's story of emplacement suggests that the very act of building can be a form of dwelling. By becoming actively engaged in his surroundings, by laying brick upon brick towards a sense of home, he was able to invest a place with meaning. Halima's urge to keep moving forward and make Australia a meaningful place for her community enabled her to gradually overcome the debilitating feelings of displacement and to become emplaced. Both Halima and Omar developed deep emotional and social ties by entering into a productive relationship with the places they inhabited.

I suggest that the affinity between building and dwelling that can be observed in Halima's and Omar's stories is not specific to them. As Heidegger points out, the Old English and High German word for building, the term *buan*, literally means to dwell, or to stay in a place (Heidegger 1975: 146). Moving from the original meaning of the term buan (now *bauen* or building), which was 'to dwell', to the question of what *ich bin* (I am) means, Heidegger points out that the term *bin* also relates to the old word *bauen*: *ich bin* or *du bist* (I am, you are) means 'I dwell' or 'you dwell': 'The way in which you are and I am, the manner in which we humans *are* on the earth, is *Buan*, dwelling. To be a human being means to be on earth as a mortal. It means to dwell' (Heidegger 1975: 147).

There is no being outside place. That does not mean that place is confined to and within itself; just as being is continuously on the move – it is always a way of becoming – emplacement can only be understood in terms of people's movements towards it. Halima's stories of the 'fantastic days' in the Mogadishu of her childhood suggest that these movements-towards, these manifold acts of building, often involve the traces of places from the past. Especially in the face of displacement, these memory places can write a place's habits and inner workings so deeply into our innermost landscapes that they can become a means for making sense of our present surroundings. Halima's stories also show that these imaginary layers, which can pave the way towards emplacement, should not be too readily discarded as nostalgia. Just like place, nostalgia needs to be understood in new ways, reflecting the act that people use idealized or imagined stories of past places as a means of making sense of their being-here. Therefore, the idea of the past as something long gone may need to be challenged. The past, Halima's experiences show, is not a foreign country; it is relevant and present for the here and now, and continues to play into and form our lifeworlds.

Omar's and Halima's stories also show that there is a limit to memory's ability to guide and transform present emplacements. Omar could not look back into a past Somalia yet disregard all that had happened to it ever since he left. He found it hard to find words for a place that, as he put it, had literally crumbled into dust, and in fact refused to indulge in memories of a beautiful past. While Halima could gain strength from looking back to the 'fantastic days' of her childhood, her memories were sometimes interrupted by the painful realization of all that was lost. Memory places do not only bring back to life beautiful and light moments, but can also take us back to places that have undergone such violent ruptures that we struggle to experientially make sense of them and integrate them into our being-here. This, it seems, is the pain of displacement.

As Halima's sadness over the papaya's lack of sweetness and the memories of pain and loss it provoked show, displacement can literally get under our skins and be felt in our bodies. At such moments, creating a story can become almost impossible. Neither Halima nor Omar were left mute, however; in trying to tell their stories, they deployed other forms of expression. By telling me detailed stories in which he pieced together Somalia's past, Omar was also making sense of it. Through the soothing rhythm of the poem and the protective boundaries of the fragment, Halima could tell me of things that were otherwise untellable. While storytelling and displacement can sometimes be experienced as opposing forces, it is important to double-listen and recognize the different expressions of 'displaced stories'. Such stories can, for example, be uttered as whispers, fragments or half-told stories. Sometimes, as Halima's story showed, they can also take on the form of heroic tales that turn losses into wins.

Storytelling, then, is the meeting point between past and present; it is another crossroad at which places and memories from the past and impressions and experiences from the present begin to leak into each other. It is at this point, where the importance of the imaginary comes to the fore, that Casey's strong emphasis on the inseparable relationship between bodies and places can be loosened and opened up towards the imaginary. Where Casey, in focusing on the importance of the lived body, emphasizes the way place is experienced immediately as *Erlebnis*, Omar's, Halima's and my own stories suggest that place is also experienced as *Erfahrung* – that is, in terms of the reflected imaginary and storied layers that form it into something meaningful. This, in turn, suggests that experience itself needs to be understood as more than merely immediate, bodily and sensory (absolute) hereness, and that our engagement with the world always involves different layers of experience.

In order to grasp the way place is experienced, we need to take into account all the political, historical, social, sensual and storied elements that shape our experiences of it. The interplay of power dynamics and place that has dominated so much modern thinking and writing on space and place is but one of the many layers that form people's place-experience. As Omar's accidental arrival in Australia shows, the state's attempt to control who is allowed in and who has to stay out can make borders and boundaries be felt in people's lives and bodies, but it does not stop people from outwitting the state in its urge to control and define places. This, again, hints at the essentially *moving* character of place, at the way people and places are continuously changing. It also suggests that place is not just a social or political construct. Because the social does not exist prior to place and it is not given expression except in and through place, it is perhaps, as Jeff Malpas (1999: 36) has suggested, only within the structure of place that the possibility of the social arises.

The different ways of being-here that wove their way through this book illuminate the all-encompassing importance of the social in our continuous struggle for emplacement. When Omar, living in an exclusionary society, decided to live one-eyed and to keep himself from experiencing the place in all its dimensions, he did so to protect himself against the painful reality of a place that marked him as an outsider. A place whose meanings he could not share and live as part of a wider whole refused emplacement. Halima's stories gave a strong sense of the way place and people leak into each other and can almost feel as one – be it through the importance of the family as the core theme of dwelling, the ways her personal suffering became embedded in the suffering of a humanized country, or her urge to create a feeling of being-at-home within her community. Human beings are born *of* and *into* the world; they dwell in each other, and together they dwell in place.

Towards the Open

At this point, so close to letting this book and the story-journeys within them come to an end, I would like to return to Tim Ingold's wayfarer, who, in travelling over land, cannot but engage with the places her movements take her through. While it is her body that takes her through these places, it is the stories she tells about them that define her experience and understanding of them. 'Inhabitant knowledge' is what Ingold (2009: 41–43) has called this form of knowledge, which is built on the practical understanding of the lifeworld, an understanding that is integrated on the way and that is 'meshworked', rather than networked (Ingold 2009: 41). Because wayfarers inhabit the world rather than travel across it, and because for inhabitants things are not classified as facts but narrated as stories, it is not just the body but our very imagination that plays into our ways of travelling through and experiencing place. Every place, Ingold (2009: 41) suggests, 'as a gathering of things, is a knot of stories'.

This book has created such a knot of stories: a gathering place for understanding the world *on the way (unterwegs)*. Becoming involved in Halima's and Omar's lives and listening to each other's stories enabled me to look at place from an inhabitant's point of view rather than trying to explain it by classifying it. By becoming Omar's and Mohamed's friend and Halima's surrogate daughter, my research became a project of talking and seeing the world *on the way*, and doing so together. In storying these paths together, it became clear that neither the places we were moving through nor the world we were trying to grasp were enclosed islands at risk of drowning in the open space of an unplaceable universe. Rather than movements across an indifferent, open space, ours were movements through bounded yet open places. The *open* I have in mind here is the openness hinted at by the crossroads in Mohamed's photograph. It is the openness of the horizon, which encloses and uncloses at the same time and which leads me at once out of this book and right into its very heart.

I would like to end with the idea of a crossroads that points towards the openness with which the stories and images shared here have spoken about place and life and the world. *Das Offene*, which Rilke so masterfully spoke about in his *Duino Elegies*, captures our continuous back and forth movements between captivity and freedom, movement and stagnation, inside and outside. Just as seeing comes before words, poetry can be a way of seeing *through* words; it is therefore fitting that this last crossroads is formed in the words of a poet.[1]

> And we: spectators, always, everywhere,
> looking *at* everything, never *from*!
> It floods us. We arrange it. It decays.
> We arrange it again, and we decay.
>
> Who has turned us around like this,
> so that, whatever we do, we always have
> the look of someone going away? Just as a man
> on the last hill showing him his whole valley
> one last time, turns and stops and lingers –
> so we live, and are forever leaving.

Note

1. Excerpt from *The Duino Elegies and the Sonnets to Orpheus* by Rainer Maria Rilke, translated by A. Poulin, Jr. Copyright © 1975, 1976, 1977 by A. Poulin. Reprinted by permission of Houghton Mifflin Harcourt Publishing Company. All rights reserved.

Bibliography

Abdi, C. 2007. 'Convergence of Civil War and the Religious Right: Reimagining Somali Women', *Signs: Journal of Women in Culture and Society* 33(1): 183–207.

Abu-Lughod, L. 1993. *Writing Women's Worlds: Bedouin Stories.* Berkeley, CA: University of California Press.

Aden, A. 1981. 'Women and Words (Somalia)', *Ufahamu* 10(3): 115–42.

Agamben, G. 1995. 'We Refugees', *Symposium* 49(2): 114–20.

Agnew, J. and J. Duncan (eds). 1989. *The Power of Place: Bringing Together Geographical and Sociological Imaginations.* London; Sydney; Wellington: Unwin.

Ahmed, C. 1995. 'Finely Etched Chattel: The Invention of the Somali Woman', in A. Jimale (ed.), *The Invention of Somalia.* Lawrenceville, NJ: Red Sea Press, pp. 157–89.

Ahmed, S. 1999. 'Home and Away: Narratives of Migration and Estrangement', *Journal of Cultural Studies* 2(3): 329–47.

Aidani, M. 2010. 'Existential Accounts of Iranian Displacement and the Cultural Meanings of Categories', *Journal of Intercultural Studies* 31(2): 121–43.

Aidid, S. 2011. 'Haweenku Wa Garab (Women are a Force): Women and the Somali Nationalist Movement, 1943–1960', *Bildhaan: An International Journal of Somali Studies* 10: 103–24.

Alexandra, D. 2008. 'Digital Storytelling as Transformative Practice: Critical Analysis and Creative Expression in the Representation of Migration in Ireland', *Journal of Media Practice* 9(2): 101–12.

Anderson, B. 1983. *Imagined Communities: Reflections on the Origin and Spread of Nationalism.* London: Verso.

Andrzejewski, B.W. 2011. 'The Poem as Message: Verbatim Memorization in Somali Poetry', *Journal of African Cultural Studies* 23(1): 27–36.

Andrzejewski, B.W. and S. Andrzejewski. 1993. *An Anthology of Somali Poetry.* Bloomington, IN: Indiana University Press.

Appadurai, A. 1988a. 'Place and Voice in Anthropological Theory', *Cultural Anthropology* 3(1): 16–20.

———. 1988b. 'Putting Hierarchy in its Place', *Cultural Anthropology* 3(1): 36–49.

———. 1996. *Modernity at Large: Cultural Dimensions of Globalization*. Minneapolis, MN: University of Minnesota Press.

———. 2006. *Fear of Small Numbers: An Essay on the Geography of Anger*. Durham, NC: Duke University Press.

Arendt, H. 1971. *The Origins of Totalitarianism*. New York: Meridian Books.

———. 1998. *The Human Condition*. Chicago, IL; London: University of Chicago Press.

Aristotle. 2007. *Physics*. Sioux Falls, SD: Nu Vision Publications (E-book).

Auden, W.H. 1976. *Collected Poems*. New York: Random House.

Augé, M. 1995. *Non-Places: Introduction to an Anthropology of Supermodernity*. London, New York: Verso.

Australian Bureau of Statistics (ABS). 2012. 'The 2011 Census: Country of Birth of Person Data'. Retrieved on 2 February 2017 from http://www. abs.gov.au/websitedbs/censushome.nsf/home/tablebuilder.

Bachelard, G. 1994. *The Poetics of Space*. Boston, MA: Beacon Press.

Baer, U. 2000. *Remnants of Song: Trauma and the Experience of Modernity in Charles Baudelaire and Paul Celan*. Stanford, CA: Stanford University Press.

Bammer, A. (ed.) 1994. *Displacements: Cultural Identities in Question*. Bloomington, IN: Indiana University Press.

Basso, K. 1996. *Wisdom Sits in Places: Landscape and Language among the Western Apache*. Albuquerque, NM: University of New Mexico Press.

Bauman, Z. 1992. 'Soil, Blood and Identity', *The Sociological Review* 40(4): 675–701.

———. 1995. *Life in Fragments: Essays in Postmodern Morality*. Oxford; Cambridge, MA: Blackwell.

———. 2000. *Liquid Modernity*. Cambridge; Malden, MA: Polity Press; Blackwell.

Becker, G. 1997. *Disrupted Lives: How People Create Meaning in a Chaotic World*. Berkeley, CA: University of California Press.

Behar, R. 1990. 'Rage and Redemption: Reading the Life Story of a Mexican Marketing Woman', *Feminist Studies* 16(2): 223–58.

———. 1993. *Translated Woman: Crossing the Border with Esperanza's Story*. Boston, MA: Beacon Press.

Benjamin, W. 2007. 'The Storyteller: Reflections on the Work of Nikolai Leskov', in W. Benjamin (ed.), *Illuminations: Essays and Reflections*. New York: Schocken Books, pp. 83–109.

———. 1999. *The Arcades Project*, Trans. R. Tiedemann. Cambridge, MA: Harvard University Press.

Berger, J. 1984. *And our Faces, My Heart, Brief as Photos*. New York: Pantheon Books.

———. 2008. *Ways of Seeing*. London: Penguin.

Berger, J. and J. Mohr. 1995. *Another Way of Telling*. New York: Vintage International.

Berger, P., B. Berger and H. Kellner. 1973. *The Homeless Mind: Modernization and Consciousness*. New York: Random House.

Berns-McGown, R. 1999. *Muslims in the Diaspora: The Somali Communities of London and Toronto*. Toronto; London: University of Toronto Press.

Besteman, C. 1996a. 'Representing Violence and "Othering" Somalia', *Cultural Anthropology* 11(1): 120–33.

——. 1996b. 'Primordialist Blinders: A Reply to I.M. Lewis', *Cultural Anthropology* 13(1): 109–120.

Biehl, J. 2005. *Vita: Life in a Zone of Social Abandonment*. Berkeley, CA: University of California Press.

Blunt, A. and R. Dowling. 2006. *Home*. London: Routledge.

Braidotti, R. 1994. *Nomadic Subjects: Embodiment and Sexual Difference in Contemporary Feminist Theory*. New York: Columbia University Press.

Browne, P. 2006. *The Longest Journey: Resettling Refugees from Africa*. Sydney: UNSW Press.

Bruner, E. 1986. 'Experience and its Expressions', in V. Turner and E. Bruner (eds), *The Anthropology of Experience*. Chicago, IL: University of Illinois Press, pp. 3–30.

Bruner, E. (ed.). 1988. *Text, Play, and Story: The Construction and Reconstruction of Self and Society*. Washington, DC: American Anthropological Association.

Bryden, M. 2003. 'No Quick Fixes: Coming to Terms with Terrorism, Islam, and Statelessness in Somalia', *Journal of Conflict Studies* 23(2): 24–56.

Buck-Morss, S. 1989. *The Dialectics of Seeing: Walter Benjamin and the Arcades Project*. Cambridge, MA: MIT Press.

Carr, D. 1986. *Time, Narrative and History*. Bloomington, IN: Indiana University Press.

——. 2014. *Experience and History: Phenomenological Perspectives on the Historical World*. New York: Oxford University Press.

Casey, E. 1976. *Imagining: A Phenomenological Study*. Bloomington, IN: Indiana University Press.

——. 1987a. *Remembering: A Phenomenological Study*. Bloomington, IN: Indiana University Press.

——. 1987b. 'The World of Nostalgia', *Man and World* 20(4): 361–84.

——. 1993. *Getting Back into Place: Towards a Renewed Understanding of the Place-world*. Bloomington, IN: Indiana University Press.

——. 1997a. *The Fate of Place: A Philosophical History*. Berkeley, CA: University of California Press.

——. 1997b. 'Smooth Spaces and Rough-Edged Places: The Hidden History of Place', *The Review of Metaphysics* 51(2): 267–96.

———. 2000. 'How to Get from Space to Place in a Fairly Short Stretch of Time: Phenomenological Prolegomena', in S. Feld and K. Basso (eds), *Senses of Place*. Santa Fe, NM: School of American Research Press, pp. 13–52.

Castells, M. 1996. *The Rise of the Network Society*. Malden, MA: Blackwell.

Chamberlain, M. and P. Thompson (eds). 1998. *Narrative and Genre*. London: Routledge.

Chambers, I. 1994. *Migrancy, Culture, Identity*. London: Routledge.

Clifford, J. 1992. 'Traveling Cultures', in L. Grossberg, C. Nelson and P. Treichler (eds), *Cultural Studies*. New York: Routledge, pp. 96–116.

Clifford, J. and G. Marcus (eds). 1986. *Writing Culture: The Poetics and Politics of Ethnography*. Berkeley, CA: University of California Press.

Coleman, S. and P. Collins (eds). 2006. *Locating the Field: Space, Place and Context in Anthropology*. Oxford; New York: Berg.

Coleman, S. and P. Hellermann (eds). 2011. *Multi-sited Ethnography: Problems and Possibilities in the Translocation of Research Methods*. New York: Routledge.

Corradi, C. 1991. 'Text, Context and Individual Meaning: Rethinking Life Stories in a Hermeneutic Framework', *Discourse and Society* 2(1): 105–17.

Crapanzano, V. 1980. *Tuhami: Portrait of Moroccan*. Chicago, IL: University of Chicago Press.

———. 1992. *Hermes' Dilemma and Hamlet's Desire: On the Epistemology of Interpretation*. Cambridge, MA: Harvard University Press.

Csordas, T. 1994. *Embodiment and Experience: The Existential Ground of Culture and Self*. Cambridge; New York: Cambridge University Press.

Das, V. 1995. *Critical Events: An Anthropological Perspective on Contemporary India*. Delhi; New York: Oxford University Press.

———. 2006. *Life and Words: Violence and the Descent into the Ordinary*. Berkeley, CA: University of California Press.

Davis, F. 1979. *Yearning for Yesterday: A Sociology of Nostalgia*. New York: Free Press.

De Blij, H. 2009. *The Power of Place: Geography, Destiny, and Globalization's Rough Landscape*. Oxford; New York: Oxford University Press.

De Certeau, M. 1984. *The Practice of Everyday Life*. Berkeley, CA: University of California Press.

Deleuze, G. and F. Guattari. 1986. *Nomadology: The War Machine*. New York: Semiotext(e).

———. 1987. *A Thousand Plateaus: Capitalism and Schizophrenia*. Minneapolis, MN: University of Minnesota.

Desjarlais, R. 1996. 'Struggling Along', in M. Jackson (ed.), *Things as They Are: New Directions in Phenomenological Anthropology*. Bloomington, IN: Indiana University Press, pp. 70–93.

———. 1997. *Shelter Blues: Sanity and Selfhood among the Homeless.* Philadelphia, PA: University of Pennsylvania Press.

Desjarlais, R. and J. Throop. 2011. 'Phenomenological Approaches in Anthropology', *Annual Review of Anthropology* 40(1): 87–102.

De Voe, P. 2002. 'Symbolic Action: Religion's Role in the Changing Environment of Young Somali Women', *Journal of Refugee Studies* 15(2): 234–46.

Dilthey, W. 1906. *Das Erlebnis und die Dichtung.* Göttingen: Vandenhoeck & Ruprecht.

Eagleton, T. 2008 [1983]. *Literary Theory: An Introduction.* Minneapolis, MN: University of Minnesota Press.

Eastmond, M. 1996. 'Luchar y Sufrir: Stories of Life and Exile: Reflections on the Ethnographic Process', *Ethnos* 61(3–4): 232–50.

———. 2007. 'Stories as Lived Experience: Narratives in Forced Migration Research', *Journal of Refugee Studies* 20(2): 248–64.

Escobar, A. 2001. 'Culture Sits in Places: Reflections on Globalism and Subaltern Strategies of Localization', *Political Geography* 20(2): 139–74.

Farah, H., A. Adan and A. Warsame. 1995. 'Somalia: Poetry as Resistance against Colonialism and Patriarchy', in S. Wieringa (ed.), *Subversive Women: Historical Experiences of Gender and Resistance.* London; New Jersey: Zed Books, pp. 165–182.

Farah, N. 2000. *Yesterday, Tomorrow: Voices from the Somali Diaspora.* London; New York: Cassell.

———. 2004. *Links.* New York: Riverhead Books.

Fassin, D. 2011. *Humanitarian Reason: A Moral History of the Present.* Berkeley, CA: University of California Press.

Fassin, D. and E. D'Halluin. 2005. 'The Truth from the Body: Medical Certificates as Ultimate Evidence for Asylum Seekers', *American Anthropologist* 107(4): 597–608.

Feld, S. and K. Basso. (eds). 1996. *Senses of Place.* Santa Fe, NM: School of American Research Press.

Fog Olwig, K. and K. Hastrup (eds). 1997. *Siting Culture: The Shifting Anthropological Subject.* London; New York: Routledge.

Foucault, M. 1975. *Discipline and Punish.* New York: Pantheon.

———. 1986. 'Of Other Spaces', *Diacritics* 16(1): 22–27.

Frank, G. 1995. 'Anthropology and Individual Lives: The Story of the Life History and the History of the Life Story', *American Anthropologist* 97(1): 145–48.

Friedman, J. 2002. 'From Roots to Routes: Tropes for Trippers', *Anthropological Theory* 2 (1): 21–36.

Gaibazzi, P. 2015. *Bush Bound: Young Men and Rural Permanence in Migrant West Africa.* New York: Berghahn Books.

Gardner, J. and A. Warsame. 2004. 'Women, Clan Identity and Peace-building', in J. Gardner and J. El Bushra (eds), *Somalia: The Untold Story: The War Through the Eyes of Somali Women.* London: Pluto Press, pp. 153–65.

Geertz, C. 1973. *The Interpretation of Cultures*. London: Fontana.

Geurts, K. 2002. *Culture and the Senses: Bodily Ways of Knowing in an African Community*. Berkeley, CA: University of California Press.

Gregorič, N. and J. Repič (eds). 2016. *Moving Places: Relations, Return and Belonging*. New York: Berghahn Books.

Griffiths, D. 2002. *Somali and Kurdish Refugees in London: New Identities in the Diaspora*. London: Ashgate.

Gupta, A. and J. Ferguson. 1992. 'Beyond "Culture": Space, Identity, and the Politics of Difference', *Cultural Anthropology* 7(1): 6–23.

Gupta, A. and J. Ferguson (eds). 1997a. *Culture, Power, Place: Explorations in Critical Anthropology*. Durham, NC; London: Duke University Press.

——— . 1997b. *Anthropological Locations: Boundaries and Grounds of a Field Science*. Berkeley, CA: University of California Press.

Hage, G. 1997. 'At Home in the Entrails of the West: Multiculturalism, Ethnic Food and Migrant Home-Building', in H. Grace, G. Hage, L. Johnson, J. Langsworth and M. Symonds (eds), *Home/World: Space, Community and Marginality in Sydney's West*. Annandale: Pluto Press, pp. 99–153.

——— . 1998. *White Nation: Fantasies of White Supremacy in a Multicultural Society*. Sydney: Pluto Press.

——— . 2005. 'A Not So Multi-Sited Ethnography of a Not So Imagined Community', *Anthropological Theory* 5(4): 463–75.

——— . 2009. 'Hating Israel in the Field: On Ethnography and Political Emotions', *Anthropological Theory* 9: 59–79.

——— . 2013. 'On Other Belongings', in K. MacCarter and A. Lemer (eds), *Joyful Strains: Making Australia Home*. Melbourne: Affirm Press, pp. 142–50.

Hartley, L.P. 1971. *The Go-Between*. London: Penguin.

Hastrup, K. 2005. 'Social Anthropology: Towards a Pragmatic Enlightenment?' *Social Anthropology* 13(2): 133–49.

Hayden, D. 1997. *The Power of Place: Urban Landscapes as Public History*. Cambridge, MA: MIT Press.

Heidegger, M. 1962. *Being and Time*. New York: Harper & Row.

——— . 1975. 'Building Dwelling Thinking', in M. Heidegger (ed.), *Poetry, Language, Thought*. New York: Harper & Row, pp. 143–62.

——— . 1977 [1956]. *Zur Seinsfrage*. Frankfurt/Main: Vittorio Klostermann.

——— . 2003 [1977]. *Seminar in Le Thor: Four Seminars*. Bloomington, IN: Indiana University Press.

——— . 2016. *Ponderings II-VI: Black Notebooks 1931–1938*. Bloomington, IN: Indiana University Press.

Hirsch, E. 2008. 'Knowing, Not Knowing, Knowing Anew', in N. Halstead, E. Hirsch and J. Okely (eds), *Knowing How to Know: Fieldwork and the Ethnographic Present*. New York: Berghahn Books, pp. 21–37.

Hobsbawm, E. 1991. 'Introduction', *Social Research* 58(1): 65–68.

Hölderlin, F. 2008. *The Death of Empedocles: A Mourning-Play*. New York: State University of New York Press.

Horst, C. 2006. *Transnational Nomads: How Somalis Cope with Refugee Life in the Dadaab Camps of Kenya*. New York: Berghahn Books.

Hough, M. 2011. 'Why Now? A Brief History of Somalia', in K. Huisman, M. Hough, K. Langellier and C. Norstrom (eds), *Somalis in Maine*. Berkeley, CA: North Atlantic Books, pp. 7–19.

Huisman, K., M. Hough, K. Langellier and C. Norstrom (eds). 2011. *Somalis in Maine: Crossing Cultural Currents*. Berkeley, CA: North Atlantic Books.

Husserl, E. 1970a [1936]. *Crisis of European Sciences and Transcendental Phenomenology*. Evanston, IL: Northwestern University Press.

———. 1970b. *Logical Investigations*. London; New York: Routledge.

———. 1981. *Husserl: Shorter Writings*. The Hague: Nijhoff.

Ingold, T. 1986. *The Appropriation of Nature: Essays on Human Ecology and Social Relations*. Manchester: Manchester University Press.

———. 2009. 'Against Space: Place, Movement, Knowledge', in P.W. Kirby (ed.), *Boundless Worlds: An Anthropological Approach to Movement*. New York: Berghahn Books, pp. 29–44.

———. 2011. *Being Alive: Essays on Movement, Knowledge and Description*. London, New York: Routledge.

Jackson, M. 1995. *At Home in the World*. Durham, NC: Duke University Press.

———. 2002. *The Politics of Storytelling: Violence, Transgression, and Intersubjectivity*. Copenhagen: Museum Tusculanum Press.

———. 2005. 'West-African Warscapes: Storytelling Events, Violence, and the Appearance of the Past', *Anthropological Quarterly* 78(2): 355–75.

———. 2010. 'From Anxiety to Method in Anthropological Fieldwork', in J. Davies and D. Spencer (eds), *Emotions in the Field: The Psychology and Anthropology of Fieldwork Experience*. Stanford, CA: Stanford University Press, pp. 35–54.

———. 2011. *Life within Limits: Well-being in a World of Want*. Durham, NC: Duke University Press.

———. 2013a. *The Wherewithal of Life: Ethics, Migration, and the Question of Well-being*. Berkeley, CA: University of California Press.

———. 2013b. *Lifeworlds: Essays in Existential Anthropology*. Chicago, IL: The University of Chicago Press.

Jackson, M (ed.). 1996. *Things as They Are: New Directions in Phenomenological Anthropology*. Bloomington, IN: Indiana University Press.

Jackson, M. and A. Piette (eds). 2015. *What is Existential Anthropology?* New York: Berghahn Books.

Jama, Z. 1994. 'Silent Voices: The Role of Somali Women's Poetry in Social and Political Life', *Oral Tradition* 9(1): 186–202.

Jay, M. 2005. *Songs of Experience: Modern American and European Variations on a Universal Theme*. Berkeley, CA: University of California Press.

Johnson, J.W. 1996. *Heelloy: Modern Poetry and Songs of the Somali*. London: HAAN.

Kapteijns, L. 1995. 'Gender Relations and the Transformation of the Northern Somali Pastoral Tradition', *The International Journal of African Historical Studies* 28(2): 241–59.

———. 1999. *Women's Voices in a Man's World: Women and the Pastoral Tradition in Northern Somali Orature, 1899–1980*. Portsmouth: Heinemann.

———. 2009. 'Memories of a Mogadishu Childhood, 1946–1964: Maryan Muuse Boqor and the Women Who Inspired Her', *International Journal of African Historical Studies* 42(1): 105–16.

———. 2010. 'Making Memories of Mogadishu in Somali Poetry about the Civil War', in L. Kapteijns (ed.), *Mediations of Violence in Africa: Fashioning New Futures from Contested Pasts*. Leiden: Brill, pp. 25–74.

———. 2011. 'Changing Conceptions of Moral Womanhood in Somali Popular Songs, 1960–1990', in M. Badran (ed.), *Gender and Islam in Africa: Rights, Sexuality, and Law*. Stanford, CA: Stanford University Press, pp. 119–48.

Keith, M. and S. Pile (eds). 1993. *Place and the Politics of Identity*. London: Routledge.

Khazanov, A. 1984. *Nomads and the Outside World*. Cambridge: Cambridge University Press.

Kirby, P.W. (ed.). 2009. *Boundless Worlds: An Anthropological Approach to Movement*. New York: Berghahn Books.

Kleinman, A., V. Das and M. Lock (eds). 1997. *Social Suffering*. Berkeley, CA: University of California Press.

Kleinman, A. and J. Kleinman. 1997. 'The Appeal of Experience; The Dismay of Images: Cultural Appropriations of Suffering in Our Times', in A. Kleinman, V. Das and M. Lock (eds), *Social Suffering*. Berkeley, CA: University of California Press, pp. 1–24.

Kleist, N. 2004. 'Nomads, Sailors and Refugees: A Century of Somali Migration', *Sussex Migration Working Papers* (Working Paper 23).

Koyré, A. 1979. *From the Closed World to the Infinite Universe*. Baltimore, MD: Johns Hopkins Press.

Lamb, S. 2001. 'Being a Widow and Other Life Stories: The Interplay between Lives and Words', *Anthropology and Humanism* 26(1): 16–34.

Langness, L. and G. Frank. 1981. *Lives: An Anthropological Approach to Biography*. Novato, CA: Chandler and Sharp.

Lefebvre, H. 1991. *The Production of Space*. Oxford: Blackwell.

Lems, A. 2016a. 'Placing Displacement: Place-making in a World of Movement', *Ethnos* 81(2): 315–37.

———. 2016b. 'Ambiguous Longings: Nostalgia as the Interplay among Self, Time and World', *Critique of Anthropology* 36(4): 419–38.

———. 2017. 'Mobile Temporalities: Place, Ruination and the Dialectics of Time', in M. Palmberger and J. Tosic (eds), *Memories on the Move: Experiencing Mobility, Rethinking the Past*. Basingstoke: Palgrave Macmillan, pp. 127–56.

Lems, A. and C. Moderbacher. 2016. 'On Being Stuck in the Wrong Life: Home-Longing, Movement and the Pain of Existential Immobility', in M. Gutekunst, A. Hackl, S. Leoncini, J. Schwarz and I. Götz (eds), *Bounded Mobilities*. Bielefeld: Transcript, pp. 113–28.

Levi, P. 1988. *The Drowned and the Saved*. New York: Summit Books.

Lèvi-Strauss, C. 1973. *Tristes Tropiques*. London: Jonathan Cape.

Lewis, I.M. 1978 [1957]. *The Somali Lineage System and the Total Genealogy: A General Introduction to Basic Principles of Somali Political Institutions*. Ann Arbor, MI: University Microfilms.

———. 1994. *Blood and Bone: The Call of Kinship in Somali Society*. Lawrenceville, NJ: Red Sea Press.

———. 1998. 'Doing Violence to Ethnography: A Response to Catherine Besteman's "Representing Violence and 'Othering' Somalia"', *Cultural Anthropology* 13(1): 100–8.

———. 1999. *A Pastoral Democracy: A Study of Pastoralism and Politics among the Northern Somali of the Horn of Africa*. London: James Currey.

———. 2008. *Understanding Somalia and Somaliland: Culture, History, Society*. Cambridge: Cambridge University Press.

Linde, C. 1993. *Life Stories: The Creation of Coherence*. New York: Oxford University Press.

Low, S. and D. Lawrence-Zúñiga (eds). 2003. *The Anthropology of Space and Place: Locating Culture*. Oxford: Blackwell.

Lowenthal, D. 1975. 'Past Time, Present Place: Landscape and Memory', *Geographical Review* 65(1): 1–36.

Lucht, H. 2011. *Darkness before Daybreak: African Migrants Living on the Margins in Southern Italy Today*. Berkeley, CA: University of California Press.

———. 2015. 'The Station Hustle: Ghanaian Migration Brokerage in a Disjointed World', in M. Jackson and A. Piette (eds), *What is Existential Anthropology?* New York: Berghahn Books, pp. 104–24.

Luling, V. 2006. 'Genealogy as Theory, Genealogy as Tool: Aspects of Somali "Clanship"', *Social Identities* 12(4): 471–85.

Malinowski, B. 1932. *Argonauts of the Western Pacific*. London: Routledge.

Malkki, L. 1992. 'National Geographic: The Rooting of Peoples and the Territorialization of National Identity among Scholars and Refugees', *Cultural Anthropology* 7(1): 24–44.

———. 1995a. *Purity and Exile: Violence, Memory, and National Cosmology among Hutu Refugees in Tanzania*. Chicago, IL: University of Chicago Press.

———. 1995b. 'Refugees and Exile: From "Refugee Studies" to the National Order of Things', *Annual Review in Anthropology* 24: 494–523.

———. 1996. 'Speechless Emissaries: Refugees, Humanitarianism, and Dehistoricization', *Cultural Anthropology* 11(3): 377–404.

Mallett, S. 2004. 'Understanding Home: A Critical Review of the Literature', *The Sociological Review* 52(1): 62–89.

Malpas, J. 1999. *Place and Experience: A Philosophical Topography*. Cambridge: Cambridge University Press.

———. 2012. *Heidegger and the Thinking of Place: Explorations in the Topology of Being*. Cambridge, MA: MIT Press.

Mansur, A. 1995. 'The Nature of the Somali Clan System', in A. Ahmed (ed.), *The Invention of Somalia*. Lawrenceville, NJ: The Red Sea Press, pp. 117–34.

Mares, P. 2001. *Borderline: Australia's Response to Refugees and Asylum Seekers in the Wake of the Tampa*. Sydney: University of New South Wales Press.

Marlowe, J. 2010. 'Beyond the Discourse on Trauma: Shifting the Focus on Sudanese Refugees', *Journal of Refugee Studies* 23(2): 183–98.

Mattingly, C. 1998. *Healing Dramas and Clinical Plots: The Narrative Structure of Experience*. Cambridge; New York: Cambridge University Press.

Merleau-Ponty, M. 2003 [1945]. *Phenomenology of Perception*. London: Routledge Classics.

Moreton-Robinson, A. 2003. 'I Still Call Australia Home: Indigenous Belonging and Place in a White Postcolonizing Society', in S. Ahmed, C. Castaneda, A Fortier and M. Sheller (eds), *Uprootings/ Regroundings: Questions of Home and Migration*. New York: Berg, pp. 23–40.

Morris, D. 1997. 'About Suffering: Voice, Genre, and Moral Community', in A. Kleinman, V. Das and M. Lock (eds), *Social Suffering*. Berkeley, CA: University of California Press, pp. 25–46.

Natanson, M. 1973. *Phenomenology and the Social Sciences*. Evanston, IL: Northwestern University Press.

Neumann, K. 2015. *Across the Seas: Australia's Response to Refugees: A History*. Melbourne: Black Inc.

Neumann, K., S. Gifford, A. Lems and S. Scherr. 2014. 'Refugee Settlement in Australia: Policy, Scholarship and the Production of Knowledge, 1952–2013', *Journal of Intercultural Studies* 35(1): 1–17.

Nielsen, K. 2004. 'Next Stop Britain: The Influence of Transnational Networks on the Secondary Movement of Danish Somalis', *Sussex Migration Working Papers* (Working Paper No. 22). Retrieved on 12 October 2016 from https://www.sussex.ac.uk/webteam/gateway/file.php?name=mwp22.pdf&site=252.

Nietzsche, F. 1957. *The Use and Abuse of History*. New York: Macmillan.

Noble, G. 2009. *Lines in the Sand: The Cronulla Riots, Multiculturalism and National Belonging*. Sydney: Institute of Criminology Press.

Oakeshott, M. 2015. *Experience and its Modes*. Cambridge: Cambridge University Press.

Ochs, E. and L. Capps. 1997. 'Narrating Lives in the Balance', Salsa V, Proceedings of Symposium about Language and Society. Austin, TX: University of Texas.

Pels, D. 1999. 'Privileged Nomads: On the Strangeness of Intellectuals and the Intellectuality of Strangers', *Theory, Culture & Society* 16(1): 63–86.

Peters, J.D. 1999. 'Exile, Nomadism, and Diaspora: The Stakes of Mobility in the Western Canon', in H. Naficy (ed.), *Home, Exile, Homeland: Film, Media, and the Politics of Place*. New York: Routledge, pp. 17–44.

Piette, A. 2015a. 'Existence, Minimality, and Believing', in M. Jackson and A. Piette (eds), *What is Existential Anthropology?* New York: Berghahn Books, pp. 178–214.

———. 2015b. *Existence in the Details: Theory and Methodology in Existential Anthropology*. Berlin: Duncker & Humblot.

Powles, J. 2004. 'Life History and Personal Narrative: Theoretical and Methodological Issues Relevant to Research and Evaluation in Refugee Contexts', *New Issues in Refugee Research* (Working Paper No. 106). Geneva: UNHCR.

Poynting, S., G. Noble, P. Tabar and J. Collins. 2004. *Bin Laden in the Suburbs: Criminalising the Arab Other*. Sydney: Sydney Institute of Criminology Series.

Prunier, G. 2010. 'Benign Neglect versus "La Grande Somalia": The Colonial Legacy and the Post-colonial Somali State', in M. Höhne and V. Luling (eds), *Peace and Milk, Drought and War: Somali Culture, Society and Politics*. New York: Columbia University Press, pp. 35–49.

Rapport, N. and A. Dawson (eds). 1998. *Migrants of Identity: Perceptions of Home in a World of Movement*. Oxford: Berg.

Rapport, N. and S. Williksen. 2010. *Reveries of Home: Nostalgia, Authenticity and the Performance of Place*. Newcastle: Cambridge Scholars.

Relph, E. 2008. 'Disclosing the Ontological Depth of Place', *Environmental & Architectural Phenomenology* 19: 5–8.

Ricoeur, P. 2004. *Memory, History, Forgetting*. Chicago, IL: University of Chicago Press.

Rilke, R.M. 2005. *Duino Elegies and The Sonnets of Orpheus*. Translated by A. Poulin. New York: Houghton Mifflin Harcourt.

Rodman, M. 1992. 'Empowering Place: Multilocailty and Multivocality', *American Anthropologist* (94): 640–56.

Rosaldo, R. 1976. 'The Story of Tukbaw: "They Listen as He Orates"', in F. Reynolds and D. Capps (eds), *The Biographical Process: Studies in the History and Psychology of Religion*. The Hague: Mounton & Co, pp. 121–51.

———. 1988. 'Ideology, Place, and People without Culture', *Cultural Anthropology* 3(1): 77–87.

Rousseau, C., T. Said and G. Bibeau. 1998. 'Between Myth and Madness: The Premigration Dream of Leaving among Young Somali Refugees', *Culture, Medicine and Psychiatry* 22(4): 385–411.

Said, E. 1979. *Orientalism*. New York: Vintage Books.

Samatar, A. 1988. *Socialist Somalia: Rhetoric and Reality*. London; New Jersey: Zed Books.

——. 2004. 'Beginning Again: From Refugees to Citizens', *Bildhaan: An International Journal of Somali Studies* 4: 1–17.

Samatar, S. 1982. *Oral Poetry and Somali Nationalism*. London: Cambridge University Press.

——. 2010. 'Somalia: A Nation's Literary Death Tops its Political Demise', in M. Höhne and V. Luling (eds), *Peace and Milk, Drought and War: Somali Culture, Society and Politics*. New York: Columbia University Press, pp. 207–20.

Schielke, S. 2015. *Egypt in the Future Tense: Hope, Frustration, and Ambivalence Before and After 2011*. Bloomington, IN: Indiana University Press.

Schielke, S. and L. Debevec (eds). 2012. *Ordinary Lives and Grand Schemes: An Anthropology of Everyday Religion*. New York: Berghahn Books.

Shaw, C. and M. Chase (eds). 1989. *The Imagined Past: History and Nostalgia*. Manchester: Manchester University Press.

Silva, S. 2015. 'Mobility and Immobility in the Life of an Amputee', in M. Jackson and A. Piette (eds), *What is Existential Anthropology?* New York: Berghahn Books, pp. 125–54.

Sontag, S. 2008. *On Photography*. London; New York: Penguin Classics.

Sossi, F. 2006. *Migrare: Spazi di Confinamento e Strategie di Esistenza*. Milan: Il Saggiatore.

Stocking, G. 1992. *The Ethnographer's Magic and Other Essays in the History of Anthropology*. Madison, WI: University of Wisconsin Press.

Stoller, P. 1989. *The Taste of Ethnographic Things: The Senses in Anthropology*. Philadelphia, PA: University of Pennsylvania Press.

——. 1997. *Sensuous Scholarship*. Philadelphia: University of Pennsylvania Press.

Throop, J. 2003. 'Articulating Experience', *Anthropological Theory* 3(2): 219–41.

——. 2009. 'Intermediary Varieties of Experience', *Ethnos* 74(4): 535–58.

Tiilikainen, M. 2003. 'Somali Women and Daily Islam in the Diaspora', *Social Compass* 50(1): 59–69.

Trigg, D. 2012. *The Memory of Place: A Phenomenology of the Uncanny*. Athens, OH: Ohio University Press.

Tuan, Y.F. 2005. *Space and Place: The Perspective of Experience*. Minneapolis, MN: University of Minnesota Press.

Turner, V. 1985. *On the Edge of the Bush: Anthropology as Experience*. Tucson, AZ: University of Arizona Press.

Turner, V. and E. Bruner (eds). 1986. *The Anthropology of Experience*. Urbana, IL: University of Illinois Press.

Van Gelder, L. 2008. *Weaving a Way Home: A Personal Journey Exploring Place and Story*. Ann Arbor, MI: University of Michigan Press.

Ward, S. 2003. 'On Shifting Ground: Changing Formulations of Place in Anthropology', *The Australian Journal of Anthropology* 14(1): 80–96.

Warf, B. and A. Santa (eds). 2009. *The Spatial Turn: Interdisciplinary Perspectives*. London; New York: Routledge.

Weiner, J. 1991. *The Empty Place: Poetry, Space, and Being among the Foi of Papua New Guinea*. Bloomington, IN: Indiana University Press.

———. 2001. *Tree Leaf Talk: A Heideggerian Anthropology*. London: Berg.

Willen, S. and D. Seeman. 2012. 'Introduction: Experience and Inquiétude', *Ethos* 40(1): 1–23.

Withy, K. 2014. 'Situation and Limitation: Making Sense of Heidegger on Thrownness', *European Journal of Philosophy* 22(1): 61–81.

Zarowsky, C. 2004. 'Writing Trauma: Emotion, Ethnography, and the Politics of Suffering among Somali Returnees in Ethiopia', *Culture, Medicine and Psychiatry* 28(2): 189–209.

Žižek, S. 2007. 'Do We Still Live in a World?' Retrieved on 15 May 2013 from: http://www.lacan.com/zizrattlesnakeshake.html.

Index

Note: Locators in *italics* refer to illustrations.

EASA Series

Published in Association with the European Association of Social Anthropologists (EASA)

Series Editor: Aleksandar Bošković, University of Belgrade

Social anthropology in Europe is growing, and the variety of work being done is expanding. This series is intended to present the best of the work produced by members of the EASA, both in monographs and in edited collections. The studies in this series describe societies, processes, and institutions around the world and are intended for both scholarly and student readership.